Behind the Walls

Law and Society Series
W. Wesley Pue, General Editor

The Law and Society Series explores law as a socially embedded phenomenon. It is premised on the understanding that the conventional division of law from society creates false dichotomies in thinking, scholarship, educational practice, and social life. Books in the series treat law and society as mutually constitutive and seek to bridge scholarship emerging from interdisciplinary engagement of law with disciplines such as politics, social theory, history, political economy, and gender studies.

A list of recent titles in the series appears at the end of the book. For a complete list, see the UBC Press website, www.ubcpress.ca/books/series_law.html.

Behind the Walls

Inmates and Correctional Officers on the State of Canadian Prisons

MICHAEL WEINRATH

UBCPress · Vancouver · Toronto

25 24 23 22 21 20 19 18 17 16   5 4 3 2 1

Printed in Canada on FSC-certified ancient-forest-free paper
(100% post-consumer recycled) that is processed chlorine- and acid-free.

Library and Archives Canada Cataloguing in Publication

Weinrath, Michael, author
Behind the walls : inmates and correctional officers on the state of
Canadian prisons / Michael Weinrath.

(Law and society series)
Includes bibliographical references and index.
Issued in print and electronic formats.
ISBN 978-0-7748-3355-4 (pbk.).–ISBN 978-0-7748-3356-1 (pdf).–
ISBN 978-0-7748-3357-8 (epub).–ISBN 978-0-7748-3358-5 (mobi)

1. Prisoners–Canada. 2. Correctional personnel–Canada. 3. Prisoners–Canada–
Attitudes. 4. Correctional personnel–Canada–Attitudes. 5. Prisons–Canada.
6. Correctional institutions–Canada. 7. Corrections–Canada. 8. Prisoners–
Canada–Social conditions. 9. Correctional personnel–Canada–Social
conditions. I. Title. II. Series: Law and society series (Vancouver, B.C.)

HV9507.W44 2016   365'.971   C2016-904134-4
                                           C2016-904135-2

Canadä

UBC Press gratefully acknowledges the financial support for our
publishing program of the Government of Canada (through the Canada Book Fund),
the Canada Council for the Arts, and the British Columbia Arts Council.

This book has been published with the help of a grant from the
Canadian Federation for the Humanities and Social Sciences, through
the Awards to Scholarly Publications Program, using funds provided by the
Social Sciences and Humanities Research Council of Canada.

Printed and bound in Canada by Friesens
Set in Zurich, Univers, and Minion by Apex CoVantage, LLC
Copy editor: Michael Kudelka
Indexer: Christine Jacobs
Proofreaders: Alison Strobel and Caitlin Gordon-Walker

UBC Press
The University of British Columbia
2029 West Mall
Vancouver, BC V6T 1Z2
www.ubcpress.ca

Contents

Figures and Tables / vi

Acknowledgments / vii

Introduction / 3

1 Canadian Prisons and Their Problems / 14

2 The Prisons and the Interviews / 55

3 How Inmates Understand Their Role / 75

4 How Inmates Relate to Others / 90

5 How Corrections Officers Understand Their Role / 124

6 Relations between Inmates and Officers / 140

7 The Effect of Policy, Architecture, and Technology / 159

8 Boundary Violations by Correctional Officers / 174

9 The Effect of Programs / 210

10 The Rise of Prison Gangs / 236

Conclusion / 267

Appendix: Interview Guide / 277

Notes / 282

Glossary: Correctional Terms and Inmate Argot / 285

References / 288

Index / 307

Figures and Tables

Figures

1.1 Canadian crime rate per 100,000, 1979–2013 / 18

1.2 Canadian incarceration rate per 100,000, 1979–2013 / 19

1.3 Incarceration rate and crime rate, 1979–2013 / 19

1.4 Canadian incarceration rates, daily counts, 1979–2013 / 23

1.5 Federal institutional violence, 2003–11 / 34

3.1 Developing the primary inmate frame / 87

4.1 The primary inmate frame / 100

4.2 The external inmate frame / 117

5.1 The primary correctional officer frame / 137

6.1 Framing relations with inmates to establish legitimacy / 157

8.1 Frame breaking and the female CO frame / 182

9.1 Behavioural program frames / 222

10.1 Prison gang frames / 254

Tables

2.1 Inmate profile / 69

2.2 Correctional officer profile / 71

Acknowledgments

First and foremost, I would like to thank my inmate and staff interview groups. All of you were most giving of your time, and I was impressed with the thoughtfulness of your answers to my many questions. To understand prison life, it is important to involve the people who experience it every day. I hope that the book and its analysis of your narratives does justice to your eloquent and heartfelt responses.

Brian Grant, former director general of research for the Correctional Service of Canada, supported the bulk of funding for this project, and I am extremely grateful for his support. Greg Graceffo, associate deputy minister of Manitoba Corrections, and the University of Winnipeg also generously contributed to this initiative. Access to inmates and staff was facilitated by Trevor Markesteyn for Headingley Correctional Centre, Christer McLauchlin at Stony Mountain Institution, James Cook for Fort Saskatchewan Correctional Centre, and Glen Brown for Matsqui Institution. A number of line staff helped make my trips to the different institutions productive ones. Thanks to all of you for taking the time and trouble to help a visitor around.

My dedicated group of transcript typists stuck with a demanding job, especially Kirsten Lezubski, who did the bulk of interviews. Others contributing who merit mention include Jillian Carrington, Gillian Weinrath, Caylene Foley, and Tanis Melnyk. I would like to thank my colleagues in criminal justice for their support over the last few years, and express my appreciation to Richard Jochelson and Kevin Walby for their comments on earlier drafts of this manuscript. External peer review is a cornerstone of good scholarship.

The two reviewers for UBC Press provided detailed and insightful critiques and improved this manuscript significantly. Many thanks to them for their time and trouble. Errors and omissions are, of course, my responsibility.

Last but not least, I am very grateful to my wife and partner, Janet Simpson, who had to listen to my ruminations over this project, its early life, half-life, and final completion. Her encouragement and support were unflagging and more than I deserved. You could not ask for a better partner.

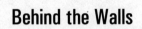

Behind the Walls

Introduction

It's 7:00 a.m., time to get up. Jones stared over at his still sleeping cellmate. He sniffed and winced; would be nice if that con took a shower, but his cellmate would probably just spend his day trying to find drugs and get high again. Jones was tired of being on remand in this institution; it meant he had to spend most of his time on one unit with little in the way of programs or even recreation. His lawyer had told him he might have a deal with the Crown soon and he would get sentenced, but it was getting tiresome spending all this time in pre-trial detention. His correctional officer worker, Ms. Markov, had said he might be able to get into a short anger management program, only a week long, but it would get him off this crowded unit a couple of times a week and maybe do him some good. Jones walked up to the staff station, hoping to get in a phone call to his girlfriend before breakfast, but his heart fell when he saw Officer Griff working. Griff was by the book, no phone calls this early, and what was worse, he seemed to enjoy saying "no." Jones smiled hopefully, looking at the phone, looking up at Griff, but the CO [correctional officer] just glared back. Well, no chit-chat with the CO this morning. Too bad, he liked talking to Markov, even though he was careful to keep it to just a few minutes. Don't want to look too friendly. Jones turned away and walked towards the unit table, maybe play a game of cards before breakfast, but he froze when he saw Dooly standing just in front of him. Jones gave the gang member a wide berth. No point getting slapped in the head for walking in the wrong place. He was not afraid of Dooly, but that old inmate code rule of fighting only one-on-one was gone, along with most of the code's better rules. Fight one gangster, you end up battling ten. He sighed; guess it was just another day in paradise.

Prison life intrigues us. And why not? The principal actors, the inmates,[1] are engaging characters: they have crossed the line of illicit behaviour that we dare not, and they are now the protagonists in a dark world full of shady characters. Institutional life conjures up for us scenes of conflict, danger, and moral drama: the chance for someone to change their life, to actively seek and obtain redemption, or, instead, to succumb to the temptations of sin and remain embedded in a wicked life. These vivid images come to us most conveniently from popular media but are also created by claims-makers actively promoting their own brand of change, or, more cynically, from politicians who simply seek to advantage themselves in their quest to gain or retain power.

What we should be more concerned about is why we do not view the prison as a place for inmates to change their behaviour for the better. Daily routines grind inexorably on, and while some inmates participate in programs or work, far too many in Canada nowadays lay idle on remand and spend their days sleeping, watching TV, playing cards or video games, or telling "crime stories" to one another. The amount of time restricted to the cell block, range, or living unit has increased recently, with less recreation and fewer opportunities to socialize in large groups in prison common areas (Porter & Calverley, 2011; Weinrath, 2009b).

If inmates play the lead, then the essential supporting cast are the correctional staff, and star among that assemblage are correctional officers (COs). While at one time stereotyped in largely negative ways as being punitive and uneducated (Willet, 1983), COs are now better educated and are more involved in prison programming in North America and England (Crawley, 2004; Crewe, 2009; Johnson, 2002a; Liebling, Price, & Shefer, 2010). But despite the fact that COs (and institutional treatment staff) are arguably better educated and trained than ever, there is little evidence that this has resulted in positive changes in prison life for inmates.

Journalists, social reformers, and scholars have been studying prisons since their use became popular in the eighteenth century (Carrigan, 1991; Rothman, 1971, 1980). Their conclusions are repetitive and often contradictory. Institutions are said by some to be inhumane and hence likely to produce hardened criminals. For others, custodial settings are too "soft" and do not deter offenders. Rehabilitation is either impossible because offenders are incorrigible, or has never really been tried due to lack of proper funding. Many claim that prisons are schools for crime and that offenders merely learn to become better criminals while serving time. Still others simply state in a general way that prisons do not work and that their use should be abolished altogether. These debates about prisons have raged almost since the first ones opened, to the point that most penologists wonder whether anyone ever considers historical accounts of prisons and their recurrent problems (Rothman, 1980).

I contend that prisons continue to be an important area of study, now more than ever. They are places that, on the surface, have seen considerable signs of progress over the past thirty years, but they continue to be beset with problems, some old, some new. Better-designed correctional institutions, more focused treatment regimes, Aboriginal programming, and improved training and expanded roles for correctional staff are just some of the progressive initiatives that I describe in this book.[2] Problems remain, however, and they include a lack of inmate solidarity, limited treatment success, COs' unrealized potential, still limited Aboriginal initiatives, and escalating violence from prison gangs. Improvements are possible, however, and I will recommend a number of policy changes that I believe would give inmates more respect, provide constructive ways for them to spend time while incarcerated, and create more opportunities for personal change and growth. In addition, I will suggest ways for COs to improve their ability to positively influence offenders.

In this second decade of a new century, we should know more about the significant evolution in Canada's use of prisons. There have been several important shifts in crime, human rights legislation, management approaches, and programming. Moreover, data from Statistics Canada shows that crime rates are down and the use of community corrections alternatives like probation and conditional sentences has increased, so inmate populations should have also declined. Perplexingly, this is not the case – inmate populations stayed steady in the 2000s and are now on the rise (Boyce 2015; Perreault, 2014; Statistics Canada, 2015).

The past thirty years have witnessed fundamental changes in prison design and inmate management in North America. In the 1970s, '80s, and '90s, Canadian corrections agencies shifted away from the traditional, intimidating fortress-style architecture in favour of linear-style prison buildings with forbidding concrete façades outside and stacked cell blocks inside (Posner, 1991). Old-style architecture was synonymous with old-style prison management – that is, with authoritarian COs and hierarchical, paramilitary staff supervision structures. Newer prisons combine modern, open-style architecture with humanistic principles of social psychology, the careful application of electronic technology, and modern management practices (Wener, 2006). To better manage inmates and staff, administrators invested heavily in new penal practices, which were carried out through "living units" and the unit management practices that flowed therefrom. This was viewed as a huge step forward for corrections in the twentieth century. Yet despite this sea change in management practices, we know surprisingly little about the impact of new-generation techniques on inmate relations and inmate–staff relations; only a small number of empirical studies have targeted this shift for inquiry (Beijersbergen, Dirkzwager, van der Laan, & Nieuwbeerta, 2012; Beijersbergen, Dirkzwager, Eichelsheim, van der Laan, & Nieuwbeerta, 2014b; Wener, 2006; Zupan, 1991).

Concurrent with these management changes, North American courts and various external bodies have been intruding more and more in the corrections system by reviewing the practices of corrections agents. In the United States this has meant civil litigation through the courts; in Canada the courts have arguably played a lesser role (Hannah-Moffat & Klassen, 2013), while the federal Correctional Investigator and provincial ombudsmen have become more actively involved in ongoing grievances and issues (Marin, 2013; Global News, 2010; Sapers, 2014). The advent of the Charter of Rights and Freedoms in 1982, the passing of the federal Corrections and Conditional Release Act in 1992, and the damning findings of the Arbour Report in 1996 all represent significant stages in the evolution of human rights within Canada's prisons (Jackson, 2002).

An emphasis on human rights is not the only trend that can be seen as promoting more progressive ways of dealing with offenders. Psychologist Steven Wormith and his colleagues have outlined how the advent of empirically based classification and treatment programs in the 1980s and 1990s signified a demonstrable commitment by governments to rehabilitation (Wormith, Ferguson, & Bonta, 2013). Moreover, Canada's corrections systems had at last distinguished themselves sharply from their counterparts in the United States. Ex-convict and scholar John Irwin (2005) has shown that rehabilitation has been in retreat and warehousing was the new raison d'être. Classification systems based on actuarial recidivism studies promised to make practitioners' decisions more objective. The shining jewel in all this change was the cognitive-behavioural therapy (CBT) model, a social learning–based regime best articulated by psychologists Don Andrews and James Bonta (2010) and aimed at addressing the "criminogenic needs" of inmates. This type of approach targets the attributes, behaviours, and psychological orientations of offenders that contribute to their offending but are amenable to change. For example, low education is a criminogenic factor correlated to crime involvement and should be targeted for improvement. Associating with a negative peer group also contributes to offending, but this too can be adjusted. CBT purports to reorient offender thinking away from predatory, impulsive thoughts and lifestyles and to promote better problem-solving as well as pro-social attitudes. CBT and correctional programming have both had an enormous impact on the academic literature. Canadian psychologists, especially those working with or for the Correctional Service of Canada, have been lauded internationally for their program designs and their published empirical evaluations of treatment initiatives (Cullen, 2005).

Behavioural treatment regimens were generally derived by white researchers from values embedded in North American culture, but what about more relevant programming for Aboriginal offenders, who are heavily overrepresented in federal and provincial prisons? Indigenous cultural programs were introduced in corrections in the 1980s and became a regular part of most institutional regimes in the 1990s and into the twenty-first century. Anthropologist Joseph Waldram's (1997) study of Indigenous spirituality–based programs and the introduction of Elders in federal penitentiaries provides a powerful account of the potential of these programs to help and heal Aboriginal inmates. Given the tragic overrepresentation of Indigenous people in custody, especially in Canada's prairie provinces (Perreault, 2009; Sapers, 2013; Statistics Canada, 2015), we need to know more about how these culturally based programs have affected the lives of Aboriginal inmates.

Changes in prison organization and inmate management have a powerful impact on the lives of inmates and on the working lives of correctional staff. Thus, staff–inmate relations should have changed greatly for the better in recent years, and today's carefully articulated rehabilitation programs should be substantially lowering recidivism. Regrettably – although perhaps not surprisingly for corrections historians – today's "progressive" practices have not translated into prison closures, reports of cheery inmate–staff relations, or significantly less violence (Harris, 2003; Jackson, 2002; Marron, 1996; Sapers, 2014). Just why these anticipated positive changes have not ensued is not clear. Many of these organizational transformations have not been carefully examined and are not well understood.

Declining Crime Rates but Rising Prison Populations

A new problem now perplexing corrections is the paradox of higher custody rates even while crime rates are declining. Crime rates have declined throughout the Western world, yet institutional populations in Canada and other countries have increased or stayed the same. More conservative decision-making and (in some cases) more restrictive laws have together resulted in more custody. Punishment-oriented interest groups – "penal populists" – attempt to influence the public through the media, resorting to "common sense" rhetoric and proffering simple (i.e., punitive) solutions to crime. According to some, penal populism is impacting trends in arrests, remand detention, and sentencing (Hough & Roberts, 2005; Pratt, 2007). Penal populists are said to use misinformation and myths (e.g., that prison life is too "soft") to promote restrictive custody and more repressive community supervision. This is an important problem for corrections, for it has resulted in more and more people being locked up than ever before. Notably, this includes a rising number of remand cases (accused, not convicted) around the world (Walmsley, 2014).

The more sophisticated behavioural programs introduced over the past twenty-five years have been criticized as ineffective (Farabee, 2005). It has been suggested that such programs fail to reduce recidivism significantly and that more emphasis should be placed on basic vocational training (Review Panel, 2007). Such training is thought to be more likely to lead to employment and successful re-entry for offenders who have been released from incarceration.

Programs are all well and good, but what about the safety of inmates when they are not in treatment or working? Violence is an old prison problem and remains a central concern for inmates and staff. Although its pervasiveness is exaggerated at times, correctional facilities can be vicious places. Some assert that violence has increased in Canada's provincial and federal prisons, and this may well be due to the emergence of prison gangs. Quite commonly now, where we find serious assaults in custodial settings, we find prison gangs (Gaes, Wallace, Gilman, Klein-Saffran, & Suppa, 2002; Ruddell & Gottschall, 2011). Clearly, there has been a rise in ethnic-based predatory prison gangs in Canada, and this appears connected in many ways to the rise of Canadian urban-based street gangs, especially in the prairie provinces (Grant & Ruddell, 2011; Grekul & LaBoucane-Benson, 2006; Nafekh, 2002; Ruddell & Gottschall, 2011). In Ontario and federal prisons, Black gangs have become a growing concern (Grant & Ruddell, 2011). Gangs can create considerable problems in correctional settings. They exacerbate the problems inherent in prison life because of their aggressive involvement in drugs, violence, and victimization of other inmates (Winterdyk & Ruddell, 2010; Wood, Moir, & James, 2009). Prison gangs are a problem throughout the Western world but, unfortunately, much of what we know about them comes from American studies, and from what Canadian correctional authorities (not researchers) tell us about gangs.

The Need for Qualitative Studies

In Canada, psychologists and sociologists dominate corrections research, and their studies tend to be quantitative – that is, survey or experimental studies based on numbers and statistics. From this we know much about recidivism rates, changes in pro-social attitudes, and staff attitudes. Canada is probably best-known for its psychological research on inmate classification, adjustment, and criminogenic needs (Andrews & Bonta, 2010; Wormith et al., 2013; Zamble & Porporino, 1988). Qualitative field studies in Canada have not been as plentiful. However, there have been many excellent fieldwork studies in corrections that have incorporated observations of daily institutional routines, interactions between inmates and staff, and in-depth interviews of staff and inmates; these studies have probed and assigned meaning to the lived prison experiences of the institutional actors. Investigations of this type have examined the custodial experiences of inmates and staff in ways that closed-ended survey questionnaires cannot (Irwin, 1970; Irwin & Cressey, 1962; Jacobs, 1977; Sykes, 1958). There have also been notable efforts by Canadian scholars over the past decade that have enriched our understanding of prison life. Efforts of note include field studies on Aboriginal inmates and associated life trauma by sociologist Elizabeth Comack (2008) and anthropologist James Waldram (1997) in the prairie provinces, and legal scholarship/case study research on correctional administrations' abuse of authority by legal scholar Michael Jackson (2002), primarily in British Columbia. More recently in Ontario, sociologist Rose Ricciardelli (2014b) has used interviews with ex-inmates to examine stigma, subcultures, and violence in Ontario federal penitentiaries, while Melissa Munn and Chris Bruckert (2013) have depicted transitions from prison back to the community using interviews with Ontario parolees. This book contributes to the growing body of fieldwork about Canadian prisons.

For this study, I relied mainly on a qualitative approach to gain an appreciation of prison life from the perspective of both inmates and prison staff, with the focus on COs in regards to the latter. In this book, I couple institutional observation with in-depth interviews of twenty-four staff and thirty-seven inmates at four prison sites across western Canada. In those interviews, I asked a series of open-ended questions crafted around salient day-to-day routines, inmate–inmate and inmate–staff relationships, programs, work, leisure, drugs, and violence to explore the impact of external and internal correctional trends on inmate and staff life. This book is not based solely on qualitative data, however; existing quantitative data from official records and other secondary sources are used to contextualize the pressing problems confronting Canadian prisons. Furthermore, I utilize these sources to triangulate my qualitative findings; this reveals consistency between many of the trends I observed and the findings of other Canadian and international scholars.

The interpretation and analysis of the data is guided by sociologist Erving Goffman's (1974) frame analysis theory and, to a lesser extent, by his early work on asylums and stigma and his dramaturgical work on impression management (Goffman, 1959, 1961, 1963). Frame analysis provides a method for understanding relations between individuals in terms of how they interpret their roles and the social and physical context of their interactions. We adjust our behaviour towards others in accordance with the type of people and the setting; frame theory can help us unravel the motivations behind our actions as well as our understanding of these situations. In this book, the frame perspective will help us grasp how a person's being physically placed in a correctional institution and that person's subsequent assignment/taking on of the role of inmate structures his or her expectations and subsequent behaviours. Inmates direct these purposeful actions towards other inmates, COs, and external others. Also considered is Goffman's (1974) notion of frame breaking – that is, the modification or defiance of expected traditional or normative behaviours. In more extreme cases – for example, walking naked in the street – frame-breaking behaviour can run dramatically against normal expectations. Or it might simply involve a modification of existing practices, such as men wearing skirts on a hot day.

The other major theoretical perspective I employ in an effort to better understand current relations between inmates and COs is the legitimacy model of prison social order developed originally by British sociologists Anthony Bottoms and Richard Sparks (Bottoms, 1999; Sparks & Bottoms, 1995). Broadly considered, legitimacy is a problem for governments: citizens must believe in the state if they are going to obey its strictures (Bottoms & Tankebe, 2012). When a government has legitimacy, citizens are more willing to obey the law and to acquiesce to the authority of government agents such as the police. Achieving and maintaining legitimacy is more likely when agents of the state act according to the precepts of procedural justice (PJ): greater compliance from citizens can be expected when legal authorities exercise their authority in a fair, even-handed manner, showing respect and courtesy to individuals, a willingness to listen, and consistency in their use of sanctions. Bottoms (1999) and Bottoms and Tankebe (2012) and others have extended the test of legitimacy to the prison – a considerable challenge when one considers the significant constraints required by the institutional management of inmates; there are many rules to enforce, and some offenders may not have a compliant nature. Empirical tests in a number of countries have provided some support for the link between procedurally fair behaviour in prison regimes and improved behaviour, mental health, and attitudes among inmates (Beijersbergen, Dirkzwager, Eichelsheim, van der Laan, & Nieuwbeerta, 2014a; Franke, Bierie, & MacKenzie, 2010; Reisig & Mesko, 2009).

This book has three main aims. First, I seek to update our understanding of the correctional institution landscape in Canada, which has been impacted by external and internal trends. Taking in roughly the past twenty-five years,

I appraise broad trends such as prison design, program changes, prison gangs, new technology, accountability measures, and the increase in remands, as well as how these developments have framed the institutional experience for inmates and staff. Second, I describe how these trends play out in day-to-day inmate and staff routines and discuss whether they have impacted the social frames in which correctional officers and inmates operate. Third and finally, I offer the views of inmates and staff with regard to procedural justice criteria, their importance in interactions, and whether Canadian COs are meeting the mark.

Chapter 1 provides a brief history of Canadian corrections and reviews important trends that have affected Canadian correctional institutions over the past quarter-century. It examines significant changes such as the rise in remand inmates, worsening overcrowding, and the reduction in early release alternatives such as parole. I also outline significant issues in Canadian corrections today, including violence and drugs, the inmate code of conduct, and prison gangs. Progressive initiatives that are reviewed include changes to prison architecture, a more interactive inmate management style by COs, and the introduction of cognitive-behavioural training and Aboriginal cultural programming. Chapter 2 outlines the theoretical and methodological base of this study and describes frame theory, procedural justice, and legitimacy in greater detail. I also discuss frame analysis and frame breaking, and provide examples. The chapter also provides background on the four prison research sites, describes the study sample(s), and discusses the study procedure and the qualitative methodology I used to gather and interpret data on inmate and staff experiences.

Chapters 3 through 10 are the heart of the book and provide the results of my site observations and in-depth interviews. Chapter 3 addresses the inmate transition into custody, the influence of the inmate code, and adaptation to prison more generally. In Chapter 4, the primary inmate frame is further developed and the decline of the inmate code is examined in detail. I also delineate how the inmate frame has affected relations with COs and describe the motivators that guide relations with family, friends, and other outsiders.

Chapter 5 discusses the CO's transition into the institution and the preliminary fabrication of the CO frame. Chapter 6 examines more closely the framing of inmate–CO relations in Canadian correctional institutions as well as how procedural justice practices influence COs' legitimacy in the eyes of offenders. Interaction between COs and inmates has long been encouraged in corrections; is progress in this being made? Chapter 7 attempts to answer this question by exploring trends in prison architecture, policy, and technology and whether they have changed inmate-CO relations. Chapter 8 addresses frame breaking by COs amidst various institutional changes over the past twenty-five years. I also consider the issue of boundary violations by COs in their relations with inmates, as well as the illegal and unreasonable use of force (and other forms of misconduct) by COs. The chapter concludes with a discussion of female COs in male inmate prisons.

Chapters 9 and 10 examine the perceived impact on inmates and staff of behavioural programs introduced in the 1980s and the emergence of prison gangs in the 1990s. I discuss the legitimacy of programs to inmates and outline the frames that guide offender conduct around other inmates and staff. The evolution of gangs in the 1990s, gang life in custody, and relations between gangs and other inmates and staff are reviewed. The Conclusion summarizes my key findings and identifies promising areas for policy development and future research.

1

Canadian Prisons and Their Problems

Early studies of prison life in the United States by sociologists presented a view of the prison as its own little world, a "total institution" that needed to be studied from the inside (Clemmer, 1940; Goffman, 1961; Irwin & Cressey, 1962; Sykes, 1958). This very internal focus changed with the publication of two seminal works in the late 1970s by sociologist John Jacobs and social historian Michel Foucault. In *Stateville*, his 1977 study of an Illinois prison, Jacobs charted how the autonomous, insular management of the old "big house" prisons in the Midwest had been irrevocably changed by social phenomena in the outside world such as civil rights and the emergence of street gangs. Foucault's (1977) sweeping historical analysis of the birth of prisons in the eighteenth century, *Discipline and Punish*, went even deeper. Foucault showed how the prison itself could be seen as part of a new strategy of social control by governments. When public spectacles of violence (e.g., corporal, capital punishment) appeared to be encouraging public insurrection rather than placating the masses, the dominant class began asserting its power through the use of knowledge instead. Emerging social sciences such as penology called for individuals to be resocialized through classification schemes (i.e., initial assessment of personal background), teaching of discipline (e.g., through daily prison routines), work, and penitence. The state sustained this by developing careful record-keeping systems. The prison was an important justification for records, but in the end was just one part of a record-keeping apparatus developed by government for schools, social services, and other areas, all of which placed most citizens under some form of monitoring.

Jacobs and Foucault, then, redirect investigators to consider the prison more broadly; yes/no surveys, drug tests, and counts of misconduct cannot tell us enough. Trends in race and gender relations, technological advances, and shifts in government policy all have implications for daily life in prisons. Thus, researchers need to contemplate the influence of external trends and events when attempting to understand the inner workings of the prison. In addition to these broad social shifts, important internal changes also need to be considered if we are to better understand the changed realities of prison life. For example, changes in technology such as the advent of computers may affect inmates and staff but this may be affected in turn by unwillingness to change or by limitations on use (because of security requirements).

Prisons in Canada: A Brief History

Indigenous Canadians practised forms of dispute resolution to deal with what today's society calls crimes. Former Crown prosecutor Rupert Ross has outlined that resolving conflicts between individuals as (opposed to punishment) was consistent with the world view of Canada's First Nations, which was based on mutuality, accommodation, and responsibility to community (Ross, 1996). European colonists brought with them a more individualistic ethos and introduced much harsher forms of penalty that mirrored punitive practices in their home countries (Carrigan, 1991; Young, 2013). Early French settlers used corporal and capital punishment, as did the English settlers who came later. Hanging, whipping, branding, and transportation (penal slavery) were meted out by authorities. In the late 1700s, Enlightenment scholars influenced political leaders to apply means other than death and overt violence to maintain social order (Carrigan 1991; Young, 2013). Foucault (1977) contends that the reduced use of capital and corporal punishment was a calculated move by elites to manage the masses, who were becoming increasingly unruly during public executions and other spectacles of gruesome physical punishment.

Like their counterparts in the United States and in the Western world more generally, Canadian politicians initially viewed prisons as a progressive intervention (Carrigan, 1991). The penitentiary in Kingston, Ontario, opened in 1835 under the Auburn system. That system, modelled on a prison in New York, emphasized penitence and required work and strict silence for most of the day. It was thought that silence and reflection would lead to penitence and reform. As was the case elsewhere (Rothman, 1971), Kingston was not open long before problems emerged there with over-crowding and with the institutional regime as a whole. This led to the Brown Commission (1849), the first investigation into Canadian prisons (but by no means the last). Its report drew a picture of overcrowding, overuse of corporal punishment (often in a vain effort to enforce silence), and feeble attempts at rehabilitation. Though the Brown Report had some impact on the prevalence of corporal punishment, that disciplinary meas-ure would remain on the books until 1972 (Young, 2013). The late nine-teenth and early twentieth centuries saw some promising reforms – for example, the Crofton system was introduced, which offered rewards to inmates as well as punishments. The former included the possibility of parole through the 1897 Ticket of Leave Act (Young 2013). These signs of progress did not persist, however.

After years of stability, the 1920s saw an increase in inmate populations and subsequent overcrowding and distress in Canada's penitentiaries. In 1938, after a series of riots and disturbances, the Archambault Commission (1938) released a report on the corrections system that criticized it for focusing too little on rehabilitation, using punishment excessively, and not granting incentives. A bit surprisingly, little came of these findings, except for easier access to visits and more recreation time (Young, 2013). Less positively, this report introduced the "medical" view of offenders, which posited that offenders were damaged as a result of difficult lives or poor socialization but could be "fixed" by proper diagnosis and treatment. Almost two decades later, the report of the Fauteux Commission (1956) emphasized rehabilitation as a guiding principle of corrections. This report generated more results than the previous ones: in the late 1950s and early 1960s a number of medium security prisons were built, an independent parole board was established, and staff training was expanded (Winterdyk & Weinrath 2013).

The entrenchment of the medical model in the 1950s and 1960s had its critics, who contended that it labelled individuals as "sick" and forced them to acknowledge deficiencies that perhaps did not exist. At the time, it was incumbent on inmates to admit problems and take treatment, or get limited privileges and no parole. Many offenders acknowledge their wrongdoing and want to serve their time and live pro-social lives on release. They see themselves as having made poor choices, but they do not see themselves as mentally ill – which the medical model requires them to do. This was one of the issues that led to the Ouimet Report (1969), one of the most influential documents ever issued by Canada's federal government on our correctional system. The report called for an earned remission system based on good behaviour; also, inmates would have the right to refuse treatment but could still work towards early release through positive performance. The same report called for shorter sentences and stronger inmate rights (Winterdyk & Weinrath, 2013). For inmates, the most significant result of the Ouimet Report was probably the introduction of mandatory release – that is, they would be released after serving two-thirds of their sentence for good behaviour, albeit under mandatory supervision for the final third of the sentence. This change is still in place, although it is now referred to as statutory release. In provincial systems, in which inmates serve no more than two years less a day, provincial authorities simply release inmates at the two-thirds point of the sentence, eschewing any form of supervision.

The Ouimet Report also argued for important changes that would directly impact provincial authorities, much more so than previous national commissions and reports. Besides shorter sentences, it called for the use of diversion at the front end of the justice process (e.g., withdrawn charges for community work or apology), greater use of probation, and intermediate sanctions such as halfway houses as alternatives to custody.

The reforms called for by government commissions have been implemented unevenly. Generally poor institutional conditions and misuse of authority are recurring issues. Some initiatives have had unintended consequences (Rothman, 1971, 1980; Young, 2013). An example already noted is the medical model of the 1950s and 1960s, which literally forced offenders to admit being "sick" and to take treatment in order to earn release.

Problematic Trends in Custody and the Conditions of Confinement

The use of custody seems to have increased over the past twenty-five years despite downwards trends in crime rates. This appears to be related strongly to federal government policy. Since 1992, the official crime rate has fallen, then stabilized (Figure 1.1). Using 1979 as a starting point, we find Canada's

FIGURE 1.1
Canadian crime rate per 100,000, 1979–2013

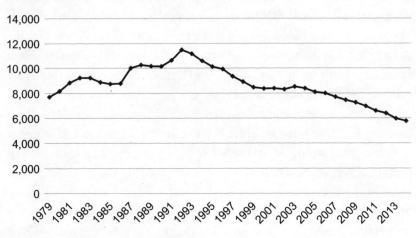

Source: Canadian Centre for Justice Statistics

police-recorded crime rate per 100,000 rose significantly during the 1980s, with a particularly marked increase in reported violent crime. In 1992, the rates for most crimes began to decrease, a welcome trend. In the first part of the twenty-first century, rates have generally continued to fall.[1] For instance, Statistics Canada data show that the overall crime rate declined 34 percent from 2004 to 2014, and the violent crime rate fell by 26 percent over the period (Boyce, 2015). Logically, incarceration rates should be tied to the crime rate, so we would expect the number of offenders in custody to have risen in the 1980s and to have declined after 1992. Contrary to this reasonable assumption, the Canadian adult inmate population has actually increased and stubbornly persisted at around 140 per 100,000, despite a clear decline in the crime rate (Figures 1.2 and 1.3).[2]

Canada's continued reliance on custody in the face of declining crime rates can be linked directly to more punitive laws. Conditional sentencing legislation was originally introduced by a Liberal federal government in 1996 with the expressed goal of reducing the number of people incarcerated.[3] This "intermediate sanction" provided judges with the opportunity to sentence low-risk offenders facing two years or less (provincial custody terms) to community supervision that included punitive

FIGURE 1.2

Canadian incarceration rate per 100,000, 1979–2013

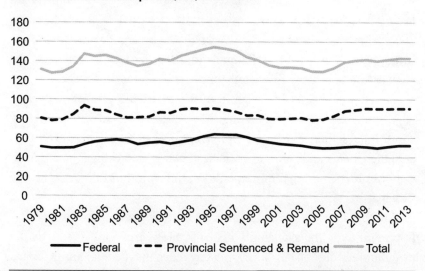

Source: Canadian Centre for Justice Statistics

FIGURE 1.3

Incarceration rate and crime rate, 1979–2013

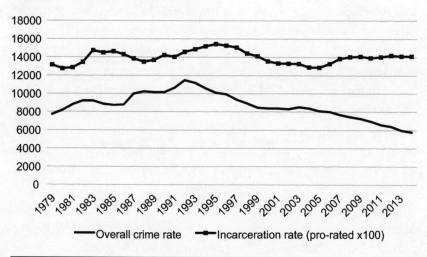

Source: Canadian Centre for Justice Statistics

elements such as curfews and community service. Criminologists Julian Roberts and Thomas Gabor found that conditional sentences contributed to a modest drop in the use of custody in the late 1990s (Roberts & Gabor, 2004). However, after a Conservative federal government came to power in the mid-2000s, things changed. In 2009, by way of Bill C-9, the Conservatives sharply restricted conditional sentences for serious personal injury offences, which significantly reduced the number of offences eligible for conditional sentencing. They followed this up by eliminating conditional sentences for non-violent offences such as theft over $5,000, auto theft, break and enter, and drug trafficking (trafficking is now subject to minimum sentence requirements) in the Omnibus Bill C-10 (Justice Canada, 2011).

But tougher sentencing is only part of the equation. For "in-counts" to remain high, the availability of "back end" early release (e.g., parole or temporary absence options) must also decline. Federal parole board decisions under the Conservatives and a greater reluctance on the part of provincial authorities to grant early releases for inmates also help explain Canada's continued high use of custody. This certainly seems to be true federally – full parole grant rates declined from 43 to 29 percent between 2000 and 2012–13 (Statistics Canada, 2014). There is also evidence that provincial corrections departments have become more punitive. Provincial parole boards in Ontario and Quebec have also reduced their grant rates – the number of inmates on parole declined 21 percent from 2003 to 2013. British Columbia eliminated its provincial parole board in 2007, requiring inmates in that province to apply to the federal National Parole Board (NPB), now the Parole Board of Canada. It takes six months for federal staff to process an inmate application, which means that inmates serving nine months or less cannot be meaningfully processed (provincial inmates generally get one-third of their sentence taken off as earned remission, euphemistically referred to as "good time"). It is not well known that provinces like Alberta and Manitoba reduced their use of temporary absences (a form of provincial parole) in the 1990s. Alberta has reduced its temporary absence pre-release program from a peak of 1,000 to an average of 100 today, while Manitoba releases inmates at the two-thirds point of their sentences, giving inmates statutory earned remission only (Alberta Solicitor General, interview with author, 2008).

It is now more difficult to be released early from provincial or federal corrections.

Further evidence of more retributive sentiment is evident in the work of the Correctional Service Review Panel (CSRP). Convened by the federal Conservatives soon after they came to power, this blue ribbon committee delivered a report that recommended more restrictive policies. The authors selectively presented Criminal Code statistics from a one-year period to suggest that violent crime was on the upswing (incorrect) and that federal penitentiaries were not doing enough to discourage recidivism (Review Panel, 2007).[4] Among its more controversial recommendations, the CSRP proposed to eliminate statutory release at two-thirds of sentence based on good behaviour. The panel was not at all clear as to how this remission plan might be implemented, which was unfortunate, because it holds huge implications for increases in the federal inmate population. Statutory release inmates numbered 3,447 per day in 2012–13, so housing even a proportion of that group for longer than two-thirds of sentence would necessitate a number of costly new federal prisons. Because parole is now harder to get, statutory releases have trended up – there was a whopping 39 percent jump from 2003 to 2013.[5]

Prisons were only one facet of the justice system that the Conservative government wanted to impact. Tough-on-crime and victims' rights rhetoric infused its political agenda and this in turn drove its justice legislation. More incarceration – an expensive and intrusive application of the justice system – undoubtedly resulted from Bill C-10, the Safe Cities and Communities Act. Conservative politicians are known for their fiscal prudence, yet the Conservatives proceeded with Bill C-10 despite cautions from the Parliamentary Budget Office that the costs of imprisonment would rise. There was some push-back from provincial governments, which had come to realize that the burden and costs of greater incarceration had fallen mostly on them (PBO, 2012).

Overcrowding had become an issue for provincial jails by the time this study was conducted. With the rise in remands, correctional institutions were double-bunking, triple-bunking, and even converting gymnasiums to dormitories to accommodate inmates. British Columbia reported that its facilities were 59 percent over capacity in 2011 (2,700 inmates for 1,692 cells), and in 2010 the Saskatchewan ombudsman warned of excessive overcrowding in the provincial system, where institutions were 65 percent over capacity (Global News, 2010; *Globe and Mail*, 2011). The federal growth rate has been slower, but by 2014 the inmate count had surpassed 15,000 and 20 percent of inmates were being double-bunked (Sapers, 2014). The rise in inmate numbers is even more difficult to accept when one considers the decline in the crime rate.

The Remand Phenomenon

Longer sentences and fewer early releases are a looming crisis for Canada's prisons, but there is another significant (albeit largely unnoticed) problem: more inmates in Canada are now serving time under more difficult cir-cumstances. Statistics Canada data show that Canada has experienced a phenomenal (and lamentable) increase in the pre-trial detention population over the past twenty-five years (Porter and Calverley, 2011; Statistics Canada, 2015).

Remanded accused – that is, those charged but not found guilty – are placed in high-security detention to await their trial or sentence. Because remand centres are maximum security facilities,[6] the accused are typ-ically confined to their unit, have no work opportunities, and usually get an hour a day for recreation (or less in some cases). The only pro-gramming provided might be educational upgrading or religious coun-selling, often delivered by volunteers. Sentenced offenders, by contrast, are assigned to a serving correctional facility, and once there staff work with them to develop a release plan. On a day-to-day basis they have greater access to recreation, programs, work opportunities, and move-ment around the institution. The irony is, of course, that remand inmates have not actually been convicted of anything, yet they must endure worse living conditions and greater uncertainty than sentenced (found or pled guilty) inmates.

Between 1979 and 2013, provincial custody totals increased by about 82 percent, from 13,458 to 24,506 (see Figure 1.4). What is most remarkable about this is the shift in the proportion of remand inmates; from 23 percent (about a quarter) to 55 percent (over half) (Statistics Canada, 2014). In other words, one in four provincial inmates was on remand previously, and now it is one in two! Statistics Canada data indicate that, in many provinces, the proportion of pre-trial cases exceeds 60 percent and is often

FIGURE 1.4

Canadian incarceration rates, daily counts, 1979–2013

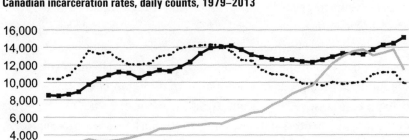

Source: Canadian Centre for Justice Statistics

close to 70 percent. This cannot be viewed as a positive development for inmates. Time in a remand unit is time away from working in the community or at least being involved in employment or treatment of some sort. At a remand centre, less time is spent off the unit, and work or treatment programs are much less accessible.

Among the explanations proffered for this shift in corrections populations, I consider only three very plausible (Beattie, 2006). First, the large increase in charges related to the administration of justice is a likely factor. Such charges are not for offences that are predatory in nature (like theft or assault); usually, they are for curfew breaches, failure to appear in court, or violations of non-contact domestic orders. In a Statistics Canada study, it was shown that these violations (breaches of the court's trust) are more likely to result in detention until trial (Taillon, 2006). Second, the entrenchment of "two for one" credit for remand time at point of sentence probably does influence some accused and/or their lawyers to delay their trial as long as they can for "extra credit," although this practice has been exaggerated by police and policy-makers (Weinrath, 2009a). The only official data related to this trend is an increase in the number of "time served" charges (Johnson, 2003). In surveys I conducted in 2006 of pre-trial cases at Headingley

Correctional Centre, I found that although some accused do delay, most inmates want to get their trials done with. They contended that it was actually the Crown that delayed, often offering last-minute two-for-one deals to avoid trial (Weinrath, 2009a). The two-for-one argument also loses appeal when we consider that remands have increased in other countries, despite there being either one-for-one credit or no credit for pre-trial detention (Manson, 2004; Roberts, 2005; Walmsley, 2014). If pre-trial detention is up in other nations, surely there must be other forces at work. Finally, this hypothesis looked even less probable after the Conservative government passed legislation to make credit generally one-for-one for remand time in 2011. Remand rates remain high, discrediting the notion that two-for-one was ever a driver of pre-trial detention (Statistics Canada, 2014; *R. v. Summers*, 2014). Note also that the government is out of step with the judiciary's view: the Supreme Court of Canada recently ruled in *R. v. Summers* that remand time is "hard time" and endorsed discretion by judges when it came to applying pre-trial credit.

The most likely explanation for Canada's increase in remands is the most straightforward one: it takes longer to get to trial now than it used to, which results in longer remands. Official data show that the mean total of days for case completion soared from 121 to 215 between 1994 and 2004 – a 77 percent increase. In addition, the number of cases exceeding eight months more than doubled, from 13 to 27 percent (Taillon, 2006). Clearly, longer trial delays result in longer remands (Boyce, 2013).

The upward spiral in remands has led to more onerous living conditions. More inmates are being housed in facilities that lack regular programming and recreation, and even those sentenced with some enhanced credit for "time served" must endure a dull and ominous day-to-day existence. Criminologist Jason Demers (2014) outlined the human costs of remand and crowding in Saskatchewan, providing qualitative data collected from a number of Saskatchewan federal and provincial correctional institutions. Prison overcrowding has a negative impact on programs as gymnasiums and classrooms are converted into housing areas. And the programs that are still offered tend to be superficial. According to Demers, inmates also reported that health care, food services, and basic needs were impaired by overcrowding.

Status of the Inmate Code of Conduct

In the twentieth century, American sociologists journeyed into prisons to conduct fieldwork, spending time observing and interviewing inmates and staff, and used their qualitative findings to construct several theories as to why correctional institutions had failed to markedly change inmate behaviour. These theories attempted to explain inmate adaptation to prison life. They all revolved around the notion of an inmate social system and how the related subcultural values that arose might hamper offender change and entrench pro-criminal attitudes (Clemmer, 1940; Goffman, 1961; Irwin & Cressey, 1962; Sykes, 1958; Sykes & Messinger, 1960).

Theories of deprivation and importation were developed largely between the late 1930s and early 1960s and remain popular to this day in the empirical work carried out by corrections scholars. Deprivation theory holds that prisons are negative places that inflict privations on inmates that generate mostly antisocial attitudes and behaviours, which form the basis for an oppositional inmate subculture (Clemmer, 1940; Goffman, 1961; Sykes, 1958). This tends to support the proposition that custodial facilities make offenders worse. Importation theory, by contrast, posits that individuals who enter prison by and large already possess criminal attitudes and values (Irwin & Cressey, 1962; Irwin, 1970; Jacobs, 1977; Mears, Stewart, Siennick, & Simons, 2013). The inmate social system and its related predatory, oppositional behaviours simply reflect a pre-existing offender subculture (Anderson, 1999). These theorists conclude that prisons have little or no effect on inmates. While holding different central premises, these theories share the view that the inmate subculture limits the ability of institutions to benefit inmates or help them improve.

The "convict code" is a codified form of the rules of the inmate subculture. Summarizing the various studies reviewed above – but with particular emphasis on Gresham Sykes and Sheldon Messinger – the convict code breaks down into rules around status, appropriate behaviour, and rules for maintaining mutual respect:

Status

- Inmates who are tough, smart, and discreet in their dealings are respected in the prison. They are often referred to as "solid" or "stand-up guys."

- Inmates who commit more serious violent crimes have more status (murder, then bank robbery).
- Inmates who are new have less status (fresh "fish").
- Informants or "rats" rank near the bottom of the inmate hierarchy and should be beaten or killed.
- Sex offenders or "skinners" are ranked at the bottom and should be beaten or killed. Among sex offenders, child molesters rank lowest.

Appropriate behaviour
- Do not talk to staff unless you have to.
- Oppose administration, or do not be agreeable to rules.
- Do not inform.
- Do your own time, and do not involve yourself in others' problems/concerns.
- Stand up for yourself, be strong, and don't be weak.
- Do not bring problems from the street (community) into prison with you. Conflicts on the street must be forgotten once incarcerated with others.

Mutual respect
- Do not stare at another inmate.
- Do not ask another inmate about their business.
- Do not look into another inmate's cell.
- Do not steal from another inmate.
- Do not call another inmate a "goof."
- Any fights between inmates are settled one-on-one.

For a "fish," the convict code provides an appropriate frame for structuring prison life.[7] A new inmate cannot change what he has been convicted of, but he should keep any record of sex offences or past informing quiet and show respect to inmates convicted of more serious violent offences. Being socially skilled, standing up for oneself, not appearing weak – all of these are important attributes to display, and an inmate who is effective at these will move up in the offender hierarchy. For a new inmate who is unsure what to do, an important lesson is to say nothing and do not trouble one's colleagues by looking at them or in their cells. Other rules of the convict code offer a sound logic for a group of men confined by others who wish to get along. Do not talk to the correctional staff, do not inform on other inmates, do not be overly cooperative, and avoid unnecessarily antagonizing anyone (Clemmer, 1940; Sykes, 1958).

Empirical work has tended to focus on comparing the importation and deprivation models (or integrated models) regarding their ability to predict inmate misconduct (Cao, Zhao, & VanDine, 1997; Dhami, Ayton, & Loewenstein, 2007; Thomas, 1977). The inmate subculture as a social system had been given less attention, reflecting the general disparity between quantitative and qualitative work in corrections research. There has been less qualitative work on the convict code; even so, a body of it has accumulated in the United States (Faulkner & Faulkner, 1997; Hassine, 1999; Hunt, Riegel, Morales, & Waldorf, 1993; Irwin, 1980; Trammell, 2009), Canada (Cooley, 1992; Ricciardelli, 2014a; Ricciardelli & Moir, 2013) and Britain (Crewe, 2005a, 2005b). Generally, this body of work has shown the code to be in decline, and a lesser influence on the day-to-day social organization of inmates.

Convict criminologist John Irwin wrote about the convict code's influence on inmate life, suggesting that it perhaps improved rather than harmed the quality of life behind bars. In his view, the rules governing inmates seemed to favour the strong; but at the same time, many of those rules – be courteous, mind your own business, don't inform on others – seemed prudent in terms of helping men living in close quarters get along and avoid violence (Irwin, 1970). Alas, Irwin also observed that by 1980 the old hierarchy had collapsed in US prisons, and that whatever camaraderie had existed under the old normative structure had disappeared. Irwin spent considerable time as a researcher in California prisons and as a community advocate. In his view, the code's downfall was the result of changes in the inmate population. Those changes included an influx of state-raised youth – that is, individuals who had long histories with the California Youth Authority and were now "graduating" to adult prison, bringing with them highly predatory values that they had learned in the system that had raised them. Irwin (1980) also saw the onset of gangs in prison as contributing to inmates' greater self-interest and predation, as well as to a general lack of solidarity within adult prisons. Likewise, Hunt and his colleagues (1993) found in their interviews with recently released

California inmates in the 1990s that the growth of new prison gangs (some started within prisons) and influx of younger inmates had exerted a negative influence on inmate culture. The increase in gangs had led to an increase in the use of confidential informants by correctional officers (COs); also, the perceived threat from gangs had provided an impetus for staff to heighten security measures. More gangs meant more conflict. The younger admissions (the "Pepsi generation") tended to be more immature, as well as less likely to follow the code and/or to offer appropriate respect to other inmates; they were just not as "solid" or dependable as offenders in years gone by.

More recent California-based research by Rebecca Trammell (2009) involving forty interviews with recently released inmates and six COs revealed that offenders followed their own informal rules, which sometimes jibed with the inmate code, sometimes not. Traditional inmate norms of not informing and acting tough were still in vogue, but offenders who were in prison gangs also had to obey the gang leaders. Trammell concluded that efforts by prison gang leaders to avoid most violence and maintain peace were motivated by their own interest in making money, but they also served the interests of the administration. In some situations, COs would actually work with inmate leaders to maintain institutional order. This diverges somewhat from Hunt and his colleagues' findings that gangs appeared more undisciplined; but note that Trammell's findings were from twenty years later.

Similar findings about the decline of the code have been reported in other parts of the United States. In their interviews with maximum security inmates in a Midwestern prison, Faulkner and Faulkner (1997) found that some of the "traditional" subcultural rules continued to exist (stand up for yourself, be smart, do your own time, don't be a snitch), but that, overall, the code had been eroded. For example, inmates were less likely to enforce prohibitions against informing, and violence was no longer required in all situations involving conflict. Staff and inmates attributed this to security improvements such as the elimination of inmate trusteeships (inmates having authority over other inmates), more restricted movement, and increased use of cell lock-up for misconduct. Research from the eastern United States likewise downplays the influence of a code. Providing an inmate's perspective from a Pennsylvania maximum security institution, the late Victor Hassine (1999), a convict criminologist, wrote that he never observed a true inmate code among his peers. Instead, he saw inmates bringing in their own street code of behaviour and using it to justify victimizing other inmates.

US research suggests that the social organization function of the convict code has weakened. This may in part be due to changing inmate profiles, but it is likely also due to efforts by correctional staff. In California, prison gangs appeared to exert some type of order, at least to control violence, but that control seemed to be directed mainly at their own members (note that most inmates are not in gangs). There is little evidence in the United States of an inmate culture that promotes oppositional views and activities against the administration. Sadly, there is even less evidence in US prisons of any inmate ethos that encourages group solidarity. Proscriptions against informing still appear to be in place but are often not followed.

Ben Crewe (2005a, 2005b) has done the most significant qualitative work in Britain. He spent ten months conducting a semi-ethnographic study of a medium security facility in the United Kingdom. He found that the inmates, although knowledgeable about the inmate code, tended to follow its rules in some situations and not in others. His respondents reported that the code had waned over the years. They attributed this to improvements in the prison environment (better living conditions, television and video games to relieve boredom) that had reduced some of the pains of imprisonment. He also observed that drug use had contributed to more stealing and less trust. Drugs (i.e., the obsession with obtaining them) and the resultant drug-related debts had contributed to an uneasy environment. Finally, the prison's use of an earned incentive system had placed pressure on inmates to cooperate with staff. That system involved COs in the ongoing assessment of inmates, and their evaluations strongly influenced security reduction and early release. To earn credit from COs, inmates were more likely to violate two of the fundamental tenets of the inmate code – specifically, they were more willing to inform on others and to tolerate the presence of sex offenders in the general population. Informing was still frowned upon, but even if someone was suspected, inmates generally did not make an issue of it unless the case was egregious. Likewise, no one took "formal" action against sex offenders in their midst, so as not to jeopardize their own release status.

Crewe found a significant shift in relations between staff and inmates: there was much more dialogue between the two groups and more amiable relations generally. In times past, this would have been against the code, and frowned upon; frequent conversations with COs would likely have led to accusations of informing on other inmates. He attributed this change to the hiring of younger prison officers, and to the role of COs in the earned incentive scheme, which compelled more interaction between the two groups.

Crewe described the solidarity between inmates as limited. Offenders' primary loyalty was to themselves, and if they did something for another inmate, payback was generally expected. However, he found limited aspects of community on a lifers wing and on a wing for drug-addicted inmates (Crewe, 2005a, 2005b).

Canadian scholars have also noted a decline in the power of the inmate code. In 1993, Dennis Cooley surveyed 117 inmates in five western Canadian federal penitentiaries as part of a study on prison violence. He found that a formal code did not exist; what rules did exist were "informal" rather than carefully policed. Like Crewe, he found the application of those rules to be situational: sometimes they were complied with, sometimes not, and whether they were or not depended on what an individual or group would gain from adherence to them. Cooley also pointed out the contradictions within many of the rules as "codified" by Sykes and Messinger (1960). For example, "do your own time," "be tough," and "don't rat" will result in a victimized inmate not seeking assistance and hence being at risk of further predations. Showing respect for all inmates is difficult over time, and the use of violence to enforce this principle contributed to conflict between inmates. Cooley found that most inmates were concerned only for themselves and expressed very little solidarity, if any. Some of this was blamed on the increased use of informants – something also reported in the United States and Britain.

In British Columbia, Curt Griffiths and Danielle Murdoch (2014) referenced the opinion of Canadian prison managers to suggest that an influx of more state-raised young inmates had contributed to the decline of the inmate code. "State-raised inmates" refers to offenders raised primarily in social service settings. This typically means being taken from their families by social services, then placed in foster homes, group homes, or institutional settings. These young inmates are viewed as living by few rules and as engaging in selfish and violent actions.

More recently, Rose Ricciardelli (2014a, 2014b) interviewed fifty-six ex-inmates from Ontario federal penitentiaries, and updated the inmate code around what she concluded was a riskier prison environment. She gleaned from her respondents that six principles of the code were still prominent: do not "rat," do not get friendly with staff, be dependable (not loyal), follow daily behaviour rules, do not interact or comment on day-to-day activities (do your own time), and be fearless (tough). She reported that there was some contact between COs and inmates but that this was guarded (don't talk for too long). Respect (or no disrespect) was an important feature of day-to-day life, as was paying one's drug debts. She indicated a heavy emphasis on enforcing inmate code violations around informing, although some of her findings appear to contradict Cooley's observations in western Canada and those reported in other jurisdictions.

Like others, Ricciardelli described an inmate society that is individualistic in nature. She found that inmates interpret the code in such a way as to ensure their own safety. Unlike others, however, her findings suggest that inmates often use violence to enforce the rules of the code. In contrast, Cooley, Crewe, and Hassine found that rule enforcement was used selectively, if at all, while Trammell reported that inmate leaders often negotiated over whether violence needed to occur. Ricciardelli couched her research around the relationship between the code and violence, and her inclusion of a disproportionate number of sex offenders may have resulted in a greater emphasis in her study on violence and lack of inmate safety.

To summarize, recent research in the United States, Britain, and Canada suggests that the force of the inmate code has declined, and so has the influence and potential benefits of an inmate subculture. Inmates appear to be more self-interested than in the past, and there appears to be greater discord among inmates. The reasons for this may well relate to the changing profile of inmate admissions (younger, less socially skilled), a more active drug trade, the presence of prison gangs, and administrative changes in security, such as greater use of informants and more active communication between inmates and staff. I have not considered the increase in inmates struggling with mental health problems, although that likely has had an impact as well (Brown, Hirdes, & Fries, 2015; Sapers, 2013). While there are differences between jurisdictions and even between prisons, there have clearly been changes.

Problems in Custody

Whether you are an inmate or a CO, a prison can be a difficult place to spend time, perhaps now more than ever. New admissions are more violent and have longer criminal histories; violence and drugs continue to be problems. Prison gangs are using violence and intimidation to try to monopolize the drug trade and gain greater control of institutions; this poses a danger to both inmates and staff. Inmate assaults and injuries are on the rise (Sapers, 2014; Review Panel, 2007).

Since the 1990s, offenders coming into the federal system have posed greater management problems (Review Panel, 2007). Empirical data and the qualitative impressions of Correctional Service of Canada managers indicate that inmates have become more difficult to manage and to prepare for release (Boe, Nafekh, Vuong, Sinclair, & Cousineau, 2003). In 1997, 14 percent of male admissions were to maximum security; in 2002, 21 percent. Around one inmate in six is now gang-affiliated; in some institutions, prison gang membership runs as high as 36 percent. Inmates are now more likely to have been incarcerated in the past in provincial or youth facilities. About 23 percent of federal inmates are now lifers, serving for homicide. This increase reflects the cumulative impact of the 1976 legislative change to 25-year minimum sentences for first degree murder (in exchange, capital punishment was abolished), and the 10-year minimum for second degree murder. The Canadian homicide rate has actually gone down substantially since 1992 (Mahoney, 2011), but the sheer number of 10- or 25-year minimum sentences has raised the proportion of lifers.

Violence

An important area to appraise for change over the past twenty-five years in Canada is violence and illicit drug use in institutions. For various reasons, this is difficult to do with any accuracy. What is available in the literature are journalists' perceptions of violence, inmate autobiographies, and the qualitative narratives of researchers. Only recently has the federal government decided to provide annual data on inmate and staff assaults. Illicit drug use is being tracked federally, and recently has showed some decline. There is more evidence that a long shadow has been cast over Canada's federal and provincial correctional institutions by the increasing presence of prison gangs. A fair-sized literature has grown around prison gangs in North America and, more recently, in Canada.

Journalists Kevin Marron and Michael Harris wrote books about Canada's federal institutions. They visited penitentiaries and interviewed staff, inmates, and their family and friends. They attempted to portray violence as a deadly fact of inmate life (Harris, 2003; Marron, 1996). Harris, who completed his book just into the new millennium, found violence still prevalent. Harris focused on the threat of violence towards staff and, not surprisingly, tended to quote heavily from his staff informants (for a critique of Harris's book, see Jackson, 2004). Canadian inmate autobiographies have informed us that prisoners must be aggressive and at least look like they're ready to fight. Former inmate and notorious escape artist Wayne Carlson (2001) indicated that he tried to demonstrate a violent nature to establish himself when first incarcerated in the 1960s. Likewise, lawyer Julius Melnitzer (1995) reported becoming an aggressor over time within the prison system. Both prisoners viewed fighting as most often avoidable if an inmate was careful in his dealings with others. Carlson viewed violence as something a shrewd inmate avoided, even in the super-maximum Marion prison in the United States. After being raised to medium security because of a fight and other issues, Melnitzer felt that it was his own improvement in getting along with others that enabled him to avoid further problems, even in a higher-security setting with (presumably) more difficult inmates.

Tracking rates of institutional violence over time is essential if we are to assess whether the situation is worsening, improving, or stable. For administrators, such tracking allows the development of benchmarks to assess individual prisons and how well they are managing their populations. Regrettably, provincial authorities do not release institutional assault statistics, while annual official rates of inmate-on-inmate and -staff assaults have only recently been generated by the Correctional

Service of Canada. CSC had been reluctant to track this information, reportedly due to concerns about consistency in definitions between institutions.

CSC began providing more data on inmate assaults on staff, inmate–inmate assaults, and inmate assaults resulting in injury in the early 2000s. From 2003 to 2011, inmate assaults on staff fell from 3.1 to 1.92 per 100 inmates per year – that is, by about one-third (Figure 1.5). Similarly, staff injuries from those assaults declined from a rate of 0.80 percent in 2003 to 0.35 percent per year in 2011; that is, injuries were cut by about half. Things were not so positive for inmates, however. Inmate–inmate assaults doubled from 2.4 to 4.96 per 100 inmates, and assault-related injuries also increased twofold, from 2.3 to 4.65. Official reports of violence are increasing. The federal Correctional Investigator has expressed alarm about this increase in inmate violence and injuries (Sapers, 2014). He is also concerned about the increasing presence of incompatibles and the use of administrative custody for inmates who feel threatened in population. Incompatibles are inmates who cannot remain in population because of conflicts with other inmates who would be likely to use violence to resolve past grievances. Administrative segregation – essentially, placement in an

FIGURE 1.5
Federal institutional violence, 2003–11

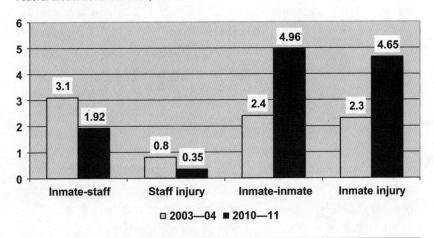

Source: Correctional Service of Canada annual reports

isolated cell under twenty-three-hour lock-up – was felt by the correctional investigator to be overused when dealing with incompatibles and other situations.

A general problem in assessing the validity of police-recorded crime is non-reporting; not every offence is reported by citizens (Boyce, 2015). Non-reporting is also a problem in assessing the scope of institutional violence. This problem is likely exacerbated by the inmate subcultural emphasis on not informing. Self-report studies, as expected, do indeed reveal higher rates of violence. In the 1995 national federal inmate survey, 26 percent of respondents reported that they had been assaulted in the prior year (Robinson, 1996). Just before this, Dennis Cooley (1993) conducted a self-report victimization survey of inmates in five medium/maximum penitentiaries and found that 34 percent of inmates had been assaulted in some way over the past year. Given that the 1995 survey included lower-risk minimum security inmates and that Cooley's work was confined to higher-risk medium and maximum penitentiaries, the two survey violence rates are likely quite comparable.

Unfortunately, little can be said about provincial correctional institutions and their violence rates, because these organizations do not release data and academic studies are unavailable; researchers investigating violence in Canadian prisons generally have been confined to federal penitentiary studies.

Illicit Drugs

Drugs are linked to problems in prison life (Review Panel, 2007). For some inmates, drug use in institutional settings continues a negative cycle of addiction. Competition over the drug market, the risks involved in moving contraband into and within a custody setting, and debts incurred to maintain a drug habit through internal or external sources inevitably lead to violence. Drug use in prisons shakes confidence in the correctional system; intuitively, one would assume that a medium security provincial or federal prison regime could keep drugs out, but empirical studies and CSC's own urinalysis regime show that high security does not keep illicit substances out.

Very little is known about drug use in provincial correctional facilities, but some studies have been done within the federal system. The

1995 federal national survey stands as one of the more helpful portraits of the national situation with respect to drug use in penitentiaries. Regarding the control of drug distribution inside, 25 percent of inmates believed that inmates were "under a lot of pressure" to smuggle drugs into their institutions. About 32 percent of inmates believed that the urinalysis program in institutions had resulted in a slight decrease in drug use; 55 percent believed that the program had had no effect; 13 percent felt that a large *increase* in drug use was associated with the introduction of the program.

Drugs were observed to be a problem by the CSC Review Committee (Review Panel, 2007) and targeted as an area demanding attention. Interdiction methods have included cell searches, inmate searches after visits, monitoring of visits, use of glass-partitioned visits where drug smuggling is suspected, ion scanning of visitors' driver's licences to catch drug traces prior to allowing entry, drug-sniffing dogs, monitoring of fence "throw-overs," and intelligence-based activities, including liaison with the RCMP and other police agencies. Urinalysis has been introduced provincially and federally. Within correctional facilities, inmates can involve themselves in drug treatment programs, and some federal and provincial institutions offer methadone maintenance programs. Around the time of my study, drug-free units with voluntary urinalysis were being introduced in institutions such as Stony Mountain in Manitoba. In the United States, James Inciardi and his colleagues (1993) survey of inmates in treatment found that visitors and staff were the most common point of entry for drugs.

Recent federal urinalysis data show a promising downward trend. Refusals of drug tests (a probable admission of guilt) have declined from 12.5 to 7.2 percent nationwide. Furthermore, over the same period, positive tests have been reduced from 13.3 to 6.5 percent (CSC, 2014). These are substantial declines and give some credence to the purported effectiveness of CSC interdiction efforts. On the other hand, these results may also indicate that inmates have figured out better ways to mask drug use.

Prison Gangs

The increased presence and influence of prison gangs, especially in prairie correctional institutions, is a concern for correctional staff and inmates.

As street gangs became a serious problem in American cities, so too they became a problem in prisons. James Jacobs (1974) linked the rise of violence in Illinois's Stateville prison to the arrival and organization of ethnic street gangs such as the Overlords and the Black Disciples. John Irwin, who wrote about the presence of an often benign thief subculture in California prisons in the 1950s and 1960s, saw his old "con culture" disappear in the 1970s and 1980s after an influx of African American state-raised youth and Black and Hispanic street/prison gangs (Irwin, 1980). Into the 1990s, California prison gangs became younger (and more violent), heavily influenced by California's Blood and Crips, and Le Neustra and Le Nortes (Hunt et al., 1993). Robert Fong (1990) and others have charted how prison gangs emerged in a big way in Texas.

Prison gangs tend to be associated with importation models of inmate adjustment – in other words, street gangs are incarcerated and become prison gangs. Salvador Buentello and his colleagues have described how prisons can spawn their own in-house gangs, which later continue their business on the streets (Buentello, Fong, & Vogel, 1991). The evolution of prison gangs has been linked to the deprivation model of inmate adjustment. Because of the threat of violence within the institution posed by other inmates or gangs, inmates band together for self-protection; that "band" then evolves into a predatory entity. The successful group gains control over the hidden inmate economy, trading in drugs and other contraband. Having succeeded in the prison, the gang continues its activities in the community as inmates are released and begin outside operations. In Texas, for example, inmates formed the Texas Syndicate initially as a self-protection group to fend off other prison gangs. They grew in numbers and organization to the point that they became a predatory prison gang in their own right. The Syndicate eventually expanded its criminal operations onto the street (Fong, 1990).

Prison gangs are also referred to as security threat groups (STGs) (Fong & Vogel, 1994–95). STGs can be any group of three or more inmates banded together for negative purposes; however, they need not be a formal or even informal gang. Prison gangs are extremely aggressive, work to control the trade in drugs and contraband, and prey on other inmates. They tend to behave more negatively towards staff (DeLisi, Berg, & Hochstetler, 2004; Gaes et al., 2002; Griffin & Hepburn, 2006; Zaitzow & Houston, 1999).

American gangs, of course, may not always translate to the Canadian situation, so let's consider the local literature. Street gangs and criminal organizations first emerged in Canada's provincial and correctional institutions in a big way in the 1990s, and their threat has escalated as they have recruited more members (Grant & Ruddell, 2011; Hughes, 1996; Weinrath, Swait, & Markesteyn, 1999). Prison is a place where recruits are found for later entry into street crime organizations (Kelly & Caputo, 2005). Federally, the number of admissions with gang affiliation has been increasing, from 12 percent in 1997 to 17 percent in 2009 – almost one in five (Grant & Ruddell, 2011). Federal prison gang members have been found to be affiliated with outlaw motorcycle gangs, traditional organized crime gangs, Aboriginal street gangs, and Asian gangs (Ruddell & Gottschall, 2011). CSC found that Canadian trends in immigration were reflected in the membership of prison gangs, especially with regard to members with Black or Southeast Asian heritage. Past studies have found that prison gang members tend to be younger and more violent and involved more in assaultive behaviour and possession of drugs (Nafekh, 2002; Ruddell & Gottschall, 2011).

Aboriginal prison gangs are a particular problem in federal and provincial facilities in the prairie provinces (Alberta Solicitor General, interview with author, 2008; Grekul & LaBoucane-Benson, 2006; Nafekh, 2002; Weinrath, Swait, & Markesteyn, 1999). In Manitoba, for example, Headingley Correctional Centre and Stony Mountain Institution both reported that 30 to 35 percent of their inmate populations had a gang affiliation, although some members were not Aboriginal. African immigrant gangs have also become a concern (Weinrath, 2009b). In a CSC study, Mark Nafekh (2002) found nationally that about 7 percent of all Aboriginal inmates were affiliated with gangs. Comparing under–twenty-five Aboriginal gang members to other under–twenty-five Aboriginal inmates, he found that prison gang members were more likely to live in a criminogenic area, to have criminal associates, and to have little or no employment history. They were also more likely to be hostile and aggressive and to have negative attitudes towards law enforcement. Jana Grekul and Patricia LaBoucane-Benson (2006) conducted qualitative interviews with Aboriginal gang members and concluded that these groups' origins appeared to reflect structural inequalities in Canadian society. Discrimination and ruptured families resulted in some Aboriginal youth seeking out a gang for social support.

In Canadian institutions, we are still dealing with long-standing problems of violence and drug use, in addition to newer problems such as increased use of remand, the emergence of incompatible inmates, and the rise of prison gangs. The weakening of the inmate code poses a bit of a puzzle: Is the lack of inmate solidarity a positive or negative in institutional life? Does it reduce the likelihood of violence and promote positive change?[8]

Signs of Progress

The Advent of the Rule of Law

The Canadian Penitentiary Service (now Correctional Service of Canada, CSC) was rocked by violent riots and disturbances in the early and mid-1970s that left many inmates injured and two inmates and one staff dead. This shook public confidence in the federal corrections system (Jackson, 2002). The resulting reforms would change the system irrevocably. Corporal punishment in prisons was abolished in 1972. In 1973 the Office of the Correctional Investigator was founded, whose task would be to investigate inmates' concerns and advocate for them. Capital punishment was abolished in 1976. In 1977, the Canadian Human Rights Act gave inmates the right to access some of the file information maintained on them. Inmates and their lawyer advocates became more active in opposing the capricious exercise of administrative power in federal and provincial institutions. This culminated in the seminal Supreme Court decision *Martineau v. Matsqui Institution Interdisciplinary Board* (1980), which compelled correctional agencies to apply the "duty to act fairly" principle into their daily operations (Jackson, 2002). *Solosky v. The Queen* (1980) was another landmark decision insofar as it established that inmates retained their civil rights while in prison and that institutional authorities had to manage them in the least restrictive manner necessary.

The disturbances of the 1970s also led to a federal standing committee being formed, the MacGuigan Commission, to investigate Canada's penitentiaries. Its report, tabled in 1977, attributed some of the violence to poor staff–inmate relations and an absence of the rule of law. It advocated the construction of newer-style prisons where more interactive, dynamic supervision of inmates would be possible. It also recommended more programs (suggested previously in the 1971 Mohr Report). It recommended that staff adhere to the rule of law and apply procedural fairness rather than the arbitrary exercise of authority. It called for an effective system of inmate grievances to be established, to provide inmates with a channel to complain through the institution to regional headquarters and finally to external bodies such as the Correctional Investigator. All of these recommendations – rule of law, interactive inmate management, more sophisticated behavioural programs, and better complaint mechanisms (e.g., inmate committees) – would be introduced in Canadian correctional institutions over the next twenty-five years.

Other appellate court decisions asserted the right of inmates to seek judicial remedy if they felt they had been unfairly placed in a more restrictive environment, such as administrative segregation or a Special Handling Unit (a restrictive high-security unit with no access to programming and limited time out of cell or off-unit). Then in the 1980s, independent adjudicators were required in all penitentiaries to hear institutional charges, rather than staff. Canada's Charter of Rights and Freedoms in 1982 provided further opportunities for inmates to apply to the courts for redress with regard to administrative actions in federal and provincial correctional institutions (Campbell, 1997). As well, the growth of provincial Ombudsman offices promoted more just relations within prisons (Ombudsman Office of Alberta, 1988; Tomkins, 2002). The federal Corrections and Conditional Release Act (CCRA) introduced by the federal government in 1992 further codified and recognized the rights of inmates, and also emphasized the duty of staff to act fairly.

After years of atrocious conditions and treatment in Kingston's Prison for Women (P4W), the *Creating Choices* report (Phelps & Diamond, 1990) was hailed as a great step forward for female offenders. The report's authors affirmed that corrections should apply a women-centred focus to the management of female offenders, one that acknowledged the past victimization of most female inmates. The same report recommended the closure of P4W, and led to the building of five regional women's prisons in the 1990s, based on next-generation unit architecture.

On the surface, the CSC seemed to have made much progress in the early 1990s. Imagine the dismay of officials when, shortly after the above changes were announced, one of the most damning incidents in CSC history occurred. At the old P4W in 1994, a disturbance by female inmates escalated into violence. After the inmates were segregated by staff, they attempted suicide by slashing themselves, and later took a hostage. The warden ordered a male emergency response team to subdue the inmates, who were then strip-searched (including cavity searches) and put in gowns and restraints. The inmates complained about excessive and rough treatment by staff, but CSC denied it, and announced that it had "unfortunately lost" a videotape of the event involving the CO response team. The videotape was subsequently "found" and generally validated the complaints of the women. This led to a Royal Commission headed by Justice Louise Arbour, whose landmark report lambasted the CSC and identified a staff culture "unconcerned" about human rights (Arbour, 1996).

Other observers doubt whether various accountability measures have succeeded. Legal activist Michael Jackson (2002) has been involved in Canada's prisons for the better part of four decades, lobbying for the rule of law and some semblance of due process rights for inmates. Based on his own involvement in BC prisons (sometimes working with prison author- ities and sometimes not), he has seen little change over time in the capri- cious exercise of coercive authority over inmates. For him, the early promise of the *Martineau* decision has not been borne out. For example, Section 7 of the Charter (on the right to life, liberty, and freedom) was used most frequently by inmates seeking relief through the courts, but Jackson found that they were most often stymied by Section 1 of the Charter, which limits rights "as can be demonstrably justified in a free and democratic society." For example, he noted that the courts have ruled that inmates do not have the same rights to privacy as other citizens (*Weatherall v. Canada (Attorney General)* 1993).

Areas of ongoing contention include the arbitrary placement of inmates in segregation and the involuntary transfer of inmates to other institutions. Jackson (2002) cites several examples from the 1990s in BC's federal penitentiaries of inmates being moved to segregation or trans- ferred on the basis of informants or inspired guesswork on the part of corrections management and staff. For Jackson, human rights for inmates have amounted to a triumph of rhetoric over reality. More recently, the suicide of Ashley Smith brought to light the poor job that federal corrections is doing in managing the mentally ill in segregated situations (Sapers, 2008). In his annual reports, the Correctional Investigator has continued to hammer away at the CSC for its overuse of segregation (Sapers, 2013, 2014).

Meanwhile, though, some observers have taken the view that inmates have *too many* rights and are not accountable, thus placing other inmates and staff at risk. In his investigation of Canada's federal prisons, reporter Michael Harris (2003) argued that the CSC administration cared little about staff safety. Having interviewed staff in federal prisons, Harris outlined instances of inmate disturbances and serious staff assaults where more concern existed for inmate rights than for staff safety. He related instances when staff who complained about a lack of safety equipment were intimidated by management. He also outlined a number of situations where he felt that serious and violent offenders had found it far too easy to obtain privileges, programs, and parole.

Direct Supervision (Dynamic Security)

Correctional systems in North America began looking to new forms of inmate management in the 1960s. The most popular innovation has been direct supervision (DS, sometimes referred to as dynamic security), originally introduced with the living unit system. This supervision style is closely linked to new-generation prison architecture. US juvenile corrections agencies experimented in the 1960s with smaller, cottage-style units, where staff could take a more therapeutic, interactive approach with young offenders (Levinson & Kitchener, 1966; Zupan, 1991). In the mid-1970s the US Federal Bureau of Prisons introduced three new living unit–style Metropolitan Correctional Centres; by 2000 there were 300 direct supervision facilities in the United States (Harding, Linke, Van Court, White, & Clem, 2001). Canadian policy-makers quickly picked up on the potential of DS to change prison practice for the better. The federal Mohr Report (1971) recommended the introduction of the living unit system in the penitentiary service, ostensibly to deal with violence and unrest and to "break down" the inmate subculture.

It seems, in Canada, that inmate violence has often been the driver behind the construction of living units. In the mid- and late 1970s, after the Mohr Report was tabled and while the MacGuigan Report was being written, new direct supervision federal penitentiaries were built in Canada. The provinces began building direct supervision facilities in the late 1970s and early 1980s. For example, Brandon Correctional Centre in Manitoba boasted living unit architecture when it opened in 1979. After a 1977 riot and the consequent inquiry (Moore, 1977), in 1981 the province of Saskatchewan opened direct supervision units in a new Saskatoon Correctional Centre and rebuilt Prince Albert Correctional Centre. British Columbia and Alberta also built a number of direct supervision facilities in the 1980s as part of a plan to move their corrections systems forward.

Ideally, direct supervision entails proper architecture and design. In his review, Wener (2006) describes new-generation facilities that feature smaller living units, single cells, and good-sized common areas for inmates to interact. In contrast to old-style linear prisons that feature long tiers of cell blocks emanating from a central hub, new-generation institutions use a podular design with smaller living units dispersed within the prison in almost a campus style. Ideally, recreation and pro-grams are run on the unit or in adjoining areas. Sight lines within the podular units allow staff to directly observe inmate activity, which dis-courages misbehaviour.

While proper institutional design is preferable, direct supervision can be (and is) run in older, traditionally built prisons (Wener, 2006; Zupan, 1991). Central to DS is the shift in the COs' approach from "static" to "dynamic" security. Since prisons first became popular in the eighteenth century, COs have carried out static or fixed security duties. This style of inmate supervision is also referred to as "indirect" because it requires distant observation of long tiers and wings from centralized control posts. COs have contact with inmates only during daily routines such as counts, searches, and the opening and closing of doors, or to respond to questions or trouble. In other words, COs and inmates have few reasons to com-municate in such systems and structures, and outside of regular routines, contact often arises only from conflicts over rule violations. This pattern of interaction relates back to the architectural design of traditional linear-style institutions built from the late 1700s to the mid-1960s. Indeed, the original Pennsylvania and Auburn systems both emphasized the maintenance of "silence" in the day-to-day lives of inmates, meaning there was even less cause for inmates and staff to interact. The original penitentiaries envisioned COs in a security role only.

With DS, the prison living area is viewed as an environment conducive to change (Wener, 2006). Staff maintain security by gaining knowledge of inmates and their activities through interaction. So staff stations are usually right in the unit, maximizing inmate–staff communication. Often a mixed model is used, with staff stations partitioned from the main unit by glass, and with an office or kiosk also on the unit. In the mixed model, staff spend considerable time on the unit but also have a place to go if tensions run high. COs on the unit communicate more actively with offenders because they have assumed some functions previously performed only by caseworkers.

New-generation architecture and dynamic security regimes represent remarkable changes in prison design and management, so it is surprising that there have been relatively few efforts to evaluate their impact. This is likely due to methodological problems in comparing truly equivalent groups (i.e., direct supervision to traditional prisons). Also, different prisons or housing units may have different inmates, staff experience, training, treatment programs, and management styles, and these differences can bias outcomes. In the thirty years since DS was introduced, a number of reasonably strong studies have accumulated that use inmate and staff surveys, misconduct data, and recidivism rates to assess impact. In his review of the literature, Wener (2006) found several positive effects: mostly lower staff and inmate assaults, greater staff and inmate perceptions of safety, lower rates of vandalism, and fewer inmate infractions overall. Staff generally reported more job satisfaction, a sense of professionalism, and lower stress levels, but this may have depended on how DS is implemented. Applegate, Surrette, and McCarthy (1999) reported that direct supervision inmates reoffended at similar rates to indirect- or traditional-style prison inmates, although their results also suggest that longer periods of time in direct supervision appear to promote less reoffence. In more recent studies, Karin Beijersbergen and her colleagues (2012) found that newer prison design in the Netherlands was associated with more favourable inmate well-being, while Americans Robert Morris and John Worrall (2014) found DS design associated with the reduction of general misconduct (but not inmate violence) in Texas prisons.

There is a dearth of research on direct supervision in Canada. Discussion on the CSC website has summarized American research on DS (Posner, 1991) or catalogued architectural shifts over time without referring to the actual impact of unit management on routine inmate life. This study hopes to investigate the impact of DS on inmates and correctional staff and how this has impacted their daily interactions, if at all.

Female Correctional Officers in Male Inmate Prisons

Direct supervision represented a large shift in prison life in the 1970s and 1980s. Another significant change was the introduction of female COs in male prisons in Canada and the United States in the 1980s. This was part of a broader change in employment in North America as women became more involved in the workforce and then in non-traditional jobs such as policing, firefighting, and corrections (Britton, 2003; Munn, 2013; Szockyj, 1989). Citing federal statistics from human resources, Melissa Munn (2013) observed a 53 percent increase in female COs between 2001 and 2010. In fact, Headingley Correctional Centre, one of my study sites, reported in 2007 that 50 percent of its CO complement was female. While generally not as physically strong as male COs, women were thought likely to provide a "normalizing" effect within an institution; it was also thought that their "natural" skills at communicating and nurturing would be of benefit (Crouch, 1985; Szockyj, 1989).

Working in a non-traditional role such as corrections, in which physicality and aggression are prized, how have female COs fared? The research suggests resistance from male colleagues. Provincial and federal research suggests that sexual harassment has been a problem for female officers (Cadwaladr, 1993; Lagace, 1994; Samak, 2003), with male co-workers identified as the main problem. How does the spectre of harassment play out on a daily shift, during which COs depend on one another for back-up in the event of physical conflict?

Programs and Risk Management

Direct supervision and female COs were concurrent initiatives in Canadian and American corrections, but with respect to programming, these two countries took fairly divergent paths in the 1980s. The United States massively expanded its correctional population in that decade, abandoning rehabilitation programming in most states and introducing legislation such as "three strike laws" that lengthened sentences and limited remission and parole. Put more simply, Americans decided to have repeat offenders serve longer sentences and to restrict early release based on good behaviour or qualifying for parole (Zimring & Hawkins, 1991). Going in a different direction, Canada's correctional organizations implemented direct supervision federally and provincially, and the federal service in particular made great strides in introducing more sophisticated methods of inmate classification, case management, and programming (Andrews & Bonta, 2010; Wormith et al., 2013).

Once sentenced, inmates need to be assessed, their security established, and a plan drawn up, be it for institutional work or for treatment. Up to the 1970s, corrections jurisdictions throughout the world used "first generation" classification, crudely assessing inmates based on practitioner experience and consideration of the offence being served and the inmate's prior record. This changed dramatically in the 1980s, and Canada led the way. The CSC created a system whereby the level of security – minimum, medium, and maximum – was determined by objective instruments. Second-generation devices like Statistical Information on Recidivism (SIR) used past research to structure decisions based on static (not changeable) past criminal and institutional behaviour and demographic characteristics (Nuffield, 1982). Third-generation instruments came next, which ranked dynamic risk and criminogenic needs (e.g., for education, employability, criminal attitudes) that could be changed over time by treatment programs, adjusting for characteristics such as gender and race. An ideal-type fourth-generation classification instrument has since been introduced that updates risk and needs assessment instruments based on empirical research on local offender populations and integrates assessment with program planning (e.g., the CSC classifies offenders, researches recidivism after offenders are released, and revises these instruments based on findings). An example of fourth-generation instruments is the Level of Service Inventory – Case Management Inventory (LSI/CMI) (Wormith et al., 2013).

Thus in the 1980s, the United States increased its use of custody while reducing its use of parole, and showed little interest in rehabilitation.

Conversely in Canada, the CSC began developing correctional programs based on social learning theory and Don Andrews and James Bonta's psychology of criminal conduct, or PCC (Andrews & Bonta, 2010). Also referred to as RNR (Risk, Needs, Responsivity) models, these cognitive-behavioural interventions attempt to address criminogenic needs. Offender needs that are critical to address in order to change behaviour are encompassed in the "Central Eight": anti-social attitudes; anti-social associates; criminal history; substance abuse; family/marital relations; use of leisure time; financial problems; accommodation problems; and emotional/personal issues. RNR programs adhere to the risk principle (high-risk offenders receive the most intensive treatment, low-risk offenders receive little or no intervention), the needs principle (target criminogenic needs, those related to recidivism), and the responsivity principle (the right program at the right time) and aim for program fidelity (the best results are achieved by well-run programs). The third-generation LSI has been checked for validity and reliability and received considerable support in the literature; CBT programs also get partial support from individual studies and multi-study meta-analysis.[9] Programs that adhere to treatment principles are generally found to reduce recidivism by 5 to 10 percent, although better designed and operated programs tend to do better (Andrews & Dowden, 2005; Aos, Miller, & Drake, 2006; MacKenzie & Hickman, 2006).

On the face of it, risk management and cognitive-behavioural programs offer a great deal: clearly defined principles, theory, supportive research, and the promise that recidivism will be reduced, which is undeniably still the bottom-line outcome for corrections. Yet this new wave of correctional programs has faced more than its share of criticisms – Hannah-Moffat (2005), for example, has observed that programs offer exaggerated claims of success, that they make the goal of risk management more important than reforming the offender, and that classification is hurtful because it blames the offender and deflects attention from the miserable social conditions that cause crime.

Anyone reading the literature on classification and the RNR model cannot help but pick up some of the enthusiasm of those who research and write in that genre. But one could well ask: since classification and cognitive-behavioural programs have been around since the late 1980s, why have we not observed huge declines in offender recidivism? The reality is that in large studies, federal and provincial inmate recidivism rates from two to five years after release run fairly consistently between 50 to 60 percent in both the United States and some Canadian jurisdictions (Farabee, 2005; Weinrath, 2000). Success rates may be high in some programs, but clearly it is difficult to achieve these rates consistently. Meta-analyses show an average decline of recidivism of 5 to 10 percent, but that is not as impressive when put in context. When we compare a treatment group recidivism rate of 40 percent to a control group reoffence rate of 45 percent, we can conclude that the treatment group does better, but not by much. Furthermore, it can be argued that the ideal implementation of RNR programs is unrealistic: strict program design and fidelity, comprehensive staff training, and delivery to the right inmate at the right time are objectives that are difficult if not impossible to achieve in the hectic world of the prison.

Programs have increased in prisons over the past twenty-five years, although provincially, remand has likely impinged on their use. How do inmates and correctional staff view prison-based programs? Are inmates cynical or optimistic about them? Is there a preference for or confidence in vocational programs versus behavioural ones?

Aboriginal Programming

Programming for mainstream offenders has been increased, especially at the federal level, but what about Canada's Aboriginal peoples? While at one time Indigenous Canadians were not prevalent in Canada's prisons (Hamilton & Sinclair, 1991), today their overrepresentation has become a sad constant. Aboriginal people are about 4 percent of the Canadian population but now comprise 24 percent of the federal inmate population (Sapers, 2013), up from 17 percent just five years ago. In the prairie provinces their overrepresentation is even higher: in Alberta, they comprise 5 percent of all adults but 33 percent of provincial adult inmates; in Saskatchewan, 13 percent but 60 percent; and in Manitoba, 15 percent but 65 percent (Statistics Canada, 2014).

Aboriginal people and other minorities are thought to be overrepresented due to extremely adverse socio-economic conditions and discrimination in Canadian society. In a broader sense, Indigenous Canadians and other minorities can be considered "racialized groups." Racialization is the practice of distinguishing groups by way of skin colour, ethnic status, religion, or language and making characterizations (e.g., smart people, good at math, lazy people, violent people) that have no scientific basis (Miles, 1989). In this sense, race can be considered a social construction. Differences in and of themselves are not a bad thing of course, but the "othering" of people of colour and of some immigrant groups typically results in identifying variations that favour those in a dominant position in society (for a recent Canadian policing study, see Comack, 2012). In North America, the dominant ones are the European settlers.

A striking example of racialization and othering is offered by Canada's Aboriginal peoples, who have been marginalized through a series of suppressive colonial practices. The Royal Commission on Aboriginal Peoples in the mid-1990s described how white settlers had focused on taking away land and dismantling existing economic systems, limiting Aboriginal mobility, and suppressing Indigenous cultural practices (RCAP, 1996). Residential schools, a failed effort at outright assimilation, have left a particularly foul legacy of physical abuse, ill-prepared parents, and cultural dislocation (Regan, 2010). Contemporary forms of colonialism include the Indian Act, which limits the autonomy of local reserve governments and their capacity to engage in economic development (RCAP, 1996). The colonial legacy has led to the persistent economic and social marginalization of Aboriginal Canadians. This can be correlated, to some extent, with their overrepresentation in the criminal justice system (Perreault, 2009). Public inquiries have identified systemic discrimination by the criminal justice system and its agents (RCAP, 1996; Cawsey, 1991; Hamilton & Sinclair, 1991; Truth and Reconciliation Commission [TRC], 2015).

Notwithstanding the findings of various inquiries, blatant racism is often difficult to detect, which can make change very difficult. No one wants to be called a racist. The inability of Euro-Canadians to perceive their own racism has been described by Peggy McIntosh (2010) as "white privilege." She outlines how Caucasians take for granted the dominance of white culture. For example, someone who is white simply assumes that he or she will treated fairly by financial institutions, the medical community, and the legal system. The subtlety of today's discrimination has perhaps been best captured by Bonilla-Silva (2006), who describes racism as "colour-blind." Most North Americans do not see themselves as racist, nor are social practices considered discriminatory. Social and economic exclusion, however, still occurs when groups use principles of meritocracy, individualism, work ethic, and moral character to explain why minorities are not progressing. Higher rates of unemployment and lack of education among Aboriginals can be explained away by declaring that they "just haven't tried hard enough." Using census and labour market survey data collected by Statistics Canada, Teelucksingh and Galabuzi (2005) found that Canada's labour market was becoming increasingly diverse (driven by more immigration and by higher birth rates among Indigenous Canadians) but that minorities still faced lower-paying jobs, lower wages for equivalent work, and higher unemployment, even after controlling for education. The authors found discrimination in the form of unrecognized credentials for immigrants and discriminatory hiring and promotion practices by organizations. These things often were not found to be intentional, but the authors note that discrimination does not have to be intentional to be real.

Similar problems of racism arise in the criminal justice system, in which Indigenous Canadians are overrepresented, as well as perhaps other racialized groups such as Blacks in Ontario. Because Aboriginal youth are stopped more often by police, they are more likely to be arrested and less likely to be granted bail (Comack, 2012). The informal mechanisms available to the police (warnings, withdrawn charges) do not appear to be used as often when it comes to Indigenous people caught misbehaving. In a clearly vicious cycle, Aboriginal youth are much more likely to come from disadvantaged backgrounds, and as a result, police are leery of providing leniency and courts are more reluctant to let them return to their homes. These young people quickly build up a lengthy criminal record, which leads to stiffer and stiffer penalties and a greater likelihood of custody (Comack, 2012).

Recent work by Sarah Turnbull (2014) and Joanne Martel and her colleagues (2011) in corrections studies has begun to unpack the rigidity of the corrections process and how subtly it continues to marginalize Indigenous identity. So before continuing, I want to summarize the history of Aboriginal programming within the federal penitentiary service.

In the 1970s and 1980s, Canadian prisons allowed Indigenous inmates to form Native Brotherhood groups. These Brotherhoods operated in a variety of ways depending on the institution, but in at least some I was familiar with they were involved in promoting group activities, raising funds, and holding events involving outsiders such as powwows. Or they might operate much like inmate committees, negotiating on rules and privileges or bringing specific Aboriginal inmate concerns to the attention of the administration. In the 1980s some Aboriginal inmates grew frustrated over the restrictions placed on their ability to engage in spiritual practices, and contended that they were being discriminated against (Waldram, 1997). This was an example of "white privilege": white inmates had access to clergy and places of worship, but Indigenous offenders did not. Two Aboriginal brothers remanded in the BC provincial system went to a BC superior court to obtain access to personal sacred items – one of the first legal victories in this area. After being sentenced, the brothers were placed in the maximum security Kent Institution. Shortly after their arrival, they joined with other inmates to petition the prison administration for pipe and sweat lodge ceremonies, as well as access to personal medicine bundles and other sacred items. They also asked that Aboriginal Elders be allowed to come in and supervise ceremonies. After several negotiations, Aboriginal spiritual practices were finally acknowledged by the Kent warden as a legitimate form of religion (Jackson, 2002).

In the 1980s, the CSC developed formal policies that allowed Aboriginal spiritual practices to grow in various ways around the country. Indigenous spiritual practices also sprang up in provincial/territorial prison systems in the 1980s, and now are quite common in corrections systems, especially in the prairie provinces, Yukon, the Northwest Territories, and Nunavut. The CSC has also attempted to incorporate culturally sensitive assessment practices when classifying Aboriginal inmates (Martel, Brassard, & Jaccoud, 2011). They have introduced Elders into their institutions, established special Aboriginal "pathways" units emphasizing Indigenous culture, and hired Aboriginal liaison program officers to help inmates develop plans to reintegrate into the community. Elders have also provided assistance during parole hearings, ideally to provide insight into Indigenous culture and address the special needs of Aboriginal inmates (Turnbull, 2014).

Aboriginal spirituality programs are described lavishly on many federal and provincial government corrections websites, but when examining their prominence in day-to-day institutional practices, they appear to fall short. During his years studying this phenomenon in the federal system, Waldram (1997) found the reality to be a sharp departure from the ideal. While the practice of Aboriginal spirituality was recognized in prison policy and procedures, Elders reported being harassed at times. Prayer bundles were searched and desecrated for no reason; security staff sometimes limited movement or delayed ceremonies. Also, Aboriginal program coordinators sometimes felt that their spiritual practices suffered from "secondary" status in prisons relative to mainstream European religions like Catholicism and Protestantism. While paid clergy have been present in federal and provincial prisons for many years, it took some time to get regular funding for Aboriginal Elders.

Waldram indicated that despite claims that they "understood" Aboriginal spirituality, corrections authorities lacked true insight into Indigenous culture and were still approaching it from a Eurocentric religious perspective. Aboriginal inmates are not a homogenous group, and their mixed belief structures (Euro-Canadian-oriented, traditional-oriented, bicultural) were not being taken into account by prison administrators. Like Bonilla-Silva, Waldram depicted a corrections administration engaging in colour-blind racism, which took the form of fitting of Indigenous cultural programs into the current treatment regimes.

According to Waldram, Aboriginal inmates had been badly traumatized by colonization, residential schools, and negative life experiences that were too often the norm for Indigenous people in Canada. Based on related trauma research, Waldram argued that spirituality had tremendous potential to alleviate trauma and help Aboriginal inmates recover to lead more constructive lives. He viewed current efforts by Canada's correctional authorities towards recognizing and supporting Aboriginal cultural practices as inadequate.

More recent work by Martel and her colleagues (2011) echoes some of these concerns. They have observed that despite efforts to increase Aboriginal reintegration, Indigenous offenders tend to be classified as high risk more often and have less access to programs in maximum security institutions. Furthermore, Indigenous culture is not being defined by the

Aboriginal community, but rather by the accreditation process controlled by the CSC. Somewhat akin to Waldram's concerns about programs ignoring the bicultural identities of some inmates, Martel and colleagues also found a tendency for federal programmers to represent Indigenous culture in relation to the dominant local tribe, instead of acknowledging the cultural distinctions of individuals (as if European-Canadian inmates were all compelled to attend Catholic services). Likewise, Turnbull (2014) found in her study of Elder-assisted parole hearings that understanding the special needs and distinct Indigenous identity of inmates took a back seat to the normative correctional practices of parole boards.

While Waldram's concept of healing for Aboriginal inmates as part of programming has been adopted by the CSC, Martel and colleagues (2011) and Monture-Angus (1999) have argued that the healing has been subjugated to the traditional risk assessment practices of corrections organizations. The Aboriginal community's definition of traditional healing is being defined within the confines of correctional policy. The Correctional Investigator (Sapers, 2013) has weighed in on this by raising serious concerns about the lack of adequate programming for Aboriginal offenders. Notwithstanding a number of CSC initiatives announced over the years, the Correctional Investigator has observed that overrepresentation continues to worsen and that programming has not improved.

Conclusion

A growing incarcerated population, overcrowding, and an increasing proportion of remanded prisoners have been negative features of the past twenty-five years. Violence and drugs still appear to be problems in Canada's correctional institutions, although this is hard to gauge, given the lack of hard data over time. Inmate culture may be less cohesive than in times past, and prison gangs have emerged as a threat to both correctional staff and offenders. Changes in human rights legislation, architectural design, and staff supervision practices, and more sophisticated rehabilitation programs, seem at first glance to be signs of substantial progress in Canadian prisons. There are significant criticisms, however, of the continued capricious exercise of administrative authority within prisons, as well as the lack of consistent efficacy shown by direct supervision and behavioural programs. At the same time, not enough is known about the use and impact of Aboriginal cultural programming.

There have been substantial transformations in Canadian prisons over the past twenty-five years, but we know little about their impact on day-to-day institutional life. Has life for inmates and staff fundamentally changed over that period, and if so, has it been for the better? In the next chapter I discuss how theoretical lenses of frame analysis and legitimacy can be applied to help us with the task at hand, and link this to my methodological approach.

2

The Prisons and the Interviews

One can investigate the broad external and internal changes that have structured and restructured prison life on many levels, but I propose that they are best understood by gauging evidence at the worker or individual level of the organization through interviews, in this case the prison being the organization and the worker/individual level being the one inhabited by inmates and staff. I have used two theoretical lenses to focus my analysis. The first is Erving Goffman's (1974) frame analysis, which is especially helpful in tying together the day-to-day threads of custodial existence and clearly depicting how the various inmate and correctional staff players organize their day-to-day experiences and interactions with others. The second lens provides a more contemporary focus on the criminal justice field – more specifically, the practice of procedural justice and its influence on the legitimacy of criminal justice actors (Bottoms, 1999; Bottoms & Tankebe, 2012; Crewe, 2007; Hulley, Liebling, & Crewe, 2011; Liebling, 2004). Social psychologist Tom Tyler (2003), a key proponent of the importance of procedural justice, asserts that a central goal of justice systems and their agents is to bring about more law-abiding behaviour from citizens. In the case of inmates, Anthony Bottoms (1999) has argued that greater compliance and better behaviour are thought likely to arise from just prison regimes and effective correctional staff. Correctional officers (COs) play a key role in attaining legitimate regimes; they have the most direct contact with inmates, and their actions impact most directly on offenders in the daily routines of the prison.

In the second part of this chapter, I link theory to methods by describing the study sites and providing an overview of how the research was undertaken. Qualitative research approaches tend to link up theory (in this case, frame analysis) with the methods applied (limited observation, depth interviews); hence the two are presented here together rather than in separate chapters.

Frame Theory

In most respects, the lowest service level is where the organizational "work" actually gets done and where goals or objectives are achieved (or not). In a correctional institution, inmates get up, eat, interact with others, and participate in programs, work, or leisure. COs conduct counts and searches, solve problems, interact with inmates, and sometimes help parole officers with some of their case preparation. How have the routines of staff and inmates been impacted by the advent of direct supervision, women in the traditionally male workplace, new programs, and legislative and organizational accountability measures? Why not directly ask the players themselves? To clearly see the end result of outside or inside influences on the prison, Peter Manning (2008) views analysis at the individual level as very worthwhile.

There are other reasons to favour such a qualitative approach. Quantitative statistics can and do miss many of the day-to-day occurrences that characterize organizational life, and may simply end up measuring how well staff keep records instead of accurately depicting institutional life. In particular, quantitative data are of little use in organizations with an active "underlife" (Goffman, 1961). These underlife activities can include staff activities or interactions that are oppositional to the stated goals of the organization, sometimes minor (e.g., not adhering to a dress code), other times more serious (e.g., employee theft) (Manning, 2008). In institutions, there are inmates who adhere to an oppositional subculture that, at its most extreme, actively resists the efforts of administration to enforce rules and promote change. Political scientist Michael Lipsky (1979) has long expressed concerns over government workers such as correctional officers, who (much like police officers and teachers) make choices with generally low visibility and limited accountability and who stymie efforts for valid assessment.

Qualitative data at the worker/inmate level allows us to investigate the potential gap between what organizations say happens and what actually does happen.

To grasp prison life from the perspective of the social actors involved, the micro-level of frame theory provides us with an interpretive perspective associated with interactionism (Goffman, 1974). Since Goffman first outlined frame analysis in the 1970s, it has proved a durable mode of inquiry for investigators studying the human condition. He explicated frame analysis by building on his past work on organizations (1961), the experience of stigma (1963), and especially his dramaturgical observations of everyday life (Goffman, 1959). He developed his early theories through fieldwork, observing individual-level interactions and interviewing subjects in public places and within institutions such as mental health facilities. Frame analysis has likely not been as widely applied by scholars as other aspects of Goffman's work, but it has been used to guide research in diverse organizational settings, such as that involved in appraising training presentations (Smith, 2009), determining how social workers construct frames around child protection decisions (Forsberg and Vagli, 2006), and understanding how social justice, medical, and market choice frames can affect how obese people are socially perceived (Kwan, 2009).

Goffman's (1974) conceptualization of frame analysis is well suited to analyses of prisons, because this perspective seeks to understand human behaviour in terms of individual social "frames" of reference through which people establish their own consistent, relied-upon patterns of actions and reactions to routine day-to-day relations and events. Social actors making sense of a strip of activity are aided by frames of interpretation, and these interpretations can vary between people. Frame analysis first considers *primary frameworks* that people work from (e.g., being an inmate, being a CO) but seeks also to examine the routine interactions and situations within that framework, such as initial behaviours and consistent responses to said behaviours, fabrications (lies), and frame breaking. The primary framework can be reworked through acts that challenge certain precepts; this is called *keying*. Examples of this might be what Michael Smith (2006) refers to as technical redoings or play acting. Another way to realign a frame is through *fabrication*, which can involve one of the parties to an interaction taking on a false understanding of the situation as a result of a con or fraud by other parties. For those who misinterpret situations (e.g., first day on the job, first day in prison), *frame breaking* may occur – that is, unintentionally inappropriate activity may occur that lies outside the bounds of expected behaviour in a particular setting. On the other hand, frame breaking may occur for reasons such as loss of control (an angry public outburst), or it may be a purposeful act for personal gain (intimidating a colleague into providing something desirable).

A typical framing of relations for inmates and COs might involve the often grudging deference of inmates to COs' authority. For instance, when told to do something by a CO, an inmate may act on the request but perform with pronounced sluggishness or great reticence. This may help him keep the respect of his peers while avoiding official repercussions from the CO. Of course, not all interactions may go as expected; if an inmate argues with a CO about the state of her cell and then starts swearing at the CO, a clear violation of the institutional rules has occurred, as well as a crack in the typical frame of deference that governs CO–inmate decorum in exchanges. Individuals may attempt to set, challenge, and perhaps even key established frame boundaries. A CO may ask an inmate a question about another inmate, in effect asking him to inform or "rat" on clandestine activity. Again, this is not a typical CO–inmate interaction; officers know not to ask inmates to talk about their peers. But the CO here may have established a relationship with the inmate such that she believes she can risk breaking the frame, or keying the frame to a more intimate, private relationship where prison secrets might be shared.

Frame analysis is used in this book to assess study subjects' accounts using two time dimensions: (1) perceptions of life in Canadian correctional institutions today, and (2) perceptions of changes in prison customs and the "why" of those changes. I intend to show that human relations have indeed changed within custodial settings over the past twenty-five years. Using interpretive frames to outline prison life and consider its variations, I examine how the interaction between inmates and correctional staff has changed as well as the informal rules and norms that now frame the boundaries of their relationships. Some of the external forces discussed in the previous two chapters will be shown to have encroached on Canada's correctional institutions and impacted its inhabitants. I contend that the interpretations of social interactions and situations within correctional institutions have indeed been affected by trends such as remand increases, government legislation, correctional policies, changes in the offender population, and even the physical design of today's prisons. Internal policy changes and new approaches in staff communication and programming are also evaluated.

Framing relations properly is critical to establishing appropriate relations. Inmates have a great drive to gain the respect of other inmates and so must conduct themselves appropriately within a primary inmate frame (Goffman, 1961; Hulley et al., 2011). But how do COs establish themselves as an influence within an inmate frame that emphasizes social distance and that probably approves of some illegitimate behaviour? I contend that for COs, procedurally just behaviours offer a promising path to legitimacy.

Legitimacy

Why do people obey the law? Why do we defer to police officers, and why do inmates obey COs? These questions have driven extensive empirical investigation into people's responses to law enforcement and legal rules. Psychologist Tom Tyler and his collaborators conclude that people adhere to rules and submit to the courts and police not because of fear of punishment, but because they view legal authorities as legitimate (Jackson et al., 2012; Sunshine & Tyler, 2003; Tyler, 2003). Tyler's work has helped establish the importance of *procedural justice* to perceptions of fairness and legitimacy; his studies and others have shown that it is not so much the outcome of legal processes or proceedings (also called *distributive justice*) that impacts people's perceptions of the law, but the fairness with which they believe their case has been handled. In other words, getting a speeding ticket from a police officer is more likely to be viewed favourably if the police officer behaves in a manner that allows the speeder to maintain her or his dignity, whatever the amount of the fine. The validity of procedural justice has huge implications for criminal justice practice: from the uniformed police officer on the street to the robed judge sitting high in the courtroom, respectful, humane treatment of people caught up in the justice system will lead to more adherences to rules. Generally, Tyler (2012) has found support for his central thesis in both cross-sectional analyses and panel studies. Procedural justice has also been used as a framework beyond the justice system – for example, Australian Kristina Murphy's (2005) use of procedural justice to help understand income tax evasion and Mark Ehrhart's (2004) application of it to explain employee behaviour.

While the scholarship on legitimacy focuses more strongly on policing (Mazerolle, Bennett, Antrobus, & Eggins, 2012; Tyler, 2004), several initiatives by British criminologists have brought legitimacy research front and centre in considering prisons and the critical question of how they maintain internal order (Bottoms & Tankebe, 2012; Crewe, 2007; Liebling, 2004, 2011; Sparks, Bottoms, & Hay, 1996). Custodial settings are arguably better suited for rigorous tests of procedural justice. It is one thing to assert that citizens obey the law because they believe in it and that they obey police because they feel they are acting fairly. But it remains that citizens may follow laws for any number of other reasons, including self-interest, and indeed, many individuals may never have encountered police and thus have only second-hand knowledge of their behaviour. It is quite different to expect that inmates – a group perhaps more prone to challenge laws and rules – will listen to COs and be influenced by COs' behaviour. COs must interact directly with inmates and enforce institutional routines and rules. In a sense, COs are "in the face" of inmates. Thus, commanding legitimacy is a greater challenge for COs in correctional facilities than it is for police in the community (Bottoms, 1999).

In his review of interpersonal violence and social order in prisons, Bottoms (1999) outlines the dilemma facing correctional authorities in trying to maintain order. Prisons are "special places" or distinct settings for six reasons: (1) they are total institutions, cut off from the outside world and more enveloping in their structuring of day-to-day living; (2) they are punitive spaces – whatever the rationale of the day, prisons are perceived by their residents as places of castigation; (3) strict routines across space and time create an atmosphere or social climate that intrudes deeply into the consciousness of keepers and kept; (4) following from (1) and (3), the carrying out of daily routines is central to the prison's nature as an institution; (5) staff–inmate relations are central to the CO's ability to ensure that the daily routine unfolds with no problems, yet COs are outnumbered by inmates, and the correctional incentives and sanctions offered inmates (visits, canteen items, remission, or cell lock-up or segregation) may have no meaning for many of them, and hence they must balance enforcing the rules with small accommodations to inmates; and (6) prisons are geo-graphical locales, each with its own history and its own style of maintaining order. This institutional culture will impact the day-to-day actions of staff in managing offenders, for the good or for the bad.

Bottoms draws from the work of Dennis Wrong (1994) to identify three methods that correctional authorities can apply to maintain order: (a) instrumental/prudential (i.e., through incentives/disincentives); (b) coercive (i.e., through physical restrictions and structural constraints); and (c) normative (i.e., through consensus/acceptance and, most significantly, legitimacy). Within a custodial setting, one can assume that a certain number of inmates will be concerned about privileges and reduced security status – or fear segregation and increased security – and will obey institutional rules so as to earn incentives and avoid disincentives. Others will behave appropriately only insofar as they are physically prevented from victimizing others (controlled movement, lock-up, observation by staff). Finally, normative consent is achieved when inmates view compliance as important because they believe in the rules or accept the prison/CO as a legitimate authority. Building on the theoretical formulations of David Beetham (1991) and research by Tom Tyler (1990), Bottoms concludes by making a case for normative consent through legitimacy as a key variable that can be acted upon by prison administration to maintain social order in custodial settings. Legitimacy will emanate from the fairness of rules and routines (cell lock-up times, recreation duration, access to canteen, visits), physical prison conditions (physical plant, food quality), and, finally, the procedural fairness of COs as they enforce rules and routines.

Since the early work by Sparks and colleagues (1996) and Bottoms (1999), the focus of legitimacy in prisons has moved away from prison organizational features and more toward the CO–inmate relationship (Bottoms & Tankebe, 2012; Crewe, 2009; Liebling et al., 2010). A prison's power is expressed in its most corporeal form by COs, who wield authority over inmates for banal routines such as getting up in the morning, but also with regard to more serious exercises of power such as formal charging and escorting an offender to segregation for a rule violation. It is how this power and authority is administered and how values are reflected in CO behaviour that has an impact on inmates. Values such as fairness, respect, courtesy, and dignity are consistent with procedural justice, so it should not be surprising that researchers have found that these values resonate with offenders; historically in the literature, respect and fairness have been central concerns for inmates upon admission and while serving time (Goffman, 1961).

At first blush, legitimacy appears to suggest that COs should be polite and non-confrontational with inmates – that offenders' compliance can be achieved by emphasizing respect, being polite, and avoiding any hint of aggression. But this is not what administering legitimate authority entails. COs must be proactive in their relations with inmates, for users of authority do not simply sit back – they are vigorous, and indeed, they must wield this authority in order to be perceived as legitimate (Bottoms & Tankebe, 2012; Hulley et al., 2011). COs must use their authority often throughout the day, mostly in routine ways, but also in situational ways. Consistency and reliability are two avenues towards gaining respect; but at the same time, legitimacy cannot be achieved by enforcing *all* the rules *all* the time, no matter how intuitively fair that may sound. The legitimating process is a dynamic one that involves interaction and accommodations between those in authority (COs) and those on the receiving end (inmates). Fair outcomes must be negotiated from the multitude of day-to-day situations that arise (Liebling, 2011).

Alison Liebling, David Price, and Guy Shefer (2010) articulate how COs can best go about achieving legitimacy among inmates. COs must distinguish between the law in the books and the law in practice. Much like police officers, no CO can enforce all the rules all the time – it is not physically possible. It is more prudent for them to underuse their power so that the institution can continue to run. This means dealing with minor violations informally and applying formal punishments only to serious transgressions. This is not to suggest that COs should avoid formally sanctioning less serious rule-breaking; the point here is that every situation is unique and requires consideration of multiple factors: the inmate's behavioural history, the CO–inmate relationship, relations with other inmates, the history of the unit, and broader institutional norms. Liebling and her colleagues (2010) found that, in practice, most COs were aware of the rule enforcement or compliance model required of them, but tended to use a negotiation model, one in which compromise over rule enforcement between staff and inmates was more the norm. The difficulty with the negotiation model, however, is that it leads to the "corruption of authority" process outlined by Sykes (1958), which posits that as time passes, COs (who are always outnumbered and vulnerable) will end up compromising in negotiations with inmates and trade off non-enforcement of rules for compliance. Inevitably, COs will be pressured to keep making concessions until they end up with nothing to barter with; at that point they relinquish their authority to inmates and find themselves having to tolerate serious illegal behaviour. At worst, COs could find themselves actually forced to engage in illegal behaviour, such as bringing in contraband for inmates.

However, those who have studied staff–inmate relations do not concede that corruption of authority is inevitable (Crewe, 2009; Liebling, 2011; Sparks et al., 1996). So long as COs maintain a professional distance, use their authority wisely, and apply the "tactics of talk," they can achieve legitimacy. Liebling articulated some of the nuances in appropriate relations between staff and inmates by distinguishing between "good" and "right" relationships. In one prison, inmate survey results revealed to her that inmates on a certain prison housing unit believed that they had a "good" relationship with staff because they were often absent from their unit and rarely spoke to them (hardly an example of proactive dynamic supervision!). In this example, the COs rated "good" were not found to be using their authority carefully or actively seeking legitimacy, despite having to manage a new regime of rules. A disturbance occurred shortly afterwards on that unit, likely because of too strict an application by COs of new unit rules. In contrast, in other units Liebling and her colleagues observed that COs were active in entreating and cajoling inmates to adjust and adapt to a new rule regime. They applied their authority (albeit not in an authoritarian way) and maintained their own legitimacy and thereby earned some legitimacy for the new institutional rules system. According to Liebling (2011, 491),

> "right" relationships sat somewhere between formality and informality, closeness and distance, policing-by-consent and imposing order. They [COs] were respectful, but incorporated a "quiet flow of power." This distinction is significant but is rarely considered, so that false assumptions are held by critics and some practitioners about less power being "good" or more legitimate and more power being "bad" and less

legitimate ... Niceness and blind faith in social harmony or the avoidance of conflicts, and naïvety, can lead to chaos.

The landmark study about legitimacy in a custodial setting was conducted by Sparks, Bottoms, and Hay (1996), who compared two British prison regimes. The two institutions, Long Lartin and Albany, differed in their day-to-day style of inmate supervision. Albany's regime was stricter in limiting inmate movement within the institution and association between inmates. The staff tended to report higher rates of institutional rule violations. The COs, however, managed to forge generally positive relationships with inmates, and the prison was known for administrative efficiency and decent food. In contrast, Long Lartin allowed considerably more freedom of movement and association, as well as more recreation time. Staff were fairly easygoing in their supervision and informally managed many of the rule infractions, resulting in reported good CO–inmate relations. The lax supervision at Long Lartin, however, allowed an active underground economy to thrive, as well as predation against vulnerable inmates. Relations may have appeared positive on the surface, but CO authority at Long Lartin was not strong enough to limit certain forms of inmate misconduct.

Building on the work of Sparks and his colleagues, Liebling (2004) conducted the largest comparative study of prison regimes and legitimacy to date. Using a quality-of-prison survey instrument, she compared five British prisons on the following dimensions: staff relationships (e.g., trust, fairness); regime (rule enforcement, fairness, order, well-being, opportunities for personal development); use of power (e.g., opportunities for inmates to act independently); inmate social life (relationships with other inmates); and overall quality of life. There were differences among the prisons, but key to quality were the inmates' perceptions of staff and their relationships. Positive evaluations of staff and their fairness in exercising their duties were correlated with high ratings of overall regime fairness. Following this up with a survey of prison officers in twelve facilities, Liebling and her colleagues found that staff who reported greater job satisfaction, administrative support, and ability to use authority tended to do better in implementing a suicide prevention program. Higher-performing institutions were also correlated with stronger relationships with staff as reported by inmates (Liebling, Durie, Stiles, & Tait, 2004). The staff and inmate survey was initially conducted in 2002 and repeated in 2004, with similar results. Liebling and colleagues noted that COs were more likely to implement the new program and act favourably towards inmates when they trusted management and felt valued on the job.

In a rare study conducted outside English-speaking Western nations, Michael Reisig and Gorazd Mesko (2009) surveyed 103 inmates in a maximum security prison in Slovenia. Using measures of self-reported and official inmate misconduct, they found that net of controls, inmate perceptions of procedural justice had a strong negative association with inmate misconduct. Legitimacy, as measured by a limited four-item scale, had only a weak direct effect, which disappeared in the controlled analysis. Similar results using a longitudinal design were obtained from the Netherlands Prison Project; Karin Beijersbergen and her colleagues conducted time one and time two interviews with newly admitted inmates three months apart. They determined that inmates who reported strong perceptions of procedural justice at time one reported less official and self-reported misconduct at time two. Anger was found to be a mediating emotion (Beijersbergen, Dirkzwager, Eichelsheim, van der Laan, & Nieuwbeerta, 2014b). Adopting a case study approach in a newly opened Australian private prison, John Rynne, Richard Harding, and Richard Wortley (2008) found that new staff who were not properly supervised or trained, and who did not feel supported by management, ultimately lost legitimacy with the inmate population. This loss of staff legitimacy led to a riot. Using an experimental design, Derrick Franke and colleagues (2010) examined legitimacy changes over time for new admissions, comparing a US boot camp prison with a typical medium security facility. In the boot camp prison, staff related to residents in a procedurally just manner, while the traditional prison offered no specialized treatment. The researchers found that opinions about the legitimacy of the criminal justice system improved for the boot camp residents at time two, but declined for the residents of the regular prison. Franke and his colleagues noted that beyond the benefits of procedural justice, avoiding "delegitimizing behaviours" was also important. In other words, disrespectful behaviour had as big an impact as respectful behaviour, if not a bigger one.

Four Prisons

A limitation of much prison research is that studies are often confined to one institution; thus, generalizations to other sites may be unwarranted. Every correctional institution has a unique design as well as its own staffing history, a distinct inmate population, unique local demographics, and even unusual geographic traits (e.g., rural versus urban); all of these may affect day-to-day prison life. This study addresses this limitation (at least partly) by including four medium security sites from three western Canadian provinces. None of the four prisons can be considered representative; together, though, they provide a fairly good view of Canadian prison life. All of these facilities are large, mainstream institutions that hold mixed racial populations, have a core of experienced staff, and offer a range of programs for inmates. Fort Saskatchewan Correctional Centre (FSCC) and Headingley Correctional Centre (HCC) are the flagship institutional facilities in Alberta and Manitoba, respectively. Both HCC and FSCC hold sentenced inmates and a large proportion of remands, as well as a high proportion of gang members. Stony Mountain Institution (SMI) is the only federal medium-security facility in Manitoba and operates as a multi-function facility because it is so remote from any other large federal facility, making transfers difficult. SMI is medium security but manages all types of inmates, runs a full array of programs, and deals with a high proportion of prison gangs in its inmate population. Matsqui Institution (MI) in British Columbia offers a good range of programs for medium security federal inmates and holds many offenders with severe addiction problems. Matsqui housed only a few gang members at the time of the study and hence served as a useful contrast to the other institutions in this study that had to manage prison gangs.

Two programs of note were operated in the federal facilities. In Stony Mountain, the Ni-Miikana Pathways unit offered cultural programming for mostly Aboriginal inmates. It held up to forty inmates at the time of the study. The program offered cultural ceremonies through institutional staff working with Indigenous Elders, such as the burning of sweetgrass (or sage) and sweats (sitting in reflection in a hothouse), and promoted involvement in Aboriginal crafts. Pathways units were originally aimed at sex offenders but are now open to all inmates. Preliminary evaluations by the CSC have been positive (Jensen & Nafekh, 2011). In Matsqui, a peer support program ran, consisting of a group of older inmates, most of them serving life sentences (lifers), who provided guidance and counselling to other inmates. The lifers would work with administration and with the Inmate Secretary (an elected inmate leader who works with the prison administration) to try and resolve problems amicably. No formal evaluation was available on this program. This approach is intriguing in that it is similar to the federal *Lifeline* program, an initiative that saw ex-offenders helping inmates who were serving life sentences (see Olatu, 2009). Despite a positive evaluation and a relatively modest cost of two million dollars per year, the national program was cancelled by the federal Conservative government in 2012.

The Interview Process

The interview guide used general, open-ended questions to allow the subjects free rein to express their feelings. The questions were derived from past research and the researcher's own experience as to what makes up the key components of institutional life for inmates and staff: transition into the prison (first time, most recent time); daily life and routines; perceived changes in prison life; relations with inmates, staff, and outsiders; programs; leisure; violence; drugs; the inmate code; the influence of prison gangs; and planning for release. Correctional staff were asked similar questions. The interview guide is located in the Appendix.

The research was vetted through the University of Winnipeg Ethics Committee and various local- and national-level correctional agency research review bodies. Inmate and staff interviews were governed by informed consent. A purposive sampling strategy was used for this study, so the sample is non-random and unlikely to be representative of Canada's inmate or correctional staff population. Because a major purpose of this study is to depict prison life and some of the key changes therein over the past twenty-five years, older, experienced inmates and COs were prioritized and hence older subjects are likely overrepresented. I did, however, interview several younger inmates and staff to help present a more immediate view on the status of prison life and inmate–staff relations. Prison gang members or affiliates were actively sought out because of the challenges gangs have created within Canadian correctional institutions.

I recruited participants by posting signs in the units or by word of mouth through staff. No financial incentive was provided. Participants were quite enthusiastic about involving themselves in the study. Excellent cooperation was received from local administrators and staff at the various institutions. Interviews were conducted in the following locations: at HCC, a private room off the unit; at Stony Mountain, a private visiting room office; and at FSCC and MI, a private office in a programs staff office area. The offices provided by administration were private and comfortable. A digital recorder was used, although it was turned off if requested. In several staff interviews, verbatim notes were taken. Many inmates and staff did not wish to use pseudonyms, and some even asked that their names be used. Staff and inmates were interviewed between June 2007 and July 2008. Transcripts were edited slightly for readability but are presented as close to the original as possible.

I toured each facility before starting my interviews. I talked informally with staff and inmates when not doing formal interviews, and spent my downtime observing the activities and flow within each institution. I had led a number of student tours previously at Headingley and Stony Mountain, and had conducted research at Headingley on a few occasions, so I was familiar with those facilities and their designs, including some significant physical changes made in the 2000s. I had toured Fort Saskatchewan previously and knew many of the staff from my previous employment with Alberta Corrections. I was least familiar with Matsqui, but spent a lot of time during the week I was there wandering around, talking informally with staff and inmates. The warden was a former university classmate of mine and spent time updating me on Matsqui's recent history and current operations. I met with senior inmate leaders at both Stony Mountain and Matsqui, enlisting their aid in recruiting older inmates for my study, and talking with them informally. While obviously it would have been preferable to spend two or three months at each place, my past experience and ability to get access to staff and inmates helped me gain a quick sense of each correctional institution.

The Inmates

The purposive thirty-seven-inmate sample reflected this study's emphasis on older offenders and inmates who had spent considerable time in prison (Table 2.1). Because of their age and experience, they were able to reflect

TABLE 2.1
Inmate profile

	N	%		N	%
Correctional facility			**Most serious offence**		
Fort Saskatchewan	3	8.1	Breach of probation	1	2.7
Headingley	18	48.6	Possession stolen property	5	13.5
Matsqui	8	21.6	Break and enter	4	10.8
Stony Mountain	8	21.6	Drug trafficking	2	5.4
Total	37	99.9	Assault causing bodily harm	1	2.7
			Domestic assault	3	8.1
Gender			Robbery	2	5.4
Male	37	100.0	Armed robbery	8	21.6
Total	37	100.0	Residential robbery	1	2.7
			Aggravated assault	1	2.7
Age			Attempted murder	1	2.7
Mean	37.5	Range 35	Sexual assault	1	2.7
Std. deviation	10.5	Min. 19	Murder	7	18.9
Total	37	Max. 54	Total	37	99.9
Race			**Legal status**		
First Nations	15	37.8	Remand	16	43.2
Metis	9	24.3	Sentenced	21	56.8
Caucasian	9	24.3	Total	37	100.0
Inuit	1	2.7			
Dene	1	2.7	**Institutional experience**		
Black	2	5.4	Provincial only	8	21.6
East Indian	1	2.7	Current or prior federal	29	78.4
Total	37	99.9	Total	37	100.0
			Prison gang status		
			Prison gang member	6	16.2
			Associate gang member	3	8.1
			Former gang member	5	13.5
			Not involved with gang	23	62.2
			Total	37	100.0

Note: Totals may not add up to 100 due to rounding.

on and carefully weigh the cultural shifts, programming changes, and other adjustments that had occurred over their years in prison. The group also included a fair proportion of Aboriginal and gang-affiliated offenders. Among this group, offence severity was high; seven of them were lifers.

None of the remands interviewed were first offenders, and most of them were experienced in prison life; many had already spent substantial time in federal penitentiaries and had much to say about the changes in the provincial systems as well as the federal one.

The average age of inmate participants was 37.5 years; their ages ranged from 19 to 54. A few younger inmates who were gang involved were also represented. More than two-thirds of the subjects were Aboriginal (67.5 percent); the next largest group, Caucasian, made up about one-quarter of the sample (24.3 percent). Over half the group were sentenced inmates (56.8 percent); the rest were on remand. Crimes against the person were prominent: slightly more than two-thirds were being held for violent crimes, the rest for property, drug trafficking, or breach offences. The high rate of violence again reflects the large number of federal inmates, or remand inmates with federal experience. Over one-third of the sample were current or former gang members. Two of the gang inmates I interviewed were high-ranking members of SMI's largest gangs, the Manitoba Warriors and the Native Syndicate. I also spoke with a former high-ranking member of a Hells Angels chapter.[1] Because of the emphasis on gangs and experienced inmates with past federal terms, the individuals in the sample were more likely to be serving on violent crimes than the general run of inmates. I contend this is a worthwhile concession, given the important and varied experience this group was able to share. Qualitative evaluator and methodologist Michael Patton (2002) would describe this sampling approach as *information rich*; decisions on inclusion were made for the purpose of maximizing the utility of the data.

Correctional Officers

The staff sample is spread fairly evenly across the different correctional institution study sites, with Stony Mountain being somewhat higher than the rest at 37.5 percent (Table 2.2). The staff were primarily male, older, and white. Most staff had started as COs and had worked in prisons for many years. Their long-term experiences as COs were important for my study.

A very high proportion of the staff sample were male (79.2 percent) and Caucasian (92 percent). The mean age was 47, but over half the sample was over 50, with a range of 28 to 72 years. Given this high mean age, it

TABLE 2.2

Correctional officer profile

	N	%		N	%
Correctional facility			**Occupational status**		
Fort Saskatchewan	5	20.8	Correctional officer	4	16.7
Headingley	5	20.8	CO supervisor	5	20.8
Matsqui	5	20.8	Keeper	2	8.3
Stony Mountain	9	37.5	Preventative security officer	1	4.2
Total	24	100.0	Parole officer	3	12.5
			Program officer	4	16.7
Gender			Program manager	2	8.3
Female	5	20.8	Psychologist	1	4.2
Male	19	79.2	Chaplain	1	4.2
Total	24	100	Warden	1	4.2
			Total	24	100

	N				N	
Age				**Current or former CO?**		
Mean	47.0	Range	44	Yes	20	83.3
Std. deviation	10.4	Min	28	No	4	16.7
Total	24	Max	72	Total	24	100

	N	%			N		
Race				**Years experience**			
Asian	1	4.2		Mean	22	Range	29
East Indian	1	4.2		Std. dev.	8.0	Min	5
Caucasian	22	91.7		Median	23.5	Max	34
Total	24	100.0		Total	24		

is not surprising that the average years of experience was also rather high: 22. Not including the warden, the sample was split in terms of security versus program duties: 50 percent of those interviewed worked in a security position, compared to 45.8 percent in programs. Regardless of current postings, over 80 percent of the group had spent time as COs, while two of the four who were not COs had worked directly with inmates as living unit officers. Because of the senior nature of the staff group, there were more supervisors (41.7 percent) than one might expect, but still, well over half (58.3 percent) of the participants were line workers. While arguably it might have been better for the study if more participants were currently serving as COs, this was a trade-off to get a higher number of respondents who were older and who thus could provide a stronger commentary on changes over the past twenty-five years. As with my inmate sample, inclusion was based to a degree on the quality and richness of information that could be obtained from respondents. Nonetheless, most of my staff sample had CO experience, which undoubtedly enriched their insights.

Qualitative Data Analysis

The constant comparative method of Barney Glaser and Anselm Strauss (1967) was applied to identify saturation points (the same people saying or describing the same things over and over) and suitable points where one could confidently extrapolate from the data. In-depth interviews with subjects were digitally recorded and transcripts later typed. Field notes and reflections were typed on a password-protected laptop after each day of interviewing. The software package NVivo was used for analysis, along with the tried-and-true method of me simply spending hours poring over field notes and typed transcripts.

Interviewing subjects and having them relate their perceptions, opinions, and life narratives provided a rich source of data to assess Canadian prisons and some of the changes over the past twenty-five years. Who better to ask than the staff and inmates who experience prisons every day? However, there are some weaknesses to a qualitative approach that relies on the memories of respondents, especially when the interviewer is asking them to reflect back decades on some issues. Respondents may not recall things accurately, or reorient past experiences to be consistent with current attitudes, or present recollections in a manner to place themselves in the most favourable light. Reactivity, or responding to the interviewer (What does he want? Do I trust him?), is a problem associated with both structured and unstructured interviews. To limit these problems, I tried to stay as objective as possible in my self-presentation, establishing rapport but avoiding leading my respondents in my questioning (Neuman & Wiegand, 2000). If they doubted their memories, I did not push the questions.

Positioning myself as a prison researcher, I bring sociological training in quantitative and qualitative methods and experience applying both strategies to studies in correctional settings, including several program evaluations. Also, my perspective is influenced by fourteen years in the public sector working in both provincial institutional and community corrections, as well as tours of institutions in Australia, New Zealand, and the United States. I have worked as both an operational and programs manager and have supervised a variety of employees from probation officers to COs. While working in corrections, I advocated for inmates as chair of an inmate privileges committee, dispensed justice as best I could as chair of a disciplinary committee, and tried to balance inmate interests with public safety while chairing a temporary absence/early release committee. I looked into formal complaints by inmates, dealt with CO labour relations issues, and conducted both internal and external investigations. I have had extensive interview experience with both inmates and staff, and not only provincial inmates. I have supervised federal offenders on parole in rural areas and dealt with many federal inmates held on exchange of services agreements in our provincial jail.

In my professional and research career, my interests have been in improving correctional practice, advocating for humane treatment for inmates. I have advocated for staff to be provided with strong training and adequate resources to offer effective programming. All of these experiences have provided me with useful insights into institutional life, so I have been able to pick up more from relatively brief observations from on-site visits than researchers with less experience. I have also been able to establish rapport relatively easily with my interview subjects. All of that said, my past life and research experiences doubtless biased some of the observations and interpretations reported here. I leave it to the reader to sort out their impact on the reliability and validity of the data.

Conclusion

In this study, frame analysis and procedural justice serve as two essential means for assessing many of the changes in institutional corrections over the past twenty-five years and their relative efficacy. This approach will also help guide us towards policies that might improve prison life and the possibility of positive change for inmates. The qualitative thrust of frame analysis and its targeting of interaction is especially well-suited for investigating changes in inmate–inmate and inmate–CO relations, the probable decline of the inmate code of conduct, and the influence of the direct supervision model of offender supervision. In other countries, procedural justice research has shown promising results in reducing inmate misconduct and shifting offender attitudes in a more pro-social direction. Procedural justice has come to be viewed as an important method for improving the behaviour and effectiveness of criminal justice personnel. Does procedural justice hold any sway in Canadian prisons? To answer that question, this study will consider the opinions and observations of inmates and correctional staff.

3

How Inmates Understand Their Role

Once inside, inmates must find ways to adjust to institutional life (Adams, 1992), and learning interpretive frames is an important part of that adaptation. Frames do not come out of nowhere; cultural frames are learned and shared and may vary according to time, place, and events (Goffman, 1974). It is important to grasp where frames originate – for instance, what are the drivers, the motivational forces behind the frames? Deprivation theorists view adaptation as very much influenced by the deficits inherent in institutional life, whereas importation theorists believe that prior life history such as involvement in crime, and personal attributes such as race or gender, are more critical to understanding how inmates settle into prisons. Both these theories identify potential institutional- and individual-level motivators for new inmates and can help us understand how adaptations work their way into the shaping of the primary inmate frame.

Constructing a Frame and the Convict Code

Setting the rules around the inmate frame, I apply here the convict code, a regime of conduct reinforced by the inmate subculture (Sykes & Messinger, 1960). Whatever its current status in Western prisons (see Chapter 1), the subculture and the precepts of the convict code still serve as useful "ideal" types from which to build a primary inmate frame. This primary frame provides important guidance to new inmates; to manage your way through conversations and interactions within the institution, it is necessary to know how to walk, talk, and act. As mentioned earlier, the convict code breaks down into rules around status, appropriate behaviour, and gaining and maintaining respect.

The convict code provides an appropriate frame for structuring the prison life of a new inmate, or "fresh fish." For example, a prisoner cannot change what he or she has been convicted of, but should keep any record of sex offences or history of informing to authorities quiet, and show respect to inmates convicted of more serious violent offences. Being socially skilled, standing up for oneself, and not appearing weak are important attributes to exhibit in interactions. If you are good at self-presentation, you will supposedly move up in the inmate hierarchy. If you are not sure what to do, it is important to say nothing and not to trouble your peers by looking at them or in their cells. Other rules of the convict code offer a sound logic for a confined group of men who wish to get along. Do not talk to the correctional staff, do not inform on other inmates, do not be overly cooperative, and avoid unnecessarily antagonizing anyone. The logical context for assessing whether the traditional code forms the basic pieces of an inmate frame is the initial placement in a custodial setting.

Transitions

Custody: Into a Liminal or Criminal Frame?
When we think of experiences so traumatic or situations so extraordinary that our personal identity could be shaken, prison inevitably comes to mind. Indeed, many inmates are no different from most of us in believing that going to prison will be an ordeal and may change us for the worse. The researcher who best captured the difficult transition facing those first incarcerated was Goffman (1961). Basing much of his analysis on mental health facilities, Goffman saw inmates as enduring humiliating experiences upon admission; he referred to these as "mortification rituals," first articulated by Harold Garfinkel (1956). These rituals included one's head being shaved, one's worldly possessions being taken away, and the assignment of an identification number. In Goffman's view, custodial institutions set up the ideal process for stigmatizing individuals, both during incarceration and after. New fish were humiliated by both inmates

and COs while inside; upon release, the "ex-convict" label deepened their pariah status.

Most prison research does not investigate the status of remand offenders, which is regrettable, because it is typically during remand that inmates get their first institutional experience (Klofas, 1990). John Gibbs's (1982, 1987) work is a notable exception: he examined the adaptation of accused individuals to the jail setting. He reported that inmates experienced considerable distress on entering custody. New inmates focused on withstanding the initial shock, maintaining communication with friends/family outside, and securing stability/safety in a potentially volatile realm. New inmates typically were in a transitional state – in limbo – and spent considerable time in their cells until they became comfortable. Ralph Weisheit and John Klofas (1990) also found collateral concerns for remands that were related to day-to-day living such as loss of job and the negative impacts on finances, family relationships, housing, and physical health. The stress of pre-trial detention on some inmates is likely reflected in the higher rates of suicide among remand admissions (Blaauw, Kerkhof, & Hayes, 2005). James Garofalo and Richard Clark (1985), as well as David Rottman and John Kimberly (1975), found that first-time accused may vary in their own crime experience (e.g., first crime, repeat offender, family involved in crime, gang member), and this in turn may affect their susceptibility to socialization within the inmate subculture. US jail research suggests that the subculture is generally weaker in pre-trial detention and that inmates who adhere to it tend to be more experienced in deviant values from either street crime activity or having served prior jail time.

Part of the shock of pre-trial custody is attributable to stigma (Gibbs, 1982; Irwin, 1985). The distress caused by being caught and no longer being able to commit crime inconspicuously as a "secret deviant" is tough to bear (Goffman, 1963). This stigma directly affects the ability of inmates to maintain friendships and family ties, especially if theirs is a repeat offence. In his study of US jails, Irwin (1985) took a very extreme view, concluding that remands were intentionally treated like a rabble, stigmatized by society generally as they were herded into jail settings with little regard for their humanity. To Irwin, the jail operated as a form of social control and worked as a social institution that further penalized an already stigmatized and marginalized underclass of the mentally ill, chronic substance abusers, the homeless, and petty offenders.

Qualitative US research by Thomas Schmid and Richard Jones (1991, 1993) and a British mixed methods study by Joel Harvey (2007) examined first-time offenders as they went through remand and sentenced status. Using a participant observation design, Schmid and Jones observed their sample of first-time, short-term (one year) drug traffickers as they went through different stages of adjustment in a maximum security setting. Initially, there was great focus on the case before the courts, until the inevitability of conviction and prison was accepted. Once in custody, inmates went through various stages of ambivalence in their relations with others. Initially, on the one hand, they wished to avoid other inmates as part of a survival strategy; on the other, they desired to make acquaintances to achieve some degree of sociability. They were quite cautious in their initial interactions, and impression management was critical throughout their incarceration. New inmates spent more time out of their cells as they became more knowledgeable about institutional life, especially how to avoid violence.

Drawing on the work of Arnold Van Gennep (1960) and Victor Turner (1995), Harvey (2007) viewed his young adult subjects as working through a "liminal state" upon admission into custody. Such a status occurs when a social actor is disengaged from a cultural state and is entering into a new one; initially, this state is ambiguous because the social expectations are unclear or unknown. The subject eventually leaves the liminal state as he or she comes to understand the cultural expectations and obligations of the new milieu. Harvey found his subjects were plagued with uncertainty; they were also preoccupied with their loss of control and freedom, their separation from loved ones, the stigma they faced as their new status became known, and their personal safety. He concluded that his subjects found it difficult to traverse this liminal state, and that those with less fear and with a strong locus of control (i.e., belief in their ability to control their fate) tended to show fewer signs of distress.

From the literature on inmate social systems and first-time prison experiences, we can conclude that transition to custody is difficult for first-time inmates and that it adversely impacts even those with an institutional history; this supports the deprivation argument. This literature is largely drawn from outside Canada. Are these findings consistent with the experience of Canadian inmates? In the next section, I try to answer this question with my study findings on the transition into a prison setting.

The First Time in Prison

A first time in prison can entail many forms of incarceration. For youth, it may include police cells, temporary detention, "open" custody in a non-secure group home, or secure custody in a high-security facility for sentenced youth. Similarly for adults, police cells are often their first experience, or they may be housed in high-security remand facilities. In other cases, offenders may get bail immediately upon arrest so that their first actual experience in prison is after sentencing to a large (800-bed) provincial facility like Headingley or a smaller federal penitentiary like Matsqui (325 beds).

Most inmates did not view police cells as their "first time"; however, they had mixed thoughts about young offender centres. Some indicated that juvenile detention "didn't count" as a first prison sentence, while others found it to be their seminal custodial experience – that is, they had developed a "jailhouse" persona while in youth detention. Everyone interviewed had a first-time custody experience to share, but each defined the setting differently. Generally, subjects outlined a hierarchy of experiences:

- Youth custody is least onerous to enter.[1]
- Remand requires the least adjustment for adults (although not always for the less experienced).
- Provincial sentenced correctional centres are more onerous than remand centres.
- Federal penitentiaries create the most anxiety prior to admission because they have the most potential for lethal violence (although they also have other longer, better programs).

In any of these settings, first-time incarcerates had to contend with the stigma of arrest and detention, and also had to manage both the ambiguous setting of custody and the attendant discomfort in dealing with new people. In most cases, subjects experienced considerable angst and trepidation on entering custody. This was managed over time, and some inmates had advantages, such as toughness or physical size, that eased the transition, like these two Headingley offenders:

> *Interviewee: It's always rough the first time. It was hard times, you know, hard times. I was in prison, a jailbird. I had bills I wasn't paying. But the human spirit has quite a way of getting through all kinds of adversities.*
> *Michael Weinrath: When you say "hard times," you're talking about mentally, or do you mean being afraid of other inmates?*
> *I: Mentally, you know, because other people knew I was a con. I wasn't afraid of the other inmates – I'm a pretty big guy. I didn't know half of what guys, you know, years younger than me knew. I guess I'm not your typical gangbanger, or stuff like that. I'm just kind of a regular guy.* (Sentenced inmate, HCC)

> *First time, I did thirty days, just a short one. Headingley was scary back then* [early 1980s], *but I had no problems. I'm a big guy, a pretty easygoing guy, and get along with most people.* (Remand inmate and ex-biker gang member, HCC)

They had certainly been influenced by popular images presented in the media of extreme institutional violence and victimization. When first entering prison, new inmates fretted over the likelihood that they would be assaulted by other inmates. Would they make friends, or would they be isolated and beaten up? This inmate found it a challenging time:

> *Yeah, you hear the stories, and you are scared when you come in. You don't want to show it, but you just never know. Eventually, you make friends and get over it.* (Lifer, MI)

Another important issue was losing contact with loved ones: inmates reported pain over losing family and friends and, in some cases, children. This inmate from Headingley found it upsetting to think he might not be able to talk to those closest to him:

The first time I was admitted was back in 1968, in Headingley, which held remand back then too. I was living here in Edmonton and just had my first daughter born. I was heartbroken being away from my family, because I was a criminal. I was mostly crying at that time at nights, hardly sleeping because I was thinking about my family and what others thought of me because I wasn't there. It was hard. It seemed like forever, 'cause all I wanted was to get out, thinking about the outside world. (Remand inmate, HCC)

Stigma was a strong concern for newcomers. Most offenders had reached the point in their criminal careers where they had previously been charged, placed on probation, or even been given a conditional sentence, but now, having been physically placed in prison, their ability to manage stigma was suddenly limited. They could no longer conceal their criminal status from others. Going to prison was a personal defeat, not just for first-time offenders but for experienced ones as well. They had to confront the fact that they had not been skilled enough to avoid capture and punishment; in the case of repeat offenders, they had become chronic "losers." This lifer was well aware that the public held incarcerated individuals in low esteem:

I: *A lot of people think of you in here as just a criminal. You know what I mean: instead of thinking of you by your name or age or who you are, they think of you as what you did, instead of who you are.*
W: *Are you talking about the staff there or are you just talking about inmates?*
I: *Both. Staff are a little bit more open. Inmates do it in a roundabout way. It is not really popular for you to ask what another guy is here for, because it isn't really any of your business. But then again, if you are too secretive as an inmate, then they think you are hiding something. The politics is just crazy sometimes.* (Lifer, SMI)

Most respondents spent the first few days of their initial custody term isolating themselves from other inmates, spending time in their own cells. Many reported crying late at night, out of sight of other inmates. Consistent with Harvey's work, offenders described a liminal, anxious state upon first entering the institution. One remand offender reported meeting inexperienced "newbies" like himself, and encountering predatory individuals, gang members, and individuals suffering from mental illness who were difficult to get along with:

> *It was scary, you know. So, when I first came in, I kept to myself – talked to a few guys, kept busy going for breaks outside and reading books and getting a job.* (Remand inmate, FSCC)

Conversely, other inmates did not experience significant personal disruption or much insecurity during their first incarceration. Social networks, even those of a deviant nature, were a powerful form of support. A former gang member with significant family support used outside contacts to help manage his very first period of custody:

> *It was tough when I first went in, but my family stuck by me, and I could call them. That meant a lot.* (Sentenced inmate and former gang member, SMI)

Offenders from criminogenic families had fathers, uncles, brothers, or cousins who were in prison and had heard a great deal about being inside. This demystified the institutional setting and eased their transition. Prison posed no problem to this Manitoba offender:

> *First trip into Headingley was like a badge of honour for me. I had family members already there. First trip into Stony Mountain was an even bigger badge of honour.* (Remand and ex-gang member, HCC)

Other means of adjustment included heavy involvement in the criminal or drug subcultures on the outside. This resulted in shared values with other inmates, which in turn facilitated an easier move into custody and reduced the number of "new rules" or frames to learn. Seeing his fellow gang members inside helped this inmate adjust:

> *Fuck. I was terrified my first time, man. I was eighteen, just fresh out of the youth centre. I watched a lot of shit about prisons in movies and shit. I thought I was going to get a beating. But it was alright, I guess. Same,*

*same, same as if you lived on the streets most of your life, eh? You tend to
see all your buddies in jail too. Know what I mean?* (Remand inmate and
gang member, HCC)

While not a gang member, this Matsqui inmate saw many of his street
friends when he was incarcerated, which eased his transition:

*The first time I went to adult was in remand. I had friends from my neigh-
bourhood who were in remand. So it was easy to transition into that because
I would hang out with them on the street. Now I hang with them inside.*
(Sentenced inmate, MI)

Friendships can run deep; this Stony Mountain inmate had criminal
associations going back to his pre-teens:

*No, I wasn't worried. I was just mad because I was in Headingley, because
I got caught. I have been in prison since I was twelve years old, 'cause my
mom didn't really ever care. She encouraged me to go out and get money for
weed. I'm not, like, a complete idiot. I know right from wrong. But you know
what? I just wanted to fit in with my friends, 'cause they all went to jail,
they're all cool, and they're all, like, yeah, man. When I get in, the first thing
I think about is getting high and finding a dealer.* (Remand inmate, HCC)

Racial background also facilitated adjustment. The disproportionate
incarceration of minorities (in western Canada, Indigenous heritage) meant
there was a clearly identifiable group to socialize with upon entry into
custody. In his review, Kenneth Adams (1992) showed that African
Americans adjusted more easily to prison than whites: they more easily
form social groups and, in some cases, gangs. This is perhaps surprising
given that whites can socialize with other Caucasians. While some of these
groupings are racially based, integration also appears to be related to networks already established, as one Indigenous inmate I interviewed related:

*Yeah, I get along with everyone, but I hang more with my people. I know
some of them from outside. Some of us go way back.* (Remand inmate and
ex-gang member, HCC)

Finally, gangs provided the most straightforward means of integration and frame learning within correctional institutions. If you were a Native Syndicate member on the street, then upon your first custody admission in either youth or adult custody, you sought out your fellow gang members. The rules of the gang, its hierarchy, and first loyalty (i.e., the "prison gang frame") all held sway within the custodial setting (for further discussion, see Chapter 10). These two Headingley gang members saw gang status as an important way to adjust:

> *My first time I was placed in remand, when I was 16, raised from young offender. I liked adult remand better than the youth centre. I wasn't frightened at all. It was pretty good. I saw other gang members.* (Remand inmate and gang member, HCC)

> *Some of them are already used to it, eh? The younger guys have been to youth centres many times. Some of them actually like it because of the gang activities, eh? They can move up fast showing how tough they are in here.* (Remand inmate, HCC)

For inmates, not only was gang status important, but it also meant trying to reside in certain parts of the prison. For this affiliated Headingley inmate, gang status was an important tool for transition: the alternative was to be lumped in with offenders who were low in the inmate hierarchy:

> *They put me in general remand population with the goofs and nobodies.[2] If you don't know nobody, then, fuck, it's gonna be really hard your first time. Thank God I was affiliated and I knew people. I was put on the gang range because my brother was in the gang, not me.* (Remand inmate and gang associate, HCC)

Inmates reported coping with fear, efforts to exploit them, stigma, and stress related to going to prison. This Fort Saskatchewan inmate recalled sidestepping efforts to immediately get him into debt and under the thumb of others:

As you first entered Fort Saskatchewan, they'd give you five bails of tobacco, and you're given this tobacco, and you go in, onto the unit, and these old-timers are sitting there, and they kind of pull you to the side and, "Oh, you got tobacco. You wanna buy this? You wanna buy that?" You gotta politely say, "No," avoid getting into debt. (Sentenced inmate, FSCC)

For some offenders, especially those involved in sex crimes, the publicity surrounding their offence could also be stressful. Consistent with observations by social scientists and inmate scholars, respondents were as likely to reference stigma from other inmates as they were from COs, other staff and those outside the prison. This remand inmate I spoke with wanted to stay in general population but was literally terrified he might be found out:

It was scary coming in here. I knew lots of guys, but my story was in the paper, you know? What if someone found out? (Remand inmate, HCC)

According to this gang associate, to avoid stigma, you had to be clever, or at least show respect to those with status within the inmate population:

I: You can't have a bad attitude. There are some tough people in here.
W: What's a bad attitude?
I: Coming in thinking you can take on anyone – you can do anything you want and fucking get away with it. You gotta show some respect. If you get outta line on certain floors, you get put in check. You get punched around for being a fuckin' goof. (Remand inmate and gang associate, HCC)

Adjustment was easier for experienced offenders and prison gang members. Gang members did not have the added burden of worrying as much about assault by other inmates. This Matsqui lifer recalled his first prison experience and emphasized the importance of the first few features of the primary inmate frame: getting/showing respect, being strong, and being smart:

I was sixteen years old, and adult-admission age in British Columbia was seventeen, so I had to lie to get in. I was told by older guys, when I was in

RCMP lock-up in Richmond, that it would be better for me to go to an adult prison rather than a youth centre. I was afraid, but you go where the big guys tell you. I ended up in Oakalla Prison [BC provincial institution], which was closed in 1993. It was over a hundred years old at that time. The cells were small. There were toilets covered with wood to keep rats from crawling up through the pipes. I'm a young-looking person now, so imagine what I looked like when I was sixteen. I don't even think I had hair under my arms. I came into the institution and was introduced to violence very quickly, in the form of an inmate being beaten half to death right in front of me. But you keep quiet, you look tough, you show respect, and you survive. (Lifer, MI)

As inmates adjusted to incarceration, they began to construct the inmate frame that would guide their relations with others. Consistent with some of the old convict code rules, getting and showing respect, being strong and not being taken advantage of, and not showing fear were all important features of the inmate frame that steered interactions among offenders. Some inmates mentioned the importance of having mentors when they were first incarcerated, and how they later became mentors themselves. At Matsqui, a number of lifers were involved as peer support group mentors and made efforts to help newcomers adjust:

It was scary because I didn't know anybody, but I was fortunate that I was taken under the wings of the old-school boys. Guys took time to teach me the ropes, the common code. (Sentenced inmate, HCC)

I have been more or less a delegated big brother in here for a lot of younger guys who come in with their heads all twisted, fucked up. I try to help them straighten it out. I tell them certain things you do in life are maybe right or wrong. Maybe you wouldn't feel so bad if you were to start doing things differently. So I might suggest going to school or taking your parole officer's advice and do a program. Maybe you will learn something new. Maybe then you wouldn't have these problems with your girlfriend. Maybe your mother would love you a little more. (Sentenced inmate and senior gang member, SMI)

Yeah, we try to make it a bit easier here for newcomers – tell 'em the rules, who to watch out for, show them the ropes. Some listen, some don't. But it helps people a bit, I think. (Lifer, MI)

Developing the Primary Frame

After their initial admission to custody, inmates develop their primary frame towards other inmates. Here, the key lenses are respect, being strong, and being smart. They develop these frames largely in order to deal with the stigma inherent in being an inmate, the loss of family, stress, and fear (Figure 3.1). The initial primary frame scripts that guide behaviour and interaction are intended to help new admissions deal effectively with other inmates. They learn to manage stigma and shock by engaging in cautionary behaviours and by observing and learning. After that, however, many initial behaviours and drivers seem very much related to values such as stoicism, aggression, and a willingness to be violent. *Gaining* respect by behaving appropriately was important, but in the initial stages it was just as important *not to lose* respect. This might best be done by acting strong, not showing fear, and being stoic, but this might not be enough; being strong might require showing a willingness to be violent. Being smart, or at least not being taken advantage of by other inmates, was also important to avoid losing respect. These three Manitoba inmates outlined how fighting or willingness to fight was a quick way to earn respect:

> *You can usually avoid a fight if you're smart. But sometimes you have to man up – or at least look like you will.* (Remand inmate, ex-biker gang member, HCC)

> *If you don't want to fight, people will treat you like a goof. You gotta be tough.* (Remand inmate and associate gang member, HCC)

FIGURE 3.1
Developing the primary inmate frame

Frame precursors	
• Crime experience	• Family member inmates
• Illicit drug use	• Social support/No social support
• Gang membership	
Liminal frame	
• Stigma	• Observe, learn
• Shock	• Be careful
Initial and enduring primary frame scripts: With other inmates	
• Get respect/Show respect	
• Be strong/Do not show fear	
• Be smart/Do not be taken advantage of	

When I did my first bit, I got into a few fights and did good. I'm a big guy,
a tough guy. It's a quick way to get respect. I try not to fight now, if I can.
(Sentenced inmate, SMI)

Conclusion

Admission experiences vary depending on inmate history; that said, first-time transitions are generally difficult. Most study respondents reported a liminal phase involving stigma, shock, and learning to manage fear. Subcultural or convict code rules appeared to guide inmate adjustment and result in the creation of initial behavioural/interactive scripts. Respondents reported liminal periods of observing and learning, avoiding mistakes, and trying to appear strong. Adjustment was affected by prior social relationships with criminal, drug, or gang networks and by current social support from outside family or others. Initial difficulty might be mediated by having family, friends, or associates already incarcerated. The experiences reported here are remarkably consistent with the literature (Adams, 1992; Gibbs, 1982; Harvey, 2007; Schmid & Jones 1991). Inmates in other studies also reported a shock phase and adjustment period during which an inmate spent significant amounts of time in his cell.

The admission experience does not appear to have changed much for inmates over the past twenty-five years. It is a troubling one, and some manage it better than others. From a policy point of view, this research indicates that in Canada, first-time inmates (and even those recently readmitted) merit careful scrutiny upon admission. Practical policies that staff advised me are in use to manage inmate transitions include orientation programs that provide inmates with information about the institution's rules and regulations, as well as its programs and services. New inmates are taken to a separate area for an hour or so, and a presentation is made. On the institutional unit itself, inmate manuals are available that explain rules and regulations. Matsqui has recently established a mentorship program, which is offered by senior inmates. In all of these potential methods for easing inmate transitions, staff are key: they are in the best position to provide inmate manuals, explain key rules and regulations, and even identify potentially vulnerable inmates who bear watching. Careful monitoring by staff of new inmates in the preliminary phase of custody would appear to be very important, but from my interviews it was unclear how well correctional authorities structured this or how consistently it was being done.

Initial scripts help us understand some of the process of adjustment for Canadian inmates admitted to correctional institutions. The next chapter builds on these preliminary findings and outlines the primary inmate frame and its operation in greater detail.

4

How Inmates Relate to Others

The initial scripts of the inmate frame demand that new inmates engage in behaviours to help manage stigma and fear; they must also endeavour to be strong and earn respect. Beyond that point, inmates must flesh out their own prison identities and develop more nuanced approaches to dealing with other inmates. External others also pose challenges. How best to communicate with family, friends, or loved ones within the margins of the new inmate persona?

Inmate–Inmate Relations

Inmate accounts of prison life outline a world of wariness, mistrust, and exploitation (Carlson, 2001; Melnitzer, 1995). Far from convict code ideals of mutual respect and support and opposition to administration, studies indicate that inmates are distrustful of their peers' intentions and cautious because of the possibility of violence or exploitation (Cooley, 1992; Crewe, 2009; Hassine, 1999; Johnson, 2002b). Researchers on this topic commonly apply Goffman's (1959) micro-theory of impression management, which encompasses dramaturgical constructs of "front stage" and "back stage" performances. Front stage, inmates talk and behave in a way they expect others to approve of; back stage, their true nature and opinions are revealed. Indeed, many of the initial responses demanded by the primary frame (i.e., be strong or look tough, observe and learn) can have an alienating quality, or at least generate caution among other inmates. Schmid and Jones (1993) found that newly admitted offenders constructed their own hardened inmate identities – an impression management tactic to gain or at least not lose respect and to discourage other inmates from harming or exploiting them. Inmates may engage in various heightened masculine behaviours to curry respect (Jewkes, 2005); however, Nick De Viggiani (2012) found that these activities, if ill-conceived, can invite derision or hostility. Boastful but grossly exaggerated stories, trying to adopt an intimidating physical presentation, or being unnecessarily violent can just as easily result in inmates losing rather than gaining respect; they can also contribute to a reduced, unpopular status. Ben Crewe (2009) found that a violent and aggressive demeanour can also incur unwanted attention from corrections staff. For various reasons, then, adopting the primary inmate frame teaches inmates to suppress emotions, which means that honest expressions to other inmates come at a premium. In Canada, Rose Ricciardelli (2014b) found that the inmate code's emphasis on "minding your own business" encouraged social distance between inmates.

Ben Crewe and his colleagues (Crewe, Warr, Bennett, & Smith, 2013) have argued that the aggressive, stoic, tough front put on by male inmates is not required at all times in institutional life. Indeed, the stoic frame can be difficult to maintain. He found that inmates, despite their best efforts, sometimes become openly distraught after difficult telephone calls. In other instances, inmates become upset over goings on outside the institution or bad news received within it, and engage in angry outbursts, sometimes destroying items in their cell or their housing unit. Drawing on the field of social geography, Crewe and colleagues outlined various situations and physical zones where individuals could engage in more honest "backstage" emotional self-expression. For example, the death of a family member was an event that would excuse crying or other overt emotional expressions. Talking one-on-one with a trusted confidant was another situation where an offender could let his guard down. The authors identified various "emotion zones" within a custodial setting where prisoners were free of the inmate frame pressures of conforming to the expectations of other inmates and staff. Visiting rooms, program classrooms, and the chapel were all areas where inmates were safe to show a softer side. These zones benefited from the presence of outsiders, people not formally with the corrections staff (correctional or parole officers), including friends, volunteers, and program staff. They also found that researchers like them were viewed as external and could act as confidants.

In his original formulation, Sykes (1958) thought that the inmate code served the function of attenuating oppressive relations between inmates. Its rules and strictures promoted civility, if not inmate solidarity and mutual respect, and directed attention towards a common foe – the prison authorities. Are the guarded relations among Canadian inmates typical, or has the situation in fact worsened over time? Recall that one objective of this study is to examine prison culture over the past twenty-five years and identify significant changes. During my interviews with inmates I sought to learn whether the convict code promoted more cordial inmate relations, or at least limited serious hostilities. I turn now to my interview findings to appraise the Canadian situation.

Inmates on Relations with Other Inmates

For prisoners, learning the inmate frame was crucial to initially getting along with their peers, which was a much greater concern than relating to staff. It was a common wisdom among inmates that the most difficult thing about doing time in prison was having to reside with other offenders, who often were found to be temperamental, judgmental, and untrustworthy. I found that while offenders could and did learn the inmate frame and understood the rules around daily interactions necessary to survival, intimacy and close friendships were rare. Inmates belonging to prison gangs were most likely to report close friendships, but even core members were hesitant to fully trust their fellow members. Surprisingly, even senior, experienced inmates reported that they trusted none of their fellow inmates. I had anticipated greater solidarity among older inmates, but found that they identified very few close associates – often none, though in some instances as many as four. This seems low, considering that each of the institutions I surveyed housed hundreds of offenders. In the federal system, Matsqui Institution's lifers' peer support group members reported the most close friends, about five or six. Stony Mountain Institution's inmate relations were quite fragmented; not surprisingly, the gangs reported the most solidarity, but even within a gang, the members were cautious. In the provincial systems at Fort Saskatchewan and Headingley, aside from the gangs, inmates reported few close relations. This likely reflected the shorter time periods spent in remand, and also the pre-trial status of inmates; they were accused but not convicted, and their long-term status was often unclear. People came and went, which made the forging of friendships difficult. This was yet another disadvantage of being a remand inmate, even if experienced, and clearly another negative feature of having so many inmates held on pre-trial status.

One way to manage the stigma of incarceration is to find support from others, but spending time with other inmates seemed to exacerbate rather than ameliorate negative feelings. Living in prison brought with it the taint of serving time with "bad people"; thus an inmate was soiled simply by his association with criminals. One method for managing stigma, then, was for inmates to reject their associates, be it subtly or directly. When interviewed, inmates would try to invoke a social distance from their peers, often describing them as stupid, incompetent, or untrustworthy. Inmates frequently differentiated themselves from their fellow inmates and their apparent slovenly or unsavoury ways. "Other" inmates were frequently observed to be inept criminals, or liars, or as having no life or work skills to speak of. They indicated that spending time with such distasteful others made their incarceration more onerous.

Inmates' day-to-day interactions with other prisoners were guided by the central tenets of the primary inmate frame. In interactions with others they would present as stoic, reserved, and nominally courteous to others; but later they would often avoid other inmates to spend time alone. Working the inmate frame with other offenders, our subjects engaged in small talk, which might consist of complaining about institutional food and rules, the correctional officers (COs), caseworkers, and program staff or of telling "crime" stories about offences committed in the past, anecdotes about their lives on the street, or even "war" stories about past incidents in prison. They generally confided little personal information to others. They were cautious in their complaints about other inmates. Ideally, they were circumspect in their communication – that is they avoided asking too many questions of their peers and kept major and minor institutional transgressions quiet. In some situations, inmates might allow their peers to be emotional, such as on the death of a family member, but such exceptions were rare. Inmates invoked a lens of wariness to manage relations with other offenders. The frame of caution saw inmates engaging in guarded interactions with others. Confidences were few and not easily shared. This remand inmate reported difficulty behaving openly around others:

> It's, like, two-faced in prison, man – where it's, like, "Yo, I'm your buddy, but you know what, I'm that guy's buddy, too. I'm gonna talk shit because I'm his buddy, too." And you're kinda like the double agent, kinda, right? It varies. But when you're in here, it's a mask. You wear a fucking mask, man, because you can't admit to being weak. Except, say, if, like, your parent passes away, or a relative or something. No one's gonna say, "Ah ha." But you can't, for instance, tell people, "Ah, fuck, man. My girlfriend just broke up with me." No, you don't – you don't go and pout and cry and shit. You'll just get told, "Fuckin' straighten out, man. Shake it out," they say. "Shake it out, man. She's just a bitch." (Remand inmate, HCC)

These two inmates at MI and HCC were generally guarded around other inmates but indicated that they did find a few individuals to socialize with, even if they were still cautious:

> I don't trust most of them. There's a lot of guys who lie to make themselves seem bigger and badder, that kinda stuff. And there are guys who are truthful, because, I figure, "I am who I am," and people won't like it regardless. So there is always someone for somebody out there. (Sentenced inmate, MI)

> W: Do you spend much time with other inmates?
> I: Yep, some guys I sit around with, play cards with, you know. They pass off certain knowledge to me – how to survive and how to go about things. Shit, you think you know it all, and then you learn things here. Some of these guys know how to make fire out of batteries, smokes without tobacco. But I don't trust any of them. (Remand inmate and gang associate, HCC)

Much as Crewe and his colleagues (2013) found in their study, inmates related to me that they were more open in private settings within the prison or with outside people. In these situations, inmates confided what they really thought about other inmates, staff, and prison life generally. External confidants might include trusted peers, corrections staff, program staff, visitors, or even researchers such as me (similar to Crewe and his colleagues' experience). In interviews I found that respondents were sometimes complimentary towards staff and the institutional regime but rarely commented favourably on other inmates. These inmates from Matsqui and Headingley were guarded around others:

I hang around with a small group. I find it hard to trust people. Sometimes, I feel insecure around people and I don't know where I fit in. Like, I have an easy time talking to you [Weinrath], but if I am talking to someone else who's killed somebody, I might not be as comfortable. Because I'm doing a short sentence – this guy has been in for, like, twelve years. He doesn't want to hear what I got to say. (Sentenced inmate, MI)

I don't talk to a lot of inmates. I kind of stay off to my own little corner. I mean, I got my group of friends that I do talk to, but generally only in that corner of the range. But I wouldn't confide in anybody in here, and I don't take anybody for their word in here. I don't trust anybody. I don't believe anybody. I didn't come here to make friends, so when I leave here, I don't take guys' phone numbers. I don't give my phone number out. I don't tell them to come and visit me. (Remand inmate and ex-biker gang member, HCC)

There's a few guys, older guys, that I talk to. There's two older guys that are closer to fifty that I really get along with really well. They mutually respect everybody, as well as I, and I confide in them, but then only in my cell. I don't trust other inmates – not as far as I can throw them. (Remand inmate, HCC)

Some inmates appeared to have become tired of applying the inmate frame during their time in custody. They did not wish to interact with other inmates. They reported spending more time on their own, often staying by themselves in their cells. Cell time spent alone can help avoid any conflicts with other inmates and getting pressured or drawn into illegal prison activities, such as moving contraband. Two of the older inmates I spoke with indicated that they did not like talking to most other inmates, mostly because they were tired of hearing about their past or future crimes, or petty issues:

I like to be around intelligent people, and they can have intelligent conversation. All a lot of these people talk about is crime and how they done crime and gotten away with it. And I'm, like, I'm getting smarter that way, but that is not good. I like being around people, but sometimes it is hard. (Sentenced inmate, HCC)

I think people in prison sicken me. I hate people in prison. I hate bullshitters. I hate guys who think they're something they're not. I just can't stand people like that – people who bullshit all the time – 'cause, me, I don't bullshit. I tell it like it is. These guys who say, "I got this much money from scores, and I got that much money, and when I got out, I was driving in my Escalade," but they don't even have a fuckin' smoke. Tell the story to someone else! Me, I'll say the truth. I got out last time – I ended up at the McLaren hotel, a fuckin' hole in the earth. I don't have nothin' to hide. I don't need the bullshit to try and look cool. (Sentenced inmate and former gang member, SMI)

Respondents from Fort Saskatchewan and Stony Mountain pointed out the problems associated with trying to establish relationships with others. Part of "being smart" in the inmate frame was predicated on avoiding relations with untrustworthy others:

I got people who will come over and talk to me sometimes, but I find it uncomfortable. I might hear something and, if the COs find out, it might get back to me. Better to know nothing. I just tell guys when they try and talk about their shit [crimes], I say, "Look, buddy, I don't want to hear about this." I say, "I'll talk to you about whatever, but not about that." (Remand inmate, FSCC)

No, I don't trust fuckin' any of them. None. And it's funny – a lot of the guys do develop trust and get burned lots in here. Would I trust them to pay me the bill [for contraband] they owe me? I don't trust them. I just know they're going to pay me because they have to. Would I give them a hundred dollars and tell 'em to drop it somewhere for me on the street after he gets out? No way. Like, I'd know that he'd fuckin' be gone with my hundred dollars and you'd never see him again. I'm not gullible. I've seen it all. I've heard all the fuckin' stories. I've seen all the cons. I wrote the book on that shit. None of it will fly with me, you know? Some people do get sucked into a lot of fuckin' stories and a lot of bullshit. I've seen guys get burned over and over in this place, and it's just 'cause they're, you know, gullible. And they do have trust in people that they shouldn't, you know. We're criminals in here. You can't trust criminals. (Sentenced inmate and former gang member, SMI)

The few examples of closeness between inmates appeared among some (but not all) prison gang members on the prairies, some of the peer support inmates serving life at Matsqui, and inmates attending the Ni-Miikana Pathways unit at Stony Mountain.

Prison gang members reported being "brothers," and senior members especially felt a strong allegiance to one another, but conversely they looked down on other inmates and had little sympathy for their problems. Even with gang members, a feeling of camaraderie was not universal:

When you come to jail with your brothers, you have solid guys around you. But we don't trust any others in the rest of the prison. (Remand inmate and associate gang member, HCC)

I have a few friends – my cousins. I trust guys in the African Mafia, my crew. I get along with most other people in here. (Sentenced inmate and gang member, HCC)

One senior gang member reported not trusting others, even core members like himself:

W: Don't you trust some inmates, like other high-ranking gang members?
I: I trust them to an extent, but it is not like I would go to them with my problems. I sometimes want to keep to myself because of my stepfather. You talk about certain things, but personal stuff like that is something I have kept in for years. (Sentenced inmate and senior gang member, SMI)

The Matsqui lifers who belonged to the peer support group appeared to take a greater interest in the welfare of fellow lifers and other inmates. The goals of the peer support program were to help inmates work out problems themselves and reduce institutional dependence. Other benevolent offenders included some of the inmates mentioned earlier at each of the four institutional sites, who either took on an informal mentoring role or knew other inmates who had done that. Still, these helpful individuals appeared to be in the minority:

> *I have some fellows I spend time with. Most of them I have known for fifteen or sixteen years, so I trust them.* (Lifer, MI)

> *We're here to stick up for other inmates, to see they don't get screwed around. We stick up for each other, too.* (Lifer, MI)

The Ni-Miikana unit, which held about forty inmates, was part of a series of Pathways units established by federal corrections for Aboriginal inmates (for an overview, see Jensen & Nafekh, 2011). The Pathways units were intended to provide Indigenous programming, including healing services, and to increase post-release success for First Nations, Inuit, and Metis offenders. This inmate found more trusting relationships in Ni-Miikana, although there was still a note of caution:

> *In this system, you can't trust anybody. Like, even on the streets, I've never trusted my own brother. But now in Ni-Miikana, I'm starting to get that trust back. You just gotta be careful what you say in here, and you'll be all right. The way you make your time is the way you're gonna do your time.* (Sentenced inmate and former gang member, SMI)

It is certainly a positive that the Ni-Miikana unit promoted stronger relationships through its programming and emphasis on Indigenous culture. But it is surprising in some ways that Indigenous inmates would say they were cautious about trusting other Aboriginals, even those related to them. The weak initial trust between Indigenous inmates is likely partly attributable to the effects of colonization, and the negative views Aboriginal Canadians are fed of their race. Similarly, in the United States, Bonilla-Silva (2006) found that African Americans often held stereotypical racist views of their peers. These negative within-group views are also associated with the concept of internalized racism, which takes the form of a negative self-identity (Cokley, 2002).

Lenses of Predation: Contraband Trade and Drug Use

For some inmates, past behaviour and prior incarcerations shaped parts of the inmate frame. Offenders involved in criminal activities outside a correctional institution might become involved in the contraband trade on the inside, and certainly that was the case for gang members. Drugs were a large part of institutional contraband. Addicts from the outside often continued that behaviour once incarcerated. For this lifer, the large number of offenders with substance abuse issues at Matsqui meant that drugs would continue to be a problem there:

> There are a lot of addicts in here. Matsqui has always been known for that. It's hard to keep the drugs out when you have that big a demand. (Lifer, MI)

Inmates used drugs for psychological escape from the tedium of prison; some of them sought steroids or other muscle enhancers to become bigger, stronger, and more intimidating. Inmates reported that many of their peers also showed an addiction to gambling and ended up with debts they could not pay. To this gang leader, enforcement and violence were a natural outcomes of bad behaviour. There are no secrets about collection strategies within correctional institutions:

> We provide a service, you know, but if you want to play, you have to pay. Some people are just stupid. They keep piling up their debt. (Sentenced inmate and senior gang leader, SMI)

Gangs used violence to control much of the contraband trade, yet I found a few independent operators who avoided gang involvement or who had sufficient family connections to avoid reprisals. "Storesmen," as these inmates called themselves, also dealt in canteen items such as tobacco and confectionary items that were allowed for inmates (but trading was illegal). They would engage in profit-making activities to attain resources and achieve what power they could, but often this profit needed to be sufficient to feed their own addiction:

> It's hard to get drugs in here. But people still need things when they don't have money, so you loan things out – chocolate bars, magazines. I have been accused of running a store here by the COs, but, hey, I am just trying to help people out, you know? Two-for-one is not so bad when the alternative is nothing. (Sentenced inmate, HCC)

The Primary Inmate Frame: Other Inmates

The primary inmate frame is first built around notions of gaining and keeping respect, and presenting oneself as strong and smart is crucial to constructing relations with others (Figure 4.1). Frames of caution and social distance gird interactions, limiting the ability of inmates to help one another. Those with experience in criminal enterprises or gang involvement may look to interactions with other inmates as opportunities to exploit and gain advantage. Still others seek out the underground economy to sate their need for illicit drugs or other contraband, and care little whether they are "victimized" by their peers. How much respect do inmates get if they can be intimidated by their peers or spend all their time trying to get drugs and get high? Not much. These offenders were sarcastically referred to as "nobodies" or "crackheads," marginal inmates who didn't have the fortitude to be "solid" inmates. Nobodies and crackheads could not be trusted and might well inform if pressured by staff, and this limited their standing within the inmate group.

FIGURE 4.1
The primary inmate frame

Inmate frame: Other inmates	Inmate frame: Correctional staff
• Get respect	• Maintain social distance
• Be strong/Do not show fear	○ Be careful about too much communication with staff
• Be smart/Do not be taken advantage of	○ Do not inform on another inmate
• Be cautious	• Be cautious/Do not trust staff
• Maintain social distance	• (For some) work with program staff to improve
• (For some) Take advantage – intimidate, manipulate, trade contraband	○ Listen to staff; try to find programs that might help for release
• (For some) Get high/Obtain drugs or gamble	

Inmates and Staff on the Decline of the Convict Code

Earlier, I incorporated some of the precepts of the inmate subcultural code as the initial building blocks for the primary inmate frame. The lack of camaraderie and cohesion among inmates that I found in my interviews was in some ways surprising, for this runs counter to the inmate subculture's claims to rules that promote solidarity among offenders. As other researchers have found, however, the inmate code of conduct in Canada has declined in influence. My respondents lived in a milieu where trust was at a premium, conversation had to be guarded, and other inmates were best kept at arm's length. So if the inmate code has declined in importance in Canadian prisons, why is this so?

I used the terms "convict code" and "inmate code" when interviewing inmates and staff on this topic. The term was used interchangeably by most respondents, but older inmates tended to prefer "convict code." Federal staff also favoured the term "convict code," more so than provincial staff. In addition, some inmates had an affinity for being identified as "cons," which they explained was a term applied only to experienced, respected inmates.

My respondents indicated that the central tenets of the inmate code were not consistently followed. On its face, the convict code promoted fraternal rules to ensure at least some harmony and solidarity among inmates. Interviews with inmates and correctional staff, however, contradicted this notion. Inmates universally believed that there had been an overall decline in the authority of the code and its rules over the past twenty years, consistent with the findings reported in other studies on inmate subculture. They gave numerous examples of inmate code violations: inmates stealing from one another, fights being many-on-one (not one-on-one), problems on the street being brought into the institution, and no consistent status hierarchy by crime being recognized. This lack of group cohesion undoubtedly had an impact on an inmate's ability to develop positive relationships within prison.

According to my subjects, the informal rules that were *supposed* to make up the ideal type of inmate code in federal and provincial prisons are largely gone. Study participants varied, however, in (a) their weighting of the code's influence today versus twenty-five years ago; (b) their view of how many inmates actually tried to adhere to the informal rules; and (c) their reasons for why the inmate code may have diminished in force. Respondents' general consensus was that there had been a number of key changes in the status and force of the code. These changes have directly affected today's inmate–inmate and inmate–staff relations.

When asked to envision what the inmate code was supposed to be comprised of, the reports of study participants did not differ substantively from what is outlined in the literature. The rule against informing was cited most frequently, followed by not becoming too friendly with COs. Inmates and staff ranked these similarly. This Fort Saskatchewan inmate reflects the consensus view – there was more talk with COs, but still a limit existed:

> *Twenty years ago, when I started, there was no talking at all, or get beat up or get a fat lip. But that is what you put yourself into. You learn to walk away and zip up, and that's it. Put your head down and walk away. You get away with a bit more talking now, but it's better to keep quiet.* (Remand inmate, FSCC)

To a lesser extent, inmates discussed rules pertaining to mutual respect, or the conventions that were supposed to exist that encouraged doing your own time, minding your own business, and not being derogatory to other inmates:

> *No, I mean, you don't have to respect me because I have this amount of years, you know. Just respect your fellow con, that's all.* (Sentenced inmate, HCC)

This SMI lifer explained that not understanding the need to be cautious in your inquiries could create problems:

> *The biggest [rule] is to keep your mouth shut, right? Mind your own business. If you come in and ask too many questions, you are in a world of hurt before you even know it, right? I just dealt with a young man who is on the mental health range, and I know he has got some issues and stuff. But he just asked question after question after question. And, you know, if you are a guy like myself, I don't really care. I just ignore it. But if you are a gang member, that is a definite no-no. "Why is he asking me all these questions? Who is this guy?" Then the next thing you know, half the gang wants to kill him. So there is that rule: Keep your mouth shut.* (Lifer, SMI)

Staff more frequently identified norms around mutual respect among inmates. Like others, this Headingley staff saw them more as rules of the past:

I think it is there, but definitely not as big as before. Years back, there used to be an inmate code of conduct, and they respected each other's privacy. Now, there is a very limited code because they are pretty much stealing from each other – unheard of back in, say, the early eighties. (Staff, HCC)

Reasons provided by respondents for the decline of the code were similar to those found by Crewe (2005a), Faulkner and Faulkner (1997), Hunt and his colleagues (1993), and Irwin (1980) in Britain and the United States and by Griffiths and Murdoch (2014) in Canada. The two biggest factors identified by offenders and staff were, first, the influx of state-raised inmates – that is, younger offenders with long histories of social services involvement and foster placement – and, second, communication with staff that had undermined some of the more negative features of the code. Generally, the decline in the inmate code was viewed as a negative phenomenon by staff and inmates, but for different reasons. Inmates were very concerned about what they perceived to be an increase in the amount of informing. They expressed anger over how this restricted their ability to solve problems within their own group. They also decried the current lack of mutual respect and courtesy: they felt that this had been an important organizing feature of inmate life "back in the day." Staff did not necessarily view the amount of informing as a problem, because of course this usually meant that COs had more knowledge of inmate activities, which improved their ability to manage their units and troublemakers. Staff felt, however, that the decline in inmate respect for one another was a negative feature of day-to-day prison life. They believed that offenders with little concern for other inmates were unlikely to show concern towards members of the community when they were released.

These inmates certainly lamented the increase in informing:

The unwritten rules of jail are basically gone. There's so much rattin' and shit on these ranges. It's fuckin' sickening. Like, when I started doing my time, you learned – and you learned fast – what jail was about. It was jail.

It wasn't what it is today. If you didn't learn fast, you got straightened out, and that was it. And then, obviously, you learned. (Sentenced inmate, HCC)

There's way too many rats, you know. I still don't think there is anything wrong with smoking, but you know, all of a sudden the guards know buddy's got tobacco. (Remand inmate, FSCC)

Informing to staff was a concern, but prisoners also were alarmed by the amount of theft by fellow prisoners. Some, like these Fort Saskatchewan and Matsqui inmates, attributed more stealing to drug-addicted prisoners:

You know, it used to be how nobody stole from each other in the old days. Now it's, like, holy fuck! You know what I mean? (Remand inmate, FSCC)

W: The old convict code had a certain nobility?
I: Yeah, but there is no nobility here, in regards to that – stealing from another inmate. That happens a lot, and it happens because of the drugs. Because of the addicts who are so bent on getting high. They are willing to take their chances of getting killed. (Sentenced inmate, MI)

Yeah, there is so little of the code in here right now. I can give you example after example of people stealing from each other, from jealousy, the envy that comes out. As we speak right now, I wouldn't be surprised if there was a lockdown because of tobacco stealing. Here, the code doesn't matter. Like, for instance, there are coffee jugs. Someone took the glass tube out of one last week, to use for a crack pipe, I guess. And that's what gives crackheads a bad name. That person, there's a day he's going to get punched out for doing that, because you know what – you're ruining the coffee for thirty guys in this range. There is no code. There is no code in here. (Lifer, MI)

Not surprisingly, my respondents indicated that older inmates were more likely to subscribe to the code, either having learned it from inmate mentors when they first were incarcerated, or having picked it up over the years using common sense and street crime experience. However, a few inmates pointed out that some younger inmates could also show that they understood the fundamentals of the code. Analogous to the "stand-up" guys and "solid cons" described in the older US literature (Sykes & Messinger, 1960; Irwin, 1970), some younger inmates were thought to have learned subcultural values from their involvement in street crime groups, and been astute enough to apply those values behind bars. Much like Irwin's (1970) distaste for "dope fiends" in his classic work *The Felon,* these Matsqui and Stony Mountain inmates asserted that drug users were not to be trusted:

> W: *Is it just the old-school guys who adhere to the inmate code?*
> I: *My best friend in the joint is now twenty-one, and we're not great friends, but he's young and he's got it.* (Lifer, MI)

> I: *There are still a lot of guys who hold true to that* [convict code]. *And I'm one of them, you know what I mean.*
> W: *Is it true more of the older guys?*
> I: *Not necessarily. Some of these younger kids are right in there, too. Some of them are very much about the code, because a lot of these kids are growing up on the street, so they know the street code. So when they come here, they follow the code here, too, which is impressive. It is more the crack kids that have no code. No code in life – they have no code in jail, right? You know, what you have out there is what you have in here, as far as I am concerned.* (Sentenced inmate and former gang member, SMI)

Inmates with COs and Other Staff

I found that the day-to-day framing of relations with COs had changed for inmates. With the convict code not holding as much sway, the social distance between inmates and COs had lessened. Talking to staff was allowed, but this was nuanced, and there were still limits on how close such relations could be. For example, as one staff explains, informing over an assault was still forbidden:

> *Parts of the code exist, and other parts are kind of minimized. You know, for example, that if a guy gets beat up, inmates are not going to talk to staff when we do an investigation. They didn't see it, or "I fell in the shower," you know? So not cooperating with staff, not listening to staff, a lot of that still exists. So there is definitely an inmate code. There always will be an inmate*

code. It's just that some of the rules, like talking to staff, have changed because times have changed. (Staff, HCC)

When interacting with staff, inmates were mindful of being scrutinized by their peers. Thus, an inmate had to avoid getting too familiar with COs and other staff. The possibility of being an informant always hung over inmates who talked too long with correctional staff. The terms "bubble hounds" and "panel mommies" were coined by offenders in Alberta to identify male and female inmates who spent too much time around staff kiosks, glassed-in officer "pods," or other CO posts. These inmates, it was said, lacked the savvy to know when it was appropriate to speak with staff, and when relations were getting too familiar.

Staff observed that the balance between talking and not talking to staff was a tricky one, and managed differently by different inmates:

I think, in any institution, there will be that sort of underlying, "Hey, you don't rat. Don't talk to the staff." It's just one of those codes that is there. Does every inmate adopt it and follow it through that all-or-nothing mentality? Absolutely not! A lot of inmates, through interaction with staff, will give information on things that are happening. Especially for their own self-interest. (Staff, SMI)

When interpreting how to behave in the inmate–staff frame, offenders may use a gendered lens. On the one hand, inmates embrace "hyper-masculine values" such as being physically aggressive, tough, and stoic, and these values can promote prison violence (Comack, 2008). On the other, the need to appear strong can lead to less aggression towards female COs. Perhaps surprisingly, female COs found that male inmates posed less of a threat to them than male COs:

The code has changed, yes and no. They steal from each other more now, there is no one-on-one for fighting, and they do talk to staff. But they don't tell us everything, and we don't expect them to. Some of them maintain more of a code than others; some inmates try to be solid. But there are still some aspects of the code inmates stick to that might surprise you. For example, male inmates don't assault a female officer. I feel safer on a male unit than a female unit. (Staff, FSCC)

Otherwise, the lens of caution, focused initially when interacting with other inmates, also came into play in interacting with COs and even program staff. They were still viewed as "the other" (i.e., non-inmate), and closeness was not encouraged or countenanced by most. A Fort Saskatchewan inmate best summed up this feeling:

I get along with staff, but I always remember I'm an inmate and they're not. (Remand inmate, FSCC)

I was left feeling that our prisons must be very lonely places for most inmates. Negative experiences with corrections staff had caused these two inmates to become guarded:

You can't get too friendly with staff. It's all good, and then they get pissed over some bullshit rule. Man, relax! I find it's better to be careful around them. (Remand inmate, HCC)

My case manager wrote a lot of incorrect things on my suspension report. When I tried to point that out, she just cut me off. (Sentenced inmate, MI)

Finally, there was general support among respondents for working with staff to find an institutional job, program, or activity. This was not universal, but even gang members expressed interest in staying active within the institution. Some, like these three inmates, were quite motivated to engage in treatment and were assisted by staff (the "program" frame will be developed further in Chapter 10):

Yeah, I talked to my worker about programs. She helped me get a job in the kitchen. (Remand inmate, HCI)

I try to tell the kids to talk to their case manager, get into programs. Sometimes they can be of use. (Sentenced inmate and senior gang member, SMI)

Staff can be helpful. Some helped me find work in here. (Lifer, MI)

Relations with People Outside Prison

For offenders, a break from the omnipresent inmate frame, and a respite from spending time with unwanted others, is offered by communication with family and friends from the community. These individuals are most often referenced by inmates colloquially as coming from either "the street" or "the outside world." There are many things inmates can gain from such outside contact. Establishing or maintaining ties with significant others is critical to managing the stigma and stress arising from initial entry into the prison (Adams, 1992; Draine, Wolff, Jacoby, Hartwell, & Duclos, 2005). Also, contact with pro-social others can push sentenced inmates to follow up on their intention to take programs and work towards an early release; determination for self-improvement may wane after the initial shock of incarceration subsides. Speaking with and writing to spouses, children, parents, or pro-social friends, or spending time in visiting areas with them, can motivate an inmate to use his or her time in custody constructively. Munn and Bruckert (2013) in Canada and Joan Petersilia (2003) in the United States have emphasized the importance of contact with others for establishing support for re-entry into the community.

Visits have generally been a poorly studied part of corrections, but since 2005 there has been a surge of investigations into visitation and its effects on inmates. Generally, researchers report positive results from contact with the outside world, perhaps most importantly in reducing post-release recidivism (Bales & Mears, 2008; Derkzen, Gobeil, & Gileno, 2009; Duwe & Clark, 2013; Mears, Cochran, Siennick, & Bales, 2012). Visits have also been found to be of benefit in maintaining institutional order. Joshua Cochran (2012), Shanhe Jiang and Thomas Winfree (2006), and Karen Lahm (2009) all found that more frequent visits were associated with a reduction in official reports of inmate misconduct. In a Florida study, Cochran and his colleagues divided inmates into categories of non-visited, late visited, early visited, and consistently visited (Cochran, Mears, & Bales, 2014). They found that increased visitation resulted in less institutional misconduct, especially for the inmates most consistently visited.

Visits have potential benefits, yet many inmates do not receive contact from the outside. In their review of prison visitations, Joshua Cochran and colleagues (2014) found that most US prison inmates do not receive a single visit. In their CSC study of federal inmates (who serve longer sentences than provincial inmates), Dena Derkzen, Rene Gobeil, and Justin Gileno (2009) found that only 46 percent of men and 54 percent of women had ever received a visit.

About half my respondents (who admittedly were not randomly selected) had received personal visits; slightly more had contact with the outside if letters and phone calls were included. Curiously, this did not vary much among remand, provincial, and federal inmates. Many remands were serving shorter periods of time, so interest in having outsiders visit in person varied (i.e., why bother, or hopefully out soon, or use of telephone is adequate). Similar sentiments were reported by inmates serving short sentences. Some federal inmates indicated that they had not received or been involved in visits because they had "burned their bridges" with significant others. Relationships were often damaged because of a family member's disappointment in an inmate's repeated bad behaviour, such as involvement in crime and illicit drug use and then compounding transgressions by lying. Beyond this, some inmates resisted outside contact for various reasons: because they had few social contacts in the community; to avoid the shame of having their family see them in prison; or a perception that life would be easier in prison (or at least less painful) if thinking about the outside was avoided at all costs.

I found that inmates used visits as opportunities to share things with close family and others and to get their minds away from the institution. For those who received visits, letters, or phone calls, making contact with community members required them to drop the primary inmate frame and adopt an external frame. Offenders related to external others in a manner that was distinct from how they might interact with other inmates or even staff, but still different from how they related to others when they had lived in the community. Each was an individual in a correctional institution, yet still connected to the outside world. The most common inmate external frame was a "pro-social" one. It was a much more personal, intimate frame used with external others, in contrast to the wary scripts used to guide conversation and behaviour with other inmates or COs. Discussion with visitors centred on the activities of family and friends on the outside. Sometimes this might involve crime or illicit activity in the community, but more often conversation revolved around personal matters such as who was working where, how was the health of an inmate's wife/girlfriend or parents, or how the children were doing. Talk inside with other inmates was taken up by all the details of institutional life; talk with outsiders was very much focused on the outside world and what went on there.

The pro-social frame is not necessarily an honest frame, especially when the topic of rehabilitation is broached. In conversations with most friends and family, inmates verbalize an acceptance of responsibility, taking on a role of "repentant con," and talk about personal change. The inmate's belief in the pro-social frame presented to outsiders is ambiguous: the inmate may feel some commitment to change but be unsure of his own follow-up on release back into the community. Rehabilitation is an important piece of the pro-social frame to invoke, however, because otherwise inmates risk losing almost all contact with the outside world. So external others need to hear the offender acknowledge his or her mistakes and express a desire to change.

Most of the time, discussions with outsiders were kept private from other inmates. Roles that popped up in this frame were associated with being a family member – a son, boyfriend, husband, or cousin. The point of such conversations was generally to keep up with "life on the street" or engage in small talk, however pressed the inmate was with day-to-day matters within the institution. Contact with others who wanted it was held dear by most inmates I interviewed. Even the promise of discussing mundane matters that grew less salient the longer the inmate was away from the community had appeal. As Crewe and his colleagues (2013) have suggested, the visiting area is an institutional zone where more personal discussions can ensue for inmates who otherwise keep things to themselves. For these two inmates, contact with outsiders brought great joy:

I talk to my family every day. Every day. I only have one number on my pin [institutional code provided for telephone use] *and that's my family. While I'm in here, my friends, all my fuckin' associates, my business associates, they can go fuck themselves. 'Cause they ain't gonna put a smile on my face. My family does. Five minutes, a half-hour of talkin' to 'em, fuck, I'd be smiling all day. I could fuckin' call 'em right now on this fuckin' phone, man, say "Hi, I love you man," tell them that I love them and that*

I'll call them right back, and I'll be smilin' all fuckin' day, man. Very rarely do you see a guy smile. But when they do, it's good, man. When you hear the guys laughing, it's loud, man. It's cool, man. (Remand inmate and gang associate, HCI)

I phone my wife every day. I write to some girls in Edmonton Max. My wife comes to visit me at least once a month with my boys. That makes things a whole lot easier. It's the only thing I look forward to, is my visits when they're booked. Yeah, I love my visits and my son. My son's birthday was last week, and they come and seen me on Thursday, so that was nice to see my boys. Growing, growing up so fast, you know. (Sentenced inmate, HCC)

Private family visits, a sometimes controversial practice in the federal system, are valued by those inmates who can make use of them. Prisoners typically spend forty-eight to seventy-two hours in a private trailer on the institution's grounds within the security perimeter. Inmates must earn this privilege through a combination of time served, good behaviour, and confirmed sponsorship. The prisoners I interviewed considered such visits an important method to maintain relationships:

Well, I used to keep in touch with people on the outside for a long time, my mom and everybody else, but pretty much, now, it's just my wife. I phone her every day. She visits me once a week. When I was at Stony, she came every second day. We used to get the PFVs [private family visits]. I am not a big writer, but I still do write to her and she still writes to me to this day, even though we visit all the time. I have kids with a different marriage, and my ex-wife won't allow any contact. Outside of my wife, I don't contact nobody. I have lost everybody from going to prison. I have hurt people so many times with this repeating drug use and this repeated going to jail, you know. So every time I get out, it is going to be different – and then I go and do it again, and here I am. (Remand inmate and ex-gang member, HCC)

I miss my wife. I miss my kids. I miss my parents. Once a month, we have a PFV here, a private family visit, so you look forward to those, pretty much. I call it "Coming up for oxygen." (Lifer, MI)

Prison gang members are thought to gain friendship and support from being part of a gang. Indeed, James Vigil (2003) has argued that the failure of family to provide support growing up is a motivator to gang joining. Yet both this gang member and an ex-gang member commented on the importance of their extended family:

> *I maintain contact with my family – all the important people to me, my grandma, my mom, one of my little brothers. My other brother just passed away, and my dad just passed away. All when I was in jail. A lot of people passed away when I was in jail.* (Remand inmate and ex-gang member, HCC)

> *I look forward every day to calling my common law and talking to my son. I am hoping to see what my other kid's gonna be. I've got one on the way. My common law doesn't like coming out here. It's bullshit coming, getting here.* (Sentenced inmate and gang member, HCC)

Surprisingly, despite the availability of relatively inexpensive calls and reasonable access to telephones, many inmates wrote and received letters. Several respondents reported using both telephone and letters. Some preferred communicating by letter. Any letters received were treasured:

> *I have my kids and my spouse and a couple other girlfriends I maintain contact with. By phone, letters, pictures, whatever. I try and limit my calls to once a day, so I write letters. I just finished writing a letter last night. I get letters from my daughters, mom, dad, stuff like that. Once a week, couple times a week, from my sisters and others. They make times easier, kinda, thinking about family. I read them over and over again.* (Remand inmate and gang member, HCC)

> *I call someone at least once a day. I talk to a couple of girls I know. They're just friends. I called my mom once today. My mom's crippled in a wheelchair with MS, so she likes for me to call her at least once a day. At least, if I call her, she hears my voice – her day goes on a little bit easier. I write letters to my daughter. Don't get letters right now. Used to. It's a highlight when you get mail.* (Remand inmate, HCC)

I phoned home three times in the last three months. I send some letters back home. Let's see, I wrote about four times now. I write to mom. Let her know I'm okay. I've been in two months – no visits. I am far away from home – Tadoule Lake, up north. It's kinda hard, sometimes. It gets lonely. No communication with my people. (Sentenced inmate, HCC)

Family and friends were not the only contacts valued; contacts with volunteer visitors were also found to be very helpful to inmates with no one else to talk to. These visitation programs clearly offer something, given the high proportion of inmates who never receive visits. This inmate valued his connection with volunteers:

Connections with the outside would be those volunteers that come here, and have come to know me over the years. I would say they have been life-altering for me. It's like friendship, someone to talk with, share stories with. They are not advocates like a lawyer, but they bring support for my parole hearing. (Inmate, MI)

Not all contact with the outside world was positive, and frequent contact was not without stress. Even when a pro-social veneer was adopted in the external frame, contact with the outside always involved having to acknowledge one's inmate status. External relations could be very positive and bring important support to inmates, but communication with the outside world could also bring pain. Earlier, I discussed the hardship that stigma placed on inmates, and that stigma could be brought on by other inmates, staff, and even themselves. Contact with friends and family also brought on stigma, reminding offenders that they were inmates and that their family/friends were outside while they were inside. For some inmates, managing the stigma brought on by contact with family members posed huge difficulties. As children grew older and started to understand that "Dad is in jail," shame and stigma began to creep into meetings, and most respondents found it difficult to see their children as time served increased. Not being able to help their partners raise their children was another embarrassment. Hearing about the success of other family members reminded inmates about their own failures. For this Matsqui inmate,

stigma grew from the indignity of being a "con" to the further humili-
ation of being a "loser":

> *I used to maintain contact with my step-mom and my step-brothers, but after*
> *coming in so much, they kind of lost hope in me. Or maybe it just hurts them*
> *too much, I don't know. They don't really specify. But I still call them sometimes,*
> *but if I lose their phone numbers, that's it.* (Sentenced inmate, MI)

Contact with those outside, and hearing about the problems of spouses
and families, reminded inmates that they had put themselves in a position
of helplessness. If a girlfriend or wife called with a woeful tale of not being
able to pay the rent, there was nothing an inmate could do. If an inmate
gave advice to a family member, there was no guarantee it would be followed. Older children might engage in school activities and graduate from
school, and inmates could only cheer them on from inside while they
missed their kids growing up. If their partner started to slip away or engage
in a relationship with another person, an inmate simply had to endure it.
If a parent or sibling passed away, an inmate was not always able to attend
the funeral, although most institutional staff made efforts to have them
attend. These were painful times for my respondents.

Inmates coped with these feelings of helplessness in different ways.
Some of them persisted in keeping outside contact and managed the stress
as best they could. They looked forward to seeing or speaking with family
and friends as often as possible. Many opted for telephone contact and
avoided glass visits, particularly when children were potential visitors.
These three inmates cited the requirement of glass visits in provincial
institutions (HCC and FSCC), as well as distance and barriers to travel, as
reasons for telephone contact in lieu of personal visits:

> *We have three kids. My wife runs a business. For her to get a babysitter, for*
> *her to come out and see me for just a glass visit, and we don't even bother.*
> *She can't bring the kids 'cause they'll freak out, right? We got a piece of glass*
> *between us. The kids are better off that I just talk to them on the phone*
> *every day. I think that is best.* (Remand inmate, FSCC)

> *I don't write letters, and I don't ask for letters. Telephones are just as good.*
> *I don't get visits, and I'd rather not anyway 'cause I don't like to see their*

faces, their emotions when they leave. It would be rough, rougher for everybody. (Sentenced inmate, HCC)

I phone my parents daily. Just to say "Hi." I just want to hear their voices, just to know that they're fine. I don't want to get visits; I don't like seeing people behind the glass. I don't write letters, and the only letter I ever received was basically money from my parents. But I don't need that much. I'm able to look after myself doing the trade [running a stores contraband system]. (Sentenced inmate, HCC)

The new security technology applied to correctional institutions' telephones may well discourage organized crime, but it also punishes those who are trying to maintain relations outside, as this inmate relates:

Phoning is tough sometimes. You can't tell your girlfriend important stuff on the phone 'cause someone is listening to you. They're recording. You can't really be alone talking with her. (Remand inmate, HCC)

Finally, some inmates chose to direct their attention back to managing the primary inmate frame, and severely limited or stopped contact altogether with family or friends. They may have liked the idea of contact, but not enough to put up with the stress, the pain, and the stigma associated with maintaining external relations. For these three inmates, the external frame could bring joy but inevitably also brought pain:

W: Do you get visits here?
I: I could, but it just hurts me when they leave, man. I don't want my family seeing me in this place. I don't want my girlfriend seeing me in this place. I sure don't want my baby in her belly hearing me talk about this place. (Remand inmate and gang associate, HCC)

I don't keep a lot of contact in here. I've closed myself off. I don't get personal visits, because everyone in my family is in Ontario. Number two, I would never ask my family to come to a federal institution. That is an embarrassment. I would never want to put them through the search, the hassle. (Lifer, MI)

When you have a girlfriend, your time goes slow because you just want to be there for her. You call her, and she's telling you her problems. But how can you deal with that when you're in jail? You can't deal with it. All you can do is sit there and take a try and listen to what she has to say, so she feels better. But it makes you feel really helpless, because there's nothing you can do about it. (Sentenced inmate and senior gang member, SMI)

Those with limited external contacts maintained that life was better when they focused on being in prison and thought only rarely of the outside. These three inmates found it easier to cope when they avoided external relations and prioritized managing the daily expectations of the inmate frame:

If your mind's on the street, then – you've heard the expression, if you're doing rough time, you're thinkin' about out there too much – just makes it rougher on you. Some nights, guys in here, I hear 'em screamin' at their women and flippin' out ... That's a sad way to do time, torturing yourself, basically. Listen, I think you're fine when you're older. You don't live by your emotions as much as when you're younger. (Remand inmate, HCC)

I have a sister I phone once a week, or I phone every Sunday. But I don't really want nothing to do with anybody else out there. I don't really wanna know what's going on out there, because I'm here to help myself. And if I talk to people out there, it's going to be that, that negative ... like, what's going on out there and ... I don't want nothing to do with it 'cause it makes my time rougher, thinking about what's going on out there instead of thinking about what's going on in here. (Sentenced inmate and ex-gang member, SMI)

I didn't get a visit once for two years because I just didn't want any. Too much contact with the outside world makes you think about the street too much, so you get depressed. If you get into this routine in here, it's our own little society. And time flies; the months drop off the calendar. But if you start thinking, start talking to people on the street all the time, thinking about your release date too much, time will just drag ... and drag. That contact makes you ponder on being in prison too much, because you do get a lot of time in your cells here. If you think too much about the street, you're going to do hard time; you'll rough it. (Sentenced inmate and former gang member, SMI)

The External Inmate Frame

I found three instances where inmates did *not* adopt a pro-social element in their external frame (see Figure 4.2) when communicating with outsiders. First, individuals with drug addictions or who were involved in the underground economy (or both) engaged in establishing or re-establishing external contacts that could help them bring in contraband. The relationships of the following three inmates tended to be focused on finding friends,

FIGURE 4.2
The external inmate frame

Family and friends	
• Maintain communication	• Reduce/Cut off communication
o Work to obtain support from family and friends	o Focus on day-to-day prison life and psychological survival
o Maintain knowledge of outside activities of significant others	o Avoid pain/stigma of having partner and children see you in prison
o Present as inmate trying to change or as inmate who will not change	
o Embrace rehabilitation goal/Reject rehabilitation goal	
o Obtain drugs/contraband	
• *Above interactions/motivations might be feigned or true*	

Others	
• Inmate as misunderstood	• Inmate as hero
o Inmate as unlucky, victim of circumstances	o Take on role and maintain contact with admirers
o Downplay, misrepresent serving offence	o Present self, using primary inmate frame values, seeking respect, being strong, masculine
o Inmate as unloved; outsider is the only one who truly understands	
o Obtain support, manipulate	

Frame breaking
• Phone bug
o Over-frequent communication with external others
o Communication to maintain control, not get support
o Act out, express anger/frustration

family members, or others who could bring in contraband – typically illicit drugs such as marijuana, cocaine, heroin, or steroids:

> *Yeah, I've used visits to get drugs in at other prisons. You need to find the right people, and yeah, sometimes you lose them if someone rats and staff find out. Good way to make money ... Well, sometimes I wanted to get high myself.* (Remand inmate, HCC)

> *It's risky, but I've had family bring in drugs. You can trust your family. I trust them more than a lot of two-faced bastards in here and on the street.* (Sentenced inmate, HCC)

> *I don't do drugs myself, but throw-overs are common here. People have their friends outside do it.* (Sentenced inmate, MI)

Second, inmates committed to a criminal identity made no effort to fake change: they refused to play the charade of pro-social dialogue; and they advised their external relations that they had no intention of quitting the criminal life. Gang inmates differed fairly consistently from other inmates, in that they tended to adopt an outside frame only partly. For them, the prison gang inmate frame (discussed later) was pre-eminent in relations with others. They contested stigma by embracing their gang status, and they saw value in being a gang member, to the point that this identity superseded their inmate status. Like this SMI senior gang member, they were more likely than other inmates to tell their external relations to accept them as gang members, or to tell external others to quit contacting them:

> *I told my girlfriend, "If you're going to be with me, you're going to have to accept me for who I am. You gotta understand that. You gotta understand that I'm a gang member. I'm in jail and when I get out, I don't know if I'll come back. I can't promise you I'm not going to come back. You gotta understand that's who I am and what I do. So, accept me for who I am and we'll get along just fine."* (Sentenced inmate and senior gang member, SMI)

Finally, some respondents reported *gaining* prestige because of their status as inmates/criminals/gang members. Some gang members were viewed as celebrities by people in the community and received many letters and invitations for contact. The "bad boy" appeal of offenders is not new; Daniel Bell (1953) wrote about the "star" status of organized crime figures, which dated back to the roaring twenties and thirties. Nonetheless, it is still perplexing that despite the stigma attached to inmates, some offenders actually experienced a gain in status once they were imprisoned. Some external others (often women) favoured their criminal activities; others viewed them as tragic figures whom they could help. These inmates, having been perceived as "misunderstood," might invoke the pro-social frame in dialogue, but they related to these women more in their inmate identity. These two gang members were almost bemused by their notoriety:

I: *I talk to my family every day, usually telephone. I get visits. I write letters to a few girls that I know on the outside. I got boxes full of letters. I get fan mail, everything.*

W: *You get fan mail?*

I: *From being in the* [biker] *club, I get people writing me letters saying, "Oh hey ——, from the club, this and that." And I got boxes of cards and letters.* (Remand inmate and ex-biker gang member, HCI)

I lost mainly all contact with my family, except for my brothers. I used to talk to my grandmother and my mother. I guess this murder conviction was the last straw. But now, I get tons of letters from girls. Like, actually, it is not a good thing to say, but I got charged for this murder and it fucking ruined my life, but it also made me, like, gangster number one. The girls, they love me, and I got probably 300 photos of 40 different girls that I talk to or write. Just from being a drug dealer alone – the girls love bad guys, it is just another worldly truth. I am fairly in good shape, and I am tattooed up, sleeve up all over. Girls love tattoos, and they love guys who are in wicked shape. I have a few girls who want to marry me and stuff, but marriage is something you get the approval from mother and grandmother before I do that. I tried to get married a couple times, and they were, like, "No, don't marry that girl." They didn't like that girl, so I wouldn't marry her. They are country girls, so they figure I should find a girl from the country. (Sentenced inmate and senior gang member, SMI)

One did not have to be a gang member to entice outside contact; this inmate found that being a misunderstood offender also might work:

> *Sometimes, I write to a strange girl. I write "Hey, you don't know me but I never did this [crime]. They made a mistake." You know, that's the whole line, "I never ever do this." Then you say, "If you're interested in writing back, it's embarrassing to write you from prison, but people make mistakes. Here I am. If you wanna write back, write back." Sometimes it works.* (Remand inmate, HCC)

Frame Breaking: The Phone Bug

Frame breaking occurs when an individual engages in behaviour that is clearly outside accepted group norms. Sometimes this involves efforts by a person to reset the frame. Other times, individuals simply exercise poor judgment. My respondents reported that some inmates managed external contact and its attendant challenges better than others. Inmates who had an obsessive need to contact their family or friends (most often their female partners) were derisively referred to as *phone bugs* by their peers. These inmates were on the telephone incessantly. They tended to be younger inmates, and often seemed be trying to control their girlfriends by telling them what to do (and getting upset when they didn't comply), or doing their best to find out exactly who they were associating with (because of feelings of jealousy). Inevitably, this resulted in greater stress, conflict with other inmates over phone use, and an eventual failure to control their family members. These three inmates found phone bugs stressful people to share a unit with:

> *I try and talk to my family once every two weeks or so. I've done a lot of time, and I found out through the years that if you are on the phone talking to your old lady every day, you will be fighting with her in no time. And before you know it, bad blood is being passed. I don't call that often, because it makes it so hard. Like, I don't call for two weeks, and then I call, just pick up on what's been going on. But after a while, you start fighting and arguing, you know. She complains that "You left me," and you got to do this. Some guys are on the phone every day, and there are other guys who couldn't be bothered, and they seem to do better.* (Remand inmate FSCC)

Some of these young guys phone their girlfriends every day. They are always on the phone. Usually, trying to tell them what to do, but it never works out. They are always pestering for the phone, so we call them "phone bugs."
(Remand inmate, HCC)

But some of these guys get on the phone fifteen times a day ... and they end up roughing it. Some of them look like they're ready to break down sometimes. I've seen guys in tears on the phone and shit. It's sad to watch them.
(Sentenced inmate and former gang member, SMI)

Conclusion

Once a prisoner has been admitted into custody, the primary inmate frame guides him to get respect, show strength, and be smart in going about his day-to-day business. There are variations on the primary inmate frame and on some of the sub-frames that play out in prison life, in relations with other inmates, correctional staff, and community members. Inmates adopted different frames for different situations but consistently maintained a fair social distance from other offenders and reported being wary around their peers. Trust was granted to only a few. This lessened the stigma received from other inmates and limited opportunities to be exploited by them. This use of social distance permeated the inmate hierarchy, from new admissions to high-ranking gang members. It is likely that the situation has worsened over the past twenty-five years, given the more frequent turnover of inmates on remand and the weakening of the convict code and its central principles. A lack of close personal friendships was another cost of imprisonment.

For some inmates, "being smart" meant taking advantage of other offenders, through intimidation or by dealing in contraband, including illicit drugs. For other inmates, the essential frames for their behaviours related to getting high, gambling, or feeding other addictions. Addicts, and inmates who were too easily intimidated, were not respected and were referred to as nobodies, goofs, or crackheads; these statuses lie just above the lower ranks, who include informants and – at the very bottom rung – sex offenders.

Offenders working the inmate frame maintained a certain social distance from their peers and adopted a cautious approach with others. More informing and a general decline in mutual respect were viewed as expressions of the convict code's decline. The interview findings presented here are consistent with the extant literature, which indicates that the lack of social cohesion in the inmate population and the decline of the inmate subculture have been observed in several US states, England, and Canada (Crewe, 2005a, 2005b; Faulkner & Faulkner, 1997; Hassine, 1999; Ricciardelli, 2014a, 2014b).

The most critical change in prisons over the past twenty-five years has been the decline of the inmate code. Solidarity between inmates has been diminished, leaving most inmates with little in the way of internal support. On the other hand, communication with staff has improved, although restrictions on overfamiliarity still gird the frame and inmates must exercise caution in managing the public impression of their relationships with COs. Many inmates found it appropriate, however, to work with staff to find constructive ways to spend their time while in custody.

From a policy perspective, the lack of solidarity between inmates is troublesome. Inmates who spend a great deal of time alone, or who have little investment in the welfare of their peers, may be more likely to become victims, prey on others, or (at worst) encounter mental health problems from too much isolation. The lifers' peer support group at Matsqui and the Pathways Unit at Stony Mountain are programs that warrant further investigation, as these initiatives appear to promote a positive type of inmate solidarity. Both these group-based programs have offered inmates a chance to take the initiative in promoting social cohesion and more favourable inmate social relations.

Inmates generally adopt a more pro-social frame when relating to community members, but this interaction often does not provide a true picture of life inside prison or an offender's true intentions. Contact with family, friends, and even volunteers certainly buoyed the spirits of some. Others found that contact with the outside increased stigma, feelings of helplessness, and day-to-day stress or distracted them from focusing on the greater priority – surviving in prison. As a consequence, some inmates opted for telephone calls and letters over personal visits. A few inmates adopted the primary inmate frame when interacting with external others and made no pretense of possible change. Offenders might also talk in an instrumental manner with external others, with the express aim of bringing in contraband, especially illicit drugs. Lastly, inmates (especially gang members) who embraced the primary frame might simply tell external loved ones to accept them for who they are, or stop contact – an honest but somewhat cold approach. A new type of inmate frame-breaking communication, perpetrated by the "phone bug," may be a result of easier access for inmates to the telephone.

Contact with outsiders poses considerable challenges to inmates because of their custody status and inmate identity. From a policy perspective, on the one hand, studies have shown that inmates who receive regular visits do better in post-release, but on the other hand the results here indicate that the management of contact with the outside world is complicated. Visits and even telephone contacts can be stressful and debilitating for some inmates. Counselling strategies that help inmates manage their external frames are recommended. Information on an inmate's external contacts is readily available to correctional staff, and strategies can be directed towards the situations offenders may encounter.

5

How Corrections Officers Understand Their Role

So far, this book has focused on inmate transitions into custody and the primary frame, but inmates are only one of the two main dance partners in correctional institutions. The next two chapters examine the transitions and working lives of correctional staff, with the focus on correctional officers (COs). Fundamental changes in frames – for example, in communication – are considered from the staff perspective; this will provide a more complete picture of life inside.

Canadian correctional history and the empirical literature can help us understand the CO's frame, including its formation and evolution over the past twenty-five years. COs' primary functions of care and control of inmates may not have changed, but other features of their role have undergone significant changes commensurate with modifications in correctional strategies and an emphasis on a more interactive style of management. Recent research into the CO role, its challenges, and how officers perform their duties has shed much light on what was once a poorly researched profession. A recent book on prison staff by Jamie Bennett, Ben Crewe, and Azrini Wahidin (2013) is a good example of the rich scholarship being invested in researching COs.

Canadian COs were strongly impacted by prison violence in the 1970s. The federal MacGuigan Commission was convened in 1976 after several serious penitentiary riots occurred across the country in the early 1970s. The MacGuigan Report (1977) was blunt in expressing serious concerns over a lack of CO accountability. Investigators regarded COs as undereducated, poorly trained, and lacking in human management skills. The inquiry findings were timely, as they were released at a time when greater scrutiny was being placed on the job of "prison guard" in the United States and Canada (Duffee, 1974; Jacobs & Retsky, 1975; Ross, 1981; Willet, 1983). Given the emergence of concerns over police corruption and lack of accountability for law enforcement in the 1970s (Sherman, 1978), it is no surprise that US criminal justice researchers such as David Duffee (1974), John Klofas and Hans Toch (1982), and Lucien Lombardo (1985) began to ponder the existence of a CO subculture. Analogous to the police subculture literature that preceded it, researchers were concerned that a negative, oppositional guard subculture existed and that this group dynamic was oppositional to prison administration, besides impeding the introduction of programs and privileges. Even worse, it was thought that some COs were abusing their authority over inmates (Crouch & Marquart, 1980; Duffee, 1974; Lombardo, 1989). The central tenets of the CO subculture included the following:

- Security and control are paramount.
- Programs are a waste of time.
- Program staff are naive "do-gooders."
- Inmate privileges must be granted cautiously.
- COs know best when maintaining order.
- At times you may have to use your own discretion in following policy.
- Physical confrontations with inmates may be necessary to manage them and should be done discreetly if necessary.
- Do not inform on another officer, even if they have violated policy.
- Social distance must be maintained from inmates.
- Do not talk to an inmate unless it is necessary.
- Do not fraternize with inmates, play games with them, or get friendly.
- Getting to know inmates will only lead to your being compromised, and in due course to doing inappropriate favours for them, letting them break the rules, or (most seriously) bringing in contraband for them.

Kelsey Kauffman (1988) and James Marquart (2001) both conducted qualitative, in-depth interviews or observational studies and found that COs would enforce compliance to the code by ostracizing staff who did not follow the central tenets of the CO culture, or marginalize them by ignoring them or treating them as weak or "deviant."

The existence of a CO subculture was challenged by others. Studies revealed considerable divergence among officers with regard to adherence to the "correctional officer principles." Some staff presented as punitively oriented, yet research also indicated that most COs maintained balanced attitudes, and supported humane treatment of inmates and the organizational goals of correctional agencies. Surveys revealed that COs' attitudes were not homogenous and that CO "types" could be identified who differentiated between more punitive and more counselling/helping approaches to doing the job (Farkas, 1997, 2000; Kauffman, 1981, 1988). Investigators found that individual COs tended to overestimate how punitive their colleagues were towards inmates (Grekul, 1999; Kauffman, 1981).

Lombardo (1985) suggested that a more nuanced view of CO culture should acknowledge the existence of a CO sub-group who perceived themselves as "subcultural custodians." This punitively oriented CO group promulgated opposition to administration and pushed the view that inmates were a constant threat. In other words, a small but sometimes influential cadre of COs was promoting a greater retributive, pro-security agenda. In reality, most COs were balanced in their approach, dependent of course on past training, supervision, leadership, local history, and environment and the broader organizational context. Lombardo cited evidence in his research review indicating that subcultural custodians would gain greater influence during times of perceived threat to the CO group (overcrowding, problems with management) and could then be more successful in promoting a more negative type of CO solidarity.

Examinations of CO culture by Farkas (1997) and Farkas and Manning (1997) identified a work group whose focus was not uniquely oppositional. Farkas found a normative code emphasizing eight principles: helping an officer in danger, limiting familiarity with inmates, not abusing authority, backing up your fellow officers, not admitting mistakes (to management), pulling your own weight (i.e., doing the work you are supposed to do on your shift), deferring to veteran COs, and minding your own business. She observed that there was some variation in importance regarding various points from prison to prison, but generally all of these principles were in play. Supporting your fellow officers was key to limiting criticism, because even more than police work, CO work is largely hidden from oversight; even with the presence of cameras on some units, the majority of their activities are usually concealed from the view of supervisors.

In the 1980s and 1990s, researchers' attention shifted away from subculture to look more analytically at COs' work experience, attitudes, and behaviour on the job. CO stress and job satisfaction have been examined extensively (for a meta-analysis, see Dowden & Tellier, 2004). The self-perceived role of COs and how it might affect their behaviour towards inmates has spawned many studies on role conflict and punitive or rehabilitative attitudes.

Research related to stress is of pragmatic interest to researchers as it has been found to be related to health problems (Söderfeldt, Söderfeldt, Ohlson, Theorell, & Jones, 2000) and to job satisfaction (Mahfood, Pollock, & Longmire, 2013), which in turn are factors related to staff turnover (Dowden & Tellier, 2004; Lambert, Hogan, & Barton, 2001). Stress studies have varied in terms of consistent predictors. Also, investigators often survey *all* correctional staff, not just COs, which further complicates generalizations (i.e., the prison counsellor experience is not the same as the CO experience). In their meta-analysis of CO stress studies, Craig Dowden and Claude Tellier (2004) found that higher stress levels were associated with being younger, white, married, less educated, or less experienced; being in a higher-security prison; having less perceived involvement in decision-making; perceiving greater institutional danger; experiencing role ambiguity; and holding a more punitive attitude. Demographic variables generally showed weak effects; job experience and prison security level likewise showed little influence; and attitudes toward custody or rehabilitation had moderate effects; while perceptions of danger and role ambiguity had the strongest effects. Stress, by contrast, tended to be the strongest predictor of job satisfaction.

The evidence tends to support the proposition that COs find institutional work stressful because of the potential danger and the ambiguous roles required of an officer on the job (Dowden & Tellier, 2004). COs now must be "helpers" and support rehabilitation, yet they must still be ready to use physical force if necessary to manage situations (Crawley, 2004; Farkas, 1997; Liebling et al., 2010). While danger may be rare, it is still a fact of institutional life.

CO Types and Legitimacy

COs have been categorized by some researchers into different types based on how they perform their job. Mary Ann Farkas outlined a CO typology based on CO interviews in the US Midwest; she identified more custody-oriented "rule enforcers" and contrasted them with officers more interested in human services. Rounding out her group were COs who balanced custody with human services ("synthetic" officers), those who followed policy closely out of fear or apathy (loners), and those who usually did not enforce rules or follow policy consistently (lax, friendly, wishy-washy). She found that negative perceptions of inmates were related to more rule-bound attitudes, and that education, age, experience, and gender influenced adaptations.

In qualitative work in Britain involving two prisons (one male, the other housing females), Sarah Tait (2011) examined CO orientation towards the care of inmates and developed a five-armed typology. The human relations-oriented CO was a "true carer" or "limited carer" who prioritized working with inmates and providing support; opposite in some ways to this type were "old school" COs who provided a safe environment for inmates but little in the way of communication and emotional support. "Conflicted" was used to describe COs who gave assistance to inmates but tended to demand respect in return and too easily became demoralized over their lack of impact. Finally, the category "damaged" described COs who no longer cared for inmates due to some job-related personal trauma or conflict with management. They tended to avoid contact with inmates and were quite negative towards management. With the exception of the damaged officers, Tait found that each type offered some advantages in managing inmates and maintaining security. For example, some inmates preferred the limited conversation offered by the old-school type, while conflicted COs tended to be better at security. Tait reported that inmates voiced a preference for caring involving respectful relations, being listened to, and encouragement. They eschewed relations based on "indifference, unfairness and status degradation" (p. 449). Tait's key points of care are similar to those principles espoused by those who support procedural justice and legitimacy to achieve inmate compliance (Bottoms & Tankebe, 2012).

A long-time observer of the US prison industry, Robert Johnson (2002b), identified a public (custody) and private (correctional) agenda of COs. A CO's public presentation emphasized a custodial orientation: showing a willingness to be tough with inmates, valuing the rules, and maintaining a certain level of social distance from inmates. This was intended for his/her peers, to make them more comfortable as co-workers and more likely to be reliable in the event of physical conflict. Summarizing the 1980s literature on the "helping role" for COs, Johnson argued that in contrast to the public agenda, the private agenda saw most COs engaging in "correctional" work that involved responding to requests and helping inmates deal with problems. This work was often behind the scenes, and showed how social distance with inmates was managed by these officers.

Just as discretion in the courts and among police officers has become a serious focus of criminal justice scholars, so too did the 1980s and 1990s see an increased interest in COs' decision-making and discretion (Hepburn, 1985). Going beyond Sykes's (1958) earlier work, investigators started to examine the cues and conditions that affected the enforcement and non-enforcement of institutional rules. Research in the United States by Lucien Lombardo (1989) and in Britain by Ben Crewe (2009), as well as by Alison Liebling, David Price, and Guy Shefer (2010), found that COs relied on their own informal authority to gain compliance from inmates and often let smaller issues go unpunished to retain legitimacy.

Studies on discretion now seek to understand how COs establish authority and maintain it through their relations and interactions with inmates. As described in Chapter 2, COs who can establish legitimate authority appear able to gain inmate compliance with less dependence on coercive measures (Beijersbergen, Dirkzwager, Eichelsheim, et al., 2014b; Crewe, 2009; Franke et al., 2010; Reisig & Mesko, 2009; Rynne et al., 2008; Sparks et al., 1996). The pathway to legitimacy appears to be best traversed using the principles of procedural justice. COs who are fair, explain their actions, listen, allow offenders to retain their dignity, and are mostly consistent in their enforcement tend to promote more pro-social and positive attitudes on the part of inmates, and observe less deviant activity. The emphasis on achieving legitimacy is based on effective interaction with inmates and the development of direct supervision prisons and a dynamic approach to security.

Adapting to Institutional Life

For new COs, the management of emotions is critical. Elaine Crawley's (2004) qualitative British study of COs examined the structured and expressive show of emotions by COs in performing their duties. Using a constructionist approach, Crawley found the prison to be a place where highly intimate, long-term, and sometimes conflict-laden relations with inmates led COs to manage their emotions and self-presentation to both offenders and other staff. The prison is often presented as a dangerous, violent place, yet Crawley observed that correctional institutions most often present as having a very domestic character in their routines. COs must pay attention to mundane but necessary routines such as getting inmates off for meals, work, school, or programs, helping schedule medical and other appointments, making sure that showers are taken, and ensuring the laundry gets done and bedsheets are changed. Crawley noted that many CO functions were not dissimilar from household management duties faced by parents. She juxtaposed the often benign work activities of correctional staff with their own portrayal of their work as dangerous, with the threat of assault hanging over all.

Crawley argued that the problem for correctional staff was the emphasis on ultra-masculine values among COs and the limitations placed on the open expression of emotions, especially the ones traditionally associated with women, such as compassion and empathy. COs must suppress feelings of disgust, anger, and pity when dealing with inmates. In tense situations they can show no fear, and they must be calm even in incidents involving physical trauma and bloodshed. Crawley viewed COs as having to engage in "emotion work" that emphasized detachment. Anxiety and fear were significant areas requiring suppression – a particularly salient problem for new recruits. Spatial zones where emotions might be more readily exposed were the hospital or the chapel. Anger at management could be legitimately expressed, albeit away from the eyes of inmates. Failure to manage emotions could result in being ostracized by one's peers (Crawley, 2004).

Helen Arnold (2005) examined the experience of new CO recruits using a multi-method approach that meaningfully incorporated her own participant observation. She believed that she and her colleagues initially gained personal confidence, greater awareness of immediate physical space, and a sudden cautiousness about giving up too much personal information. Most serious for recruits was fear around being able to perform effectively in the event of violence. As the time came closer for placement on the job, the fear of making mistakes became greater, and confidence decreased.

Within the first six months of the job, however, confidence increased as institutional knowledge grew and practice led to competence in performing tasks (e.g., searches, securing/opening cell doors). Fear lessened, and inmates were viewed more as "human beings" as opposed to dangerous "others." Still, being assertive and able to remain firm and say no was important in establishing authority. Hyper-vigilance continued to develop as a trait. Some reported enjoying the CO role and their ability to help inmates. Outside the job they had become more observant but also more suspicious of others, and they adopted a more aggressive approach in dealing with others. Officers also became more emotionally detached and able to suppress feelings on the job as they faced inmate violence or inmate self-injury or distress.

Officers in later stages of their careers became less analytical and more focused on the day-to-day routines. Arnold found, like Lombardo (1989), that COs just wanted to get through the day. Vigilance out in the external world was also heightened. Their experiences allowed them to "cue" to discrepancies in behaviour on the unit, and they used this knowledge to identify and then deal with problematic situations. They were not as optimistic as newer recruits about their ability to help inmates, and saw their position as a job that needed to be done each day. Like Crawley's, Arnold's subjects reported that they had found it vital to desensitize themselves to the more negative goings on in the prison, and to be detached in their reactions to suicide attempts, violence such as stabbings, or unhappy news that inmates received from the outside community.

To summarize, the literature on COs has evolved from a fairly critical one to one whose goal is to understand their work culture and decision-making, the impact the work environment has on their job performance, and how COs' activities affect inmates. These findings can be coupled with information on the early phases of their socialization and this study's qualitative data to gain insight into how COs initially construct their primary correctional frame.

Transitions

Most of the correctional staff I interviewed did not have working in a prison as their first career goal. Most appeared to drift into the job, but once there, found that the position suited them. This finding was not surprising, as most of my sample were senior staff who had worked in corrections for many years. Younger staff that I interviewed tended to have either a university degree or some post-secondary education. Newer staff also reported receiving more training than those hired in the 1970s. Even in the 1990s, training and support from co-workers varied. The maxim appeared to be "sink or swim" in the 1970s and early 1980s; you either were a CO or were not. These two staff reported that training and orientation were much better now. Like other respondents, they commented on the importance of properly training new recruits:

> *First day on shift* [late 1970s] *when I started, there was no formal training. Basically, you were just paired up with a senior officer. Everything was on-the-job training, basically. Some of it was fairly organized; some of it seemed fairly disorganized. And you couldn't show you were scared.* (Staff, HCC)

> *The training now is definitely better. Safer for staff coming in; safer for others who have to work with them. But you never really know how someone is going to work out until you see them manage on a unit by themselves.* (Staff, FSCC)

Recruits learned the CO frame as they strived to fit in and become competent in their position. That meant knowing the formal rules and routines, as well as the informal and unwritten rules of how to interact with inmates and other staff. Most important for a new CO to learn was the management of fear, and how to frame relations through an appearance of strength. New staff quickly needed to learn to interact with other staff and inmates in a calm, assertive manner that would not display the anxieties of a new recruit. From the first day and during the initial adjustment period, new COs had to come to terms with the relative risks associated with working in a prison. A correctional institution is a setting where violence can and does occur, including potentially serious assaults against COs. For staff initially, it was crucial for them to overcome and not show any overt fear of inmates, to demystify their "dangerous" status, and to understand that they were, in most ways, just people. This was not always easy. This officer found some inmates would attempt to intimidate him on his first shift just by staring:

> *I started on the morning shift there, and one of the guys said, "Here is a set of keys – go all the way down to the very end of the tier." I had never been there before. It was a long walk because everybody on that whole unit, they realize you are the rookie, you are the newcomer. They try to intimidate you. Inside, there was probably a lot of butterflies. You had to walk by a pool table and all the way down to the end, not really knowing what was at the other end. I got finished the job of opening the main door and then was waiting. You could hear people coming down. You count them through, then lock the door, and then you walk back all the way through, and then you are told to count again. I will never forget that. It was probably something I knew about or read about, but I was now experiencing it.* (Staff, FSCC)

Can training alone allow an easy transition into a CO role? This former officer felt that some natural attributes, like a thick skin, were important:

> *I: My first shift in a BC provincial jail was very nerve racking, because as you know, there is no literature of what prison life is like, so you don't know what you are getting yourself into. So, first shift I worked was the graveyard shift, and it was very nerve racking, and you muddled your way through and didn't let anyone know you were nervous.*
> *W: So you may have had some thoughts on not staying. What made you stick it out?*
> *I: Well, you either are the type of person who takes things personally or you're not, then you're going to be stressed out. So I'm not one who takes things personally, so I was able to do it.* (Female staff, MI)

As Arnold (2005) suggested, this officer found that demystifying the threat that inmates did or did not pose was an important part of transition:

> *It was almost funny because you think that they're animals. You right away think they're animals, until you actually spend some time with them. You*

know, you sit down with them and realize they are human beings like everybody else. (Staff, HCC)

Besides simply managing the general fear of working in a prison, COs have to take control of situations where inmates are reluctant to comply with institutional rules. New or not, COs must enforce the prison's rules and manage its routines – which is difficult if inmates say no. For new staff, every situation weighs heavily. When an inmate refuses to comply in front of other offenders, a recruit can lose face and it can become even more difficult to get cooperation from inmates in the future. The CO frame requires that staff present as strong – as firm and assertive (perhaps even aggressive) with inmates – and that they not back down. This may mean saying "no" to an unreasonable inmate request despite being pressured, or getting a resistant offender to comply with a rule or reasonable request. Two officers I spoke with had been hired thirty and fifteen years ago respectively prior to being interviewed, and they considered their training weak. They managed to establish authority by not giving in to external pressure from inmates:

We had three days of training and then you were pretty much thrown in the fire. You had to learn quickly and had to prove yourself – definitely had to prove yourself to the full-time staff. So in my mid-twenties, I got a key, a radio, and was put in an area where there were a lot of gangs, the segregation area, and some predators. They all knew I was a rookie – a fish, if you want to use jargon. It was intimidating, but you either succeeded or you didn't, at that time. It was definitely intimidating at the beginning, but you couldn't back down. Training is much better now. (Staff, HCC)

I was a doorman in a bar and, one night, this guy came in, and he was wearing a corrections shirt. I didn't even know what corrections was, but I knew about Headingley jail, so we talked for a few minutes. I dropped my application off and by the next Monday, I was in for three-day orientation. Wednesday, I was midnight shift. I was standing on the main floor with a set of keys. You were hired here because you were a big man, you didn't take any shit, and this was the way it was. There was no casework. You

were a prison guard. There was no counsellor. There was no facilitator.
They expected you to keep a lid on the place. (Staff, HCC)

There were several background characteristics and experiences that mediated fear. New recruits with military backgrounds were familiar with higher-risk surroundings. Those with social service backgrounds or who had family members who worked as COs had some insight into what inmates might be like and what was expected of new officers. A few of the older staff I interviewed who came from rough, working-class backgrounds reported knowing many inmates previously and confessed to being rough individuals themselves (more so in their younger days!):[1]

I probably knew between a third and half the inmates here when I started.
I wasn't the nicest kid in the world, either. I was working in a gas station,
and a guy that is now retired from here said, "You are out there freezing
your butt off. You should apply to Stony." So I got hired in 1976. I grew up
in the North End, and I was one of those types who fought all the time. So
I was leery, cautious, and watching carefully, but I wasn't really afraid.
(Staff, SMI)

I worked in a foster-home/group-home system for ten years, and then I
went to the Manitoba Youth Centre (MYC) for ten years. My first experience
with the adult institution was pretty shocking. You walk in there, and just
the whole set-up of people being locked up, and them giving you keys and
saying you have to unlock them. But I knew some of what was going on
from MYC, so I adjusted pretty quickly. (Staff, HCC)

Staff felt a need to believe in their own competence to gain the respect of their fellow COs and other correctional staff. For correctional staff, making it through the first few months was crucial. Some of the job was like most occupations: there was a need to become familiar with individuals in the workplace, both inmates and staff, and with what was required day to day. Becoming competent led to greater confidence. But the pressure to conform and perform was perhaps higher in a correctional institution because of two things. First, inmates were constantly in contact with officers, so any errors or mistakes would be prominent not just to an individual offender but to the entire unit of offenders, not to mention the prison's informal social network. Second, CO activities were highly visible to their partners and co-workers because of the close quarters in an institutional setting. Errors might be kept from supervisors and management, but maintaining secrecy from co-workers for any faux pas was difficult to impossible.

These three officers found that effort and time aided their transitions in provincial facilities at Headingley and Fort Saskatchewan, as well as the federal penitentiary at Stony Mountain:

> *I had a fairly smooth transition, coming in. Not saying that it was all sunshine or anything like that. Part of it is getting to know the people and routines. I find that what you put out comes back to you, and that was my way.* (Staff, SMI)

> *In some ways, the initial social setting is pretty close to anywhere else. People have to get used to you, and you have to learn the routines.* (Staff, FSCC)

> *It was tough at first. You had to get the routines down and know who was who. The informal rules they don't tell you about are important, too. Once you know how the place runs, the job gets easier and you will be accepted by the inmates and other staff.* (Staff, HCC)

Framing appropriate relations with inmates was another skill that COs had to develop. Initially, COs walked a fine line communicating with inmates. Given the initial premise of most recruits – that all inmates are dangerous and manipulative – it is not surprising that correctional staff were quite guarded with inmates when they began. A CO had to get to know inmates, and eventually establishing relationships and cultivating sources of information on the unit were priorities.

Managing social distance was also important when dealing with supervisors, in order to maintain the respect of peers. As these two officers reported, being too friendly with superiors or management was looked down on:

> *It was tough, sometimes, trying to look like one of the gang but also impressing the managers. If you were on probation, you had to make efforts to look*

like you were listening to the boss, but if you got too friendly, you could lose the respect of other officers. (Staff, FSCC)

Some people are a bit slow at realizing that no one likes a suck-up. You have to be professional, even friendly maybe, with supervisors but not overdo it. (Staff, SMI)

Shaping the Correctional Officer Frame

Just as with inmates, a CO's adaptations to prison life were influenced by their backgrounds (see Figure 5.1). It was advantageous to have work experience in related organizations like the military or social services.

FIGURE 5.1
The primary correctional officer frame

Frame precursors	
• Social background • Work experience, military, social service	• Training
Liminal frame	
• Managing fear • Learning about inmates	• Observing routines, learning formal and informal rules
Initial and enduring primary frame scripts: With inmates	
• Get respect/Be able to exercise authority • Be strong/Do not show fear • Be smart/Help inmates, but do not be taken advantage of	
Primary frame	
Inmates	**Other correctional staff**

• Get respect/Be able to exercise authority
• Be strong/Do not show fear
• Be smart/Help other inmate but do not be taken advantage of
• Manage social distance
  o Do not become overly friendly with inmates
  o Establish and maintain appropriate boundaries with inmates
	• Be strong/Do not show fear
	• Manage inmates, do not let them manage you
	• Be competent
	• Be ready to aid and support other officers
	• Do not embarrass another officer in front of an inmate
	• Maintain proper social distance from inmates
	• Do not inform on another officer to management
	• Do not be too supportive of management
	• Use offender relationships to influence behaviour, obtain information, and manage unit/area

Experience in lower-income or working-class situations helped some officers in this study relate better to inmates when they started their careers. Training prior to entering the institutional world had improved and was viewed as helpful: newer staff appreciated the quality of training, while older respondents were pleased that recruits were better prepared than in the days when COs were hired for physical stature/prowess and received little or no training.

From these precursors, COs (like inmates) moved into a liminal frame where they occupied a role as new staff and were treated differently by inmates and other staff. During this pivotal transition period, COs had to frame interactions around not showing fear, learn more about inmates, and realize that offenders were not perpetually violent predators. Once through this initial stage, COs ideally got respect from inmates and became effective at exercising authority. It was also important to grow knowledgeable about the institution and to help inmates solve problems. They learned to establish familiar relationships that could prove helpful in managing offenders, but they were also careful to establish behavioural boundaries when dealing with inmates (i.e., not too close). For example, more familiar relations could lead to inmates telling them about activities in the unit, including potential trouble.

To be accepted by other COs, new staff had to be able to manage inmates and do their job competently. Showing support for fellow officers meant at least appearing to be ready to physically back them up in case of trouble, being astute enough not to embarrass or undermine them in front of other inmates, and keeping social distance from inmates generally. Informing on another officer to management, or even being too friendly with management, would cost a CO credibility with peers.

Conclusion

The transition for new recruits into the CO position continues to be challenging but has become less so due to better training – an important positive change over the past twenty-five years. More recent times have seen, overall, more educated staff hired. New COs must still learn the correctional frame and build their interpersonal relations around the projection of calmness, mental strength, and firmness in decision-making. The construction of the CO frame shares some similarities with inmate transitions: officers need respect from inmates, at least enough to exert influence/control over them. There are several substantive differences between inmate and CO adaptations, however. Management of fear is different for staff, for example, because as soon as they enter the unit they are immediately outnumbered, and this situation does not change. More so than for new inmates, there is pressure on rookie COs to be competent at their job, and they must appear so to both staff and inmates.

This study's findings are consistent with much of the extant and emerging literature on COs and their transitions into the workplace (Arnold, 2005; Bennett et al., 2013; Crawley, 2004). Dealing with fear, being able to manage inmates, and gaining workplace competence resonate as the most vital areas for COs to focus on when they start their jobs.

The biggest change over the past twenty-five years for COs seems to relate to the quality of selection, orientation, and training. Recent recruits generally valued what they were taught, while veteran staff saw significant improvement in training quality from the time they began. From a policy perspective, this study's findings indicate that staff training can do much to facilitate the adjustment of correctional staff. Helping new staff manage fears and realistically assess the "danger" posed by inmates should facilitate adjustment and, in the long term, reduce turnover. In terms of on-the-job training, mastering correctional facility policies, local procedures, and institutional routines should be a priority. Also, knowledge testing should be done often the first year on the job.

6

Relations between Inmates and Officers

The primary CO frame emphasizes that COs manage their interactions to present as being strong and knowledgeable. Also, they manage their social distance from inmates and management as they adjust to institutional life. In this chapter, I develop the CO frame to more explicitly detail inmate–CO relations and the characteristics that earn a CO respect and legitimacy. As noted earlier, a remarkable change has occurred in Canadian correctional institutions: COs and inmates talk far more than they used to, and this communication is framed by different norms and rules than in the past. Following from the procedural justice and legitimacy research touched on in Chapters 2 and 5, in this section I outline the traits and behaviours of the "good," effective, and legitimate CO and compare them with more negative observations by inmates and staff.

The study participants, both inmates and staff, overwhelmingly concurred that greater inmate–CO interaction has been the most significant shift in human relations within Canadian correctional institutions over the past twenty-five years. The commandments of the old CO code – don't talk to inmates, maintain extreme social distance, never trust inmates, and so on – clearly do not hold as much sway as in the past. Some participants believed that younger inmates and staff were more likely to communicate, but I found that the shift in relations was also evident among older inmates and COs. Prison inhabitants have all had to change their views to accommodate this development. One long-time federal staff discussed the sometimes dramatic changes in the strength of the inmate code:

I'd definitely say the inmate and officer's code – they are the same thing, you know – are not as strong as they used to be. Both of them changed a lot. When I started in 1989, inmates didn't talk to me, and if they did, they needed something. They said it politely and in front of a lot of other people, and loudly so everybody could hear what they were talking about. Inmates were told not to talk to staff, either. Only the heavies got to talk to COs, or the inmate leaders that were running the show. They didn't address you by your first name; there was some distance. Now, today, it's all one big happy family, "Hey Joe, how you doin'." You can shake hands. I've seen staff hugging inmates [laughs]. (Staff, SMI)

This lifer inmate reflected on how things have changed, and for the better. Significantly for him, the increase in communication also gave him a chance to relate to staff in a positive way:

I think COs and inmates talking more is good. I can talk to them about my quitting smoking and other things I've done. Since I've changed during my last parole, I have more in common with some of the officers than the other inmates. (Lifer, MI)

This long-time officer at Fort Saskatchewan recalled when he and others did not talk to inmates. Times had changed for him and other staff:

I: Communicating, there is a big difference now. Back in the old days, inmates never cracked to staff. If you cracked to a staff, they figured you were a rat and they may beat you up. Today, they go up to the panel [a CO station on the unit at FSCC] *and talk to the staff, and staff talk to the inmates. If a staff is making a round* [patrol around the unit], *inmates talk to them. I have reached that stage in my life where I get a lot of respect from the inmates. They know I am strict. They know what I am like, but they talk to me. And I talk to them now, as before I wouldn't ever talk to an inmate.*
W: But wasn't there a correctional officer code, sort of, too – you weren't really supposed to talk to inmates?
I: Right, exactly, it was like us and them. They did their thing; we did ours. But not today – inmates and staff talk today. (Staff, FSCC)

Staff and inmates both noted that a unit's physical configuration influences inmate activity. At one time, walking up to the staff station (a bubble behind glass in many cases) was forbidden. Today, staff kiosks are more often located out in the common area. Talk in a unit is viewed as normal activity within the inmate frame and is positively influenced in some correctional institutions by direct supervision architecture requiring that COs be on the unit. This inmate served quite a bit of time in institutions and found that being able to go up to the "bubble" had become easier for him:

> *I see a lot of the younger correctional officers here, and they seem like pretty good guys. They seem like they could be my neighbours back home, you know, and we would get along just fine, you know. I got to know some of them personally, a little bit. One guard bought a new bike and is going fishing soon – we can talk about that type of stuff. I have way more in common with these officers than I do with the other inmates in here. We had similar lives, except for the years I was in jail, and we get to know each other, and you get a feeling and a way of knowing each other. The bubble* [staff station] *is a problem for some inmates, but for me, it is not a problem.* (Remand inmate, FSCC)

How far have the barriers come down between inmates and staff? This Headingley CO observed that interaction had increased to the point that COs were playing games such as cards with the inmates:

> *It was almost unheard of to go out of your way to socialize with an inmate; it was them and us. In the direct supervision units, officers are in with the inmates at all times. We are actually playing cards with them now, playing Nintendo. The inmates actually will come right in your office and sit down and talk with you. There seems to be definitely a lot more interaction with the inmates than there ever was before.* (Staff, HCC)

Working towards Legitimacy

The research evidence indicates that COs and institutional management can be more effective at gaining behavioural compliance if inmates perceive them as legitimate (Beijersbergen, Dirkzwager, Eichelsheim, et al.,

2014b; Beijersbergen, Dirkzwager, Molleman, van der Laan, & Nieuwbeerta, 2013; Hulley et al., 2011; Liebling, 2011; Reisig & Mesko, 2009). To recap from Chapter 2, legitimacy is derived largely from actions of justice system agents that follow the precepts of procedural justice. Criminal justice actors are more likely to achieve legitimacy if the individuals they come in contact with perceive themselves as being treated with respect, are allowed to maintain their dignity, have their concerns dealt with fairly and consistently, are listened to and find that the judge, police officer, or CO dealing with them is competent (Franke et al., 2010; Tyler, 2003, 2012). In a similar vein, Liebling and colleagues (2010) contend that the pinnacle achievement by COs is establishing the "right relationship" with inmates. This relationship is based on COs showing respect for inmates and dealing with them fairly. The right relationship influences inmate behaviour in favourable ways. Inmates valued officers who were good listeners and easy to talk to, who had a sense of humour, who were mature, motivated, intelligent, and careful, and who were capable of using authority and "keeping an eye on you" while being compassionate.

My Canadian study data generally supported the tenets of legitimacy and procedural justice found in the literature from other nations. Inmates identified respect, fairness, courtesy, and an impartial, even-handed use of authority as central to the perception that a CO was "good" or legitimate. Inmate and staff respondents were consistent in these views at both provincial and federal institutions. COs perceived favourably by inmates and other staff displayed humanistic qualities such as a sense of humour, a willingness to listen, empathy, and most importantly, an ability to withhold judgment for past criminal behaviour and to show respect. This inmate valued a CO's willingness to help for even small requests:

> *I like a correctional officer that has a sense of humour, but also one who knows what's going on, is good at their job. They will give you a straight yes or no answer. They don't pass the buck or slough you off when you're trying to get something. It may not mean something to them, but if it's something that you require, like another towel or something, chivalry is important.* (Remand inmate, HCC)

Being accommodating may not come naturally for all COs, and for some it may take time to learn how important this quality is to offenders. This inmate observed that many COs became more helpful over time:

> *It's funny how officers change. I see all the rookies that come in as correc-tional officers, want to make a name for themselves, want to be Joe tough guy, Joe bad guy, don't make friends with the inmates. Then it's funny, because I've known a lot of them over the years, and now the guys that were total assholes are really good guys now, 'cause they've changed over the years. They've come to realize that, when we ask them for something, we ask them because it's out of our reach, out of our grasp. We're in a cage, so we're not asking them just to bug them, waste their time, or make their day go worse. We can't do it ourselves or we would.* (Remand inmate, HCC)

Respect, not stigmatizing inmates, and allowing them to retain their dignity was valued by these three inmates:

> *One who doesn't talk down or ignore you. Well, I like* ———. *She's, like, awesome, man. You ask her if you can make a phone call in the office, no problem. You don't have to fill out a request form, or go through your case worker, or whatever.* (Sentenced inmate, HCC)

> *A good officer is someone that knows how to be humorous, with a good attitude, a good spirit. Right? Just because you're an officer with a uniform on, doesn't mean that you're better than the person that's locked up, or it doesn't mean that you have the right to let that power go to your head. 'Cause if I'm the guard and you're the inmate, I know I got control over you.* (Sentenced inmate and former gang member, SMI)

> *A good correctional officer shows you respect, not somebody who talks down to you like you're a piece of garbage. That's the biggest thing, you know. Some of these guards say "Please, thank you." That means a lot to me. Even with the younger generation, the younger officers, that means a hell of a lot to me.* (Remand inmate, FSCC)

While there was widespread agreement about the increase in com-munication and generally positive feelings among both inmates and staff, there was considerable divergence as to how substantive conversations were, and the efficacy of COs in their approach to inmates. In other words, more talk did not translate into meaningful conversation or useful inter-action. This lifer found that many correctional staff still penalized inmates by the type of crime that they committed:

> *The most negative thing, I think, is probably the fact that a lot of people think of you in here as just a criminal, a number. Instead of thinking of you by your name, or age, or who you are, they think of you by what you did.* (Lifer, SMI)

This Stony Mountain resident and former gang member felt there were still very judgmental officers who intensely disliked inmates:

> *I like a guard that's been there, done that – somebody that doesn't judge you, like black and white on paper, sees you as a friend. Somebody to talk to. There's a lot of good guards in here that aren't biased or racial. But there are also a lot of the staff here only for their paycheque. They don't understand that we're doing our time. We're paying our debt to society. It's bad enough we're in here, being away from our families and stuff. The good ones are sociable. They can joke around with you, talk to you as a human. But then there are other staff that think that you're just a piece of shit, you're an animal, and they treat you like an animal, and they would prefer if you were just locked up and had nothing. I dread certain shifts coming on. I just, I despise them, I can't fuckin' stand them, because it seems that they try their hardest to make hell for us in here.* (Sentenced inmate and ex-gang member, SMI)

Three inmates pointed out that COs could communicate in a manner hurtful to building relationships and that in some cases their talk could stigmatize or antagonize offenders. Strict or aggressive rule enforcement was another way to aggravate inmates. Negative relationships could be built as easily as positive ones:

> *I don't like people who just talk down to you. Some people, you can't ask questions or it's "Holy cow!" A guard turns around and yells at this guy; well, now the inmate is mad. He's going to have a bad day now, and before you know it, ten guys are having a bad day.* (Remand inmate, FSCC)

Bad guards go out of their way to start conflicts. There's some guards that provoke inmates. They say certain things. You can't say certain things back to them 'cause you're an inmate. You're the one that gets in trouble. (Sentenced inmate and former gang member, SMI)

A good correctional officer knows their job, does their own time when they are at work. They're not getting in your face. They speak up if they have to. The old-school guards are the ones I can relate to more. I can talk to them. Bad correctional officers are always fuckin' pickin' at shit for nothin'. They come in and will go by the book, or worse, make up their own shit as they go. The biggest killer is where they got the attitude, you know. "It's my fuckin' house and I'm running this thing. Fuck off," you know. But a lot of these guys are honestly trying to help you, I believe. There are some that are only here for the buck, but you can see the difference. (Sentenced inmate, HCC)

These two inmates believed that COs could gain the support of inmates by providing simple courtesies:

Little things to them are important to us. I had to pay my insurance once, not let the claim expire. I had a hell of a time to arrange getting it paid. People treat you like it's an inconvenience. But I can't do it myself. I depend on them for help. (Sentenced inmate, MI)

If a guard is nice to you, you feel better. Some guards in here are cool, like the —— guy, fuckin' big guy. You can sit down and talk to them. They play cards with you, you know. They watch TV. They joke with you. They play games with you. The other guards are always in the office, all fuckin' by the book, man. It's like, "Can I get this please?" They say, "Hold it. No, I'm busy." You always get one fucking rotten apple outta the bunch, kind of thing. The majority are pretty nice. But good officers talk, interact more with the inmates; they don't judge the inmates by their paperwork. I'm in here for a fucking horrible, horrendous shit, where I'm like, you know, like, fuck, I hang my head every day, and my friends on the street read about my shit. Some guys [officers] *will tell other inmates what you are in for.* (Remand inmate, HCC)

Over and over, inmates expressed the belief that COs held the power in the institution. This gang member was constantly surprised that officers did not seem to grasp that innocuous requests for phone calls, pillows, bedding, or others supplies were, in reality, big requests for inmates, who were utterly dependent on staff for these things:

> *Good correctional officers, you ask them a favour and they do it for you. Say you called your family and you didn't get hold of them. They give you another chance later. But some of them don't; they say "You had your turn." Bad correctional officers, they are on a power trip, they don't give a fuck about the inmates. They just kill the mood in the unit.* (Remand inmate and gang member, HCC)

Earlier I alluded to an increase in reported mental health concerns among inmates in federal and provincial institutions. Inmates are aware that some of their peers have such difficulties, or go through considerable stress at times. This inmate was surprised when COs showed neither insight nor patience for troubled prisoners:

> *A lot of the staff here are pretty good, but some of them are asses, to be honest. Some of them let their jobs go to their heads. They like being able to tell someone what to do and that person has to do it or you can charge them. Officers should treat every individual for who they are and how they act, not to just paint everybody with the same brush. That is a good officer. I think open minded would probably be the biggest thing I would look for in a guard. I think that they should be able to take some mental-health training. Believe it or not, some of the peer support people in our prison who help other inmates out, they got better training in mood disorders and different mental illnesses than most of the staff.* (Lifer, SMI)

Mental health is a concern, but stress can be an issue generally for inmates, especially those awaiting sentence, as this Fort Saskatchewan inmate on pre-trial detention explained:

> *I don't like an officer who walks into the unit and he's got that controlling attitude. You can feel it – the torn speech, he comes on the mike and barks "Lock up time." You can feel that vibe right now. That's where the inmates get kind of low down. We are here to do our time. We don't know*

if we are going to be getting out because this is remand. It's very hard
for an inmate. A guard has got to know these things. (Remand inmate,
FSCC)

Many of the qualities of a "good" CO were linked to fundamental
employee work values and principles of effective supervisory and interpersonal communication that are not unique to the prison setting. Bringing
your personal problems to work, be they domestic or alcohol-related, was
a definite liability, as this Headingley inmate pointed out:

W: *What makes a good correctional officer, to you?*
I: *Gee, they're all pretty good. Sense of humour, someone who don't take*
   themselves too seriously, and someone who's compassionate. You gotta
   show empathy.
W: *What makes a bad correctional officer?*
I: *The kind of people who bring their domestic or other problems to*
   work. We had one guy there, he used to come in smelling like booze
   every once in a while. A bit of an alcoholic himself, you know?
   (Sentenced inmate, HCI)

Inmates like this offender at Matsqui expected a professional performance by COs once they began their day on the job:

A good officer is one who can leave his home life at home, and doesn't hate
the person because he's a convict but respects the person because of who he
is. If he's an asshole, treat him like an asshole. If he's a hard case, treat him
hard. Bad officers are bitter and should be on this side of the fence instead
of the other side. (Sentenced inmate, MI)

Dynamic or direct supervision (DS) is predicated on COs being physically on the units rather than in an office adjoining a cell block. But unless
COs are physically on the unit doing their rounds or available at unit kiosks,
their presence is limited. DS has obviously contributed to an increase in
inmate–CO interaction, but many inmates expressed concerns about some
COs spending most of their shift in their offices and not spending much
time out and about in the units. These three inmates observed that many

officers "hid" in their offices or glassed-in staff stations, or felt that they were too lazy to come out:

Some of the correctional officers spend most of their shift in the office instead of out in the unit. It's better when they are out. They keep inmates calm. (Remand inmate and ex-gang member, HCI)

They are supposed to be on these units all the time, but some guards are better than others. You can tell some just don't want to spend any time around us. (Remand inmate, FSCC)

I prefer to see officers out and about. Means they know a bit about what is going on. (Sentenced inmate, MI)

According to one lifer, the adoption of strict guard and inmate roles hindered honest and effective communication. Seeing beyond stereotypes was offered as a method to achieve more honest and respectful communication:

I try my hardest not to treat people by their roles – correctional officer, inmate, we are all just people. Otherwise, we are playing the game of us and them, and I won't play that game. Guards are seen as the problems by inmates; inmates are seen as the problems by guards. Management thinks that the CO union is the problem. It's all a mirage; it's all been created in someone's brain. It all happens in our head. Don't make me start acting like an inmate, sneaking around. Remember the Zimbardo prison experiment back in 1972, where students simulated a prison, taking on guard and inmate roles. It left me with a great conclusion: People don't have to play those roles. We need to do more of this, do what you are doing right now, just talking to people. (Lifer, MI)

Much of this study took place in western Canada, where there is a high proportion of Aboriginal inmates in custody, so it is not surprising that race emerged as an issue for some inmates. Some Indigenous respondents felt that COs simply did not understand their culture. Indicative of a "white privilege" perspective, most COs might go as far as treating inmates equally, but saw no need to give Indigenous cultural values an equal footing, unless it was in a required Aboriginal program. Much like most Canadians who come from a dominant Euro-Canadian cultural perspective, many COs saw no need for any special accommodation for Indigenous inmates. COs understanding their culture was important to these two inmates:

> I: *Some inmates think guards are bad just because they don't give in to what they want. But I understand that, they have a job to do. But to me, a big thing is to respect inmate culture. It's a big thing in Manitoba, to the Native people, is our culture.*
> W: *So you feel that guards can be a bit racist?*
> I: *Not racist, they just don't understand our culture. It's not racist. Because what they don't know, they don't understand. That's what I think makes a bad correctional officer. Other than that, they're all right.* (Remand inmate and ex-gang member, HCC)

> *Some of the guards on this unit don't seem to understand our culture and what we are trying to do. They get on shift and get aggressive. What is wrong with them?* (Sentenced inmate and ex-gang member, SMI)

Aboriginal inmates felt that COs could show greater sensitivity to their culture, and expressed a desire to have more Indigenous COs on the units, or at least some Aboriginal staff to run spiritual ceremonies. In the absence of an Indigenous CO, this former gang inmate recommended more communication:

> *I'd like to see a Native guard on every range, you know? Maybe it doesn't even have to be a Native guard, but have a guard on the range, instead of sitting in the office all the time. When they're communicating with the inmates, that calms everything right down. If not, maybe have a Native person or even a chapel guy on the range. Keeps us calm.* (Remand inmate and ex-gang member, HCC)

Colour-blind racism is visible in some respects among correctional staff. It is all well and good that overt racism is not common, but respectful relations are not achieved when Aboriginal inmates are just "treated like everyone else." When they do not respect cultural differences such as communication or spiritual practices, COs are discriminating against Aboriginal inmates. It takes more than a few sweetgrass ceremonies and one special federal unit to show a true commitment to understanding and respecting Indigenous culture. This definitely limits CO ability to achieve legitimacy.

Surprisingly, overt racism still existed. Racism was not voiced as a pervasive concern (surprising), but when inmates experienced it, COs lost considerable respect and legitimacy. At least one black inmate had experienced taunting from COs:

> *I'm not expecting these people to be nice to me, you know, 'cause I'm a criminal. But I'm a person, too. Say "Please" and "Thank you," maybe ask if I want stuff. Some are racist. Some say, "What's up brother?" You can tell by the way they say it that, inside, they hate you. Two years ago, at the remand centre, someone called me "Nigger." Racism is always bad.* (Remand inmate and gang associate, HCC)

Greater communication should lead to successful dynamic security. Getting to know inmates and gleaning information from them allows staff to be proactive in responding to potential trouble in a unit. Most staff respondents found value in this strategy, and those who had been COs previously had applied it to varying degrees when they worked in security. This Fort Saskatchewan CO balanced respect for and concern about inmates against the need to collect information from them to help limit misconduct on her unit:

> *Today, the difference between staff and inmates has gotten very narrow. But the inmates still got a bit of a code, unless you work with them all the time. And the way it works in the prison system, Mike, as you probably know, is that when an inmate gets comfortable with you, he or she will tell you things, but you either don't tell, or you don't get it back to him that you have passed it on. So they trust you. Like, when we were having this incident just yesterday and the day before. These inmates came and told me, named all the names. So I passed it to management, but in a way that nobody connects that I was talking to them. So we moved the troublemakers around, and the unit is quiet. But it takes a while; they will feel you out.* (Female staff, FSCC)

Inmates had mixed feelings about communicating more and having COs know more. They recognized that staff had to make others safe, but many were concerned that greater communication had resulted in too many informants. Informing sometimes had unfair consequences for inmates falsely accused. There was a particular distaste for "group punishments" administered because of informants. Other inmates felt that increased communication had resulted in too much CO involvement in their daily lives. While most acknowledged that there were definite safety benefits to greater CO involvement with inmates, these Matsqui inmates felt they were not being allowed to manage their problems on their own:

> *There are some positives* [with more interaction] *when it comes to safety; anyone would be fool to say "No." No one deserves a shit-kicking. So there is a benefit to it, but some of it goes too far. An example being, on a canteen day that was payday, we were told we couldn't go. Someone apparently said "something" may happen. Now, can you imagine, you want to go to canteen and they say "No," because they think someone is going to get beat up? Then we have to lock up.* (Lifer, MI)

> *W: What makes a good correctional officer?*
> *I: One that will stay back and let us do whatever we got to do here. Like, just stay out of our affairs, right? Because things will work themselves out. They are trying to integrate the prison to make it so there is no protective custody, but there is the other perspective. They create this atmosphere where now guys are running to them over nothing. Just because a guy got punched in the head, they take him out of here, for fear of his safety. Hey, this stuff goes on. We're not here to try to kill people. There's a reason for that, and there have to be pretty strong reasons to kill somebody. So, when they lock down the racquetball room because there is a fight in there, it doesn't stop fights going on in the units, fights going on in other places in jail. But you are limiting us, by stopping our exercise.* (Sentenced inmate, MI)

Not all inmates desired close contact with COs, nor did they wish them to be heavily involved on their units. Some inmates voiced a preference for COs who kept their interactions business-like and to the point. These inmates wished to have personal space, to avoid informing on their peers, and to also avoid engaging in idle talk. Those desiring little contact included both younger and older inmates. For example, this middle-aged inmate liked conversation kept to a minimum:

> *I prefer officers who more or less leave you alone. I had the perfect COII – when I talked to him, our conversation is like three minutes, I hear about you, you hear about me. 'Cause I told him I've been around. This is, like, my fourth time, and that's a lot of time coming to prison, and I'm low maintenance, and he's low maintenance, too. But it is different for others, and I guess this goes along with the new staff and inmates who are coming in, the new generation – they like to talk more.* (Lifer, MI)

Staff respondents shared inmates' concerns about the effectiveness of some of their colleagues. Inmates and staff inhabited the same institutional world, and most staff seemed to grasp what was needed to maintain or improve their relations with inmates. They expressed concern that their punitive, aggressive co-workers were creating needless conflict and sometimes putting others at risk of inmate violence. Regardless of age, staff participating in this study with CO experience prided themselves on giving inmates basic respect, not holding a grudge, and being positive when they came to work. They saw the value in extending small courtesies to inmates. Many saw the "grey" in enforcing rules and granting privileges, and even those COs (or former COs) who viewed themselves as sticklers for rules prided themselves on being at least consistent and honest with inmates. These three COs from Fort Saskatchewan, Stony Mountain, and Matsqui reflected the consensus of my respondents:

> *I enjoy my job. I am always good, always happy. Inmates love me 'cause I am never grumpy, I am always happy and it bounces off of me onto them. As soon as I come in, they are happy. They are watching the panel because I am there. But you know, Mike, I don't bug them. I don't harass them. I don't swear at them. Staff sometimes don't help them, so they come to me, and those first three days on shift are pretty busy. One guy says, "I'm trying to get a hold of legal aid on that phone." I says, "When do you want to do it? I will do it right now. You come in the office, and we'll dial the number. I'll punch, and you pick up that phone and talk." And you know what, he is happy and I am happy, and I like a happy unit.* (Staff, FSCC)

As I've worked in the system, the irony is that the older officers in the system, the "cowboys" in the old days, are often the ones that I can build a quicker rapport with than the younger officers. They've seen a lot, they've been through a lot, and once you've seen so much in life, you have a different perspective. The things that get other people upset really quickly just don't bother you anymore. You begin to see that people are human. That everybody has their faults and everybody has their issues and problems, and that the best way to deal with people is try to treat them like a human being. Those that have learned the lesson make extremely good correctional officers. (Staff, SMI)

I'd put correctional officers and parole officers on the floor at all times [physically on the unit with the inmates]. Parole officers in all jails would be on the living units on the floor. Accessible, everyone would be accessible at all times, be there to answer questions. No one wants to deal with inmates. As a supervisor to parole officers, I'm having a big problem having my staff on the floor. But then it becomes political. As a supervisor, it's my responsibility to make sure we're moving forward. The idea is that the inmates are dangerous and we need protection. But the biggest protection we have is our mouth. Use your mouth and your brain, and see what's going on. (Staff, MI)

Among inmate respondents, many gang members tended to be fairly negative towards COs. They generally saw them as adversaries and not as potential sources of assistance. I assess this adversarial framing further in Chapter 10.

These two remand inmates at Headingley were quite critical of COs:

W: How do you get along with correctional officers?
I: Some, not very well. I don't really like them. The only ones I get along with, they are just here for their job. I don't like the ones who think that they are fucking cops. (Remand inmate and gang member, HCC)

I don't get along with COs. When I need something, I ask them. Stay out of my way, I'll stay out of your way. If I ask you for something, you know, they're supposed to be there to fuckin' help you out and stuff. (Remand inmate and gang member, HCC)

Finally, inmates and staff shared the perception that COs who engaged in legitimatizing behaviours were better at managing inmates, gaining compliance, and limiting tension and the potential for disorder. This provides at least some support for applying procedural justice when performing the CO role. These three inmates were certain that "good" COs, particularly those who showed respect to inmates, were effective at maintaining order:

Yeah, there are some officers I respect and will listen to. The ones who don't judge you, talk to you like you are a human being. Some of the others I avoid or do the minimum, eh? You know, we can't help ourselves, we can't do some of these things. Why make such a big deal out of helping us? If you're going to be an asshole, why should I listen to you? (Remand inmate, HCC)

The unit is quiet when certain officers are on. They're good humoured and know their job. The ones on a power trip, they bring the whole unit down. It sucks. (Remand inmate, FSCC)

Some officers are good and I'll talk to them, try to work things out for myself or other inmates. Others, I just avoid. (Lifer, SMI)

Staff felt strongly that fair treatment, good communication, and professional relationships resulted in better-managed units and greater personal safety. For these three officers, talking to inmates and showing inmates respect had its own rewards:

I think it holds true that you're firm, fair, and friendly, but not their friend. The man that taught us that years ago in Kingston, I remember him telling the class, "Don't start to use jail house jargon. Don't swear. Don't act like them." And I remember that. I always thought of that, because really, if you treat people with respect, they'll do the same. So when I came back from Kingston, everyone was surprised that our unit ran fine, because other officers had problems. But even though we were new, just treating them fairly, showing some empathy sometimes, it made a difference. Coming as a woman, you don't know what kind of relationship they had with their mom or sister, so you could be that person. The same for men – don't make the situation any worse for them, because so many of them are social casualties. Try to be a force for positive things. (Female staff, MI)

Like I say, Mike, if you get along with inmates, they will tell you things and do what they ask. Other officers have problems, but it's all how you treat people. I show them respect and help them, and I have a happy unit. (Female staff, FSCC)

I have never been assaulted in twenty-seven years. That doesn't mean I never had to get physically involved with inmates; I have lots of times. But I've avoided getting jumped because of experience, level headedness, maturity, and showing respect to inmates. I have always said to an inmate, "You want to be treated like a man, I will treat you like a man. You want to be treated like an asshole, I will treat you like an asshole." And I have met inmates on the street that say, "You know what, Mr. J.? You always treated me fairly." In situations where we do have uprisings, some of these inmates will say, "Let's deal with Mr. J. He has always given me a fair chance. He has pepper-sprayed me, he has thrown my ass into the hole, but it's nothing I didn't deserve when it happened." Patience is important for new staff, and looking to senior staff for help. (Staff, HCC)

At the same time, aggressive staff could create problems for others. Such staff might improve with experience as they learned how to better manage the "grey" areas of inmate discipline. These two staff commented on having to deal with problems created by others:

I didn't like working with other staff who get carried away with themselves. They get pushy with the inmates, they are petty about doing things for them, and the whole unit gets tense. I had to spend my time putting out fires, calming things down. When I complained, they called me a "con lover." (Staff, SMI)

You can see the difference sometimes with the younger and older staff. The younger staff get too aggressive; they don't want to look like pushovers. But the inmates don't like it when staff enforce every rule, and things can get tense and [they] act out. The older staff tend to be more patient. They usually only charge inmates when they deserve it. Things are calmer. But it can take time to learn that. (Staff, HCC)

Framing for Legitimacy

For staff, several important features emerge as vital for framing inmate relations (see Figure 6.1). COs need to engage in procedurally just behaviours – especially important are respect, fairness, courtesy, empathy, and a willingness to listen. An understanding of inmate cultures is important, particularly when it comes to Indigenous inmates. Spending time physically on the unit and being knowledgeable and competent in enforcing inmate rules and regulations are two features not normally thought of as helpful, but inmates view them as essential. Likely even more critical to successfully exercising authority is avoidance of negative behaviours that can impair legitimacy. Being demeaning, punitive, unwilling to listen, and apathetic about an inmate's culture, and not knowing institutional rules, limits an officer's ability to manage inmates. Worse, bringing personal problems to work or engaging in illicit behaviours stand to diminish an officer's influence dramatically.

FIGURE 6.1
Framing relations with inmates to establish legitimacy

Strategies
▪ Get respect/Be able to exercise authority
▪ Be strong/Do not show fear
▪ Be smart/Help inmates, but do not be taken advantage of

Legitimizing behaviours	Delegitimizing behaviours
• Shows respect to inmates	• Treating inmates in a demeaning manner
• Fair in exercising authority enforcing rules	• Punitive in exercising authority and enforcing rules
• Courteous	• Rude and discourteous
• Willing to listen	• Not willing to listen
• Empathetic	• Judging inmates on their crime(s)
• Sense of humour	• Does not know or care about inmate's culture
• Not judge inmates on crime(s)	• Incompetent at rules and regulations
• Be knowledgeable or try to understand inmate's cultures (e.g., Indigenous background)	• Never being physically on unit
• Knowledgeable of institution and its rules and regulations	• Bringing personal problems to work
• Being physically out on the unit (not hiding)	• Engaging in illegal behaviour

Conclusion

Inmates and correctional staff confirm there have been changes in inmate–staff communication over the past twenty-five years. This study's subjects have outlined how these changes can best be translated into more positive or legitimate relations between COs and inmates. More pessimistically, there are limits to the positive impact of some of these changes. Punitive and disrespectful CO talk and behaviours still exist and can result in the "delegitimization" of staff. Franke and his colleagues (2010) have noted that for COs, avoiding inappropriate behaviour is probably more important than behaving in a procedurally just manner. In other words, the correctional frame of legitimacy is hard to build but easily broken. This study's results are generally consistent with and support most previous research findings (Beijersbergen, Dirkzwager, Eichelsheim, et al., 2014a, 2014b; Beijersbergen et al., 2013; Franke et al., 2010; Hulley et al., 2011; Liebling, 2011).

From a policy perspective, this study's findings indicate that COs should engage in procedurally just behaviours whenever possible, but that they should also avoid negative actions. Procedurally just processes promote legitimating behaviours, so staff should be trained in these. On the job, it is recommended that COs be physically on the inmate housing unit as much as possible. COs should work hard at developing positive interaction with inmates but should avoid becoming overly familiar; indeed, they should provide personal space to inmates who do not want close relationships. Learning about other cultures and about mental health problems are important aspects of training, and emphasizing both will add to inmate perceptions of staff competence. Finally, COs need to keep their personal problems out of the workplace in order to do their job professionally.

7

The Effect of Policy, Architecture, and Technology

Communication and relations between inmates and COs have improved in some ways, but why? What has driven the change? Three important factors to consider are direct supervision (DS), dynamic security initiatives, and new-generation prison design and technology. Canadian federal and provincial correctional jurisdictions as well as US prison systems have had different degrees of success in implementing dynamic forms of security – that is, having COs manage inmates through interaction and by forming relationships with them. Corrections organizations have been attempting to incorporate direct supervision styles since the 1970s, albeit very slowly. The implementation of DS has been limited by the availability of properly designed facilities, entrenched attitudes of managers and staff, and outright resistance by staff (Hughes, 1996; Wener, 2006; Zupan, 1991). Some study participants told me that even between 1998 and 2008, they had seen marked improvements in CO–inmate communication. It seems to have taken a surprisingly long time for DS to result in the more active engagement of either inmates or staff with each other. Promoting such a policy on its own had little initial effect.

My interviews and on-site observation (albeit restricted) lead me to assert that the keys to a change in staff–inmate relations have been case management policy, DS architecture, and new technology. These three often-overlooked organizational and physical features of correctional facilities have changed over the past twenty-five years so as to restructure the role, activities, and behaviour of COs. As policy and practice, dynamic security is no longer a platitude. For instance, policy changes have required

COs to assume some day-to-day case management activities – a job modi-fication that has led to more inmate contact. New prison designs are requiring staff to work in close contact with inmates and making it harder for them to avoid inmate contact. Finally, the introduction of new com-puter technology into the federal and provincial corrections systems has given COs access to offender records. This background knowledge now forms a basis for casual or more in-depth case-related conversation. The related literature gives additional support for the notion that policy, archi-tecture, and technology can influence behaviour and practice within a correctional setting.

Correctional Policy, Technology, and Transformation

As Michael Lipsky (1979) has documented, criminal justice agents often avoid scrutiny and can resist change; that said, policy changes can and do impact behaviour. Lucien Lombardo (1989) interviewed COs at Auburn prison in 1976 and 1986 and evaluated some of the adjustments he observed in CO behaviour and their probable causes. He found that CO involvement in solving problems for inmates had actually declined over ten years. An increase in counselling positions and a policy requiring referral to other staff had mandated COs to be less involved with inmates. Also, the intro-duction and expansion of the sergeant's position (rank above CO) provided a means for inmates to bypass COs and go directly up the institutional hierarchy to resolve issues. In sum, Lombardo found that policy clearly had affected the job duties performed by the COs, as well as inmates' perceptions of the COs' role.

More recent examples of the potentially significant impact of policy change on CO practice are offered by British corrections. In her assessment of inmate–staff relations, Alison Liebling (2004) saw management imple-mentation of the earned remissions scheme as critical to changing the culture. This policy saw an inmate's potential early release linked to ongoing staff assessment of inmate behaviour on the units. In later work, Ben Crewe (2009, 2011) voiced concerns over this arrangement. COs' new input into release decisions and earned remission evolved into a "soft power" that could enhance, but also hurt, officers' influence over inmates. Inmates reported to Crewe that they had to be careful what they said or did around COs. Crewe (2011) felt that at times, the soft power had developed to a stage that it could be a detriment to CO influence; inmates upset over their ratings could end up disliking officers and see them as less legitimate.

Katja Aas (2004) viewed the introduction of technology and computerized offender databases in corrections as likely to depersonalize relationships between correctional staff and inmates. Aas contended that before automation, staff would meet and talk with offenders to get to know them, thereby constructing a unique "narrative identity." As a result of automation, COs were categorizing offenders by automated rankings of risk or other groupings, and this reduced their interest in or willingness to establish relationships, besides allowing "governance at a distance." Aas builds from an emergent literature on technology and social relations to caution about the negative impacts of technology on staff–inmate interaction.

Policies Changing the CO's Role and Responsibilities

The staff interviewed in this study indicated that policy changes and their new case management duties had a clear and lasting effect on inmate–CO communication. There was a clear link between the creation of the COII position (or its provincial equivalent) and interaction between the two prison groups. The COII position required an officer to meet with the inmates on their caseload and participate in case meetings. Two former officers recalled how caseloads impacted the CO role:

> When they involved the correctional officers in casework, that really got staff on the units talking more to inmates. (Staff, FSCC)

> Yes, having caseloads appeared to change correctional officer approaches to inmates. They definitely talked more. (Staff, MI)

In the federal system and (to an extent) in provincial jurisdictions, policies were introduced that specifically required "range walks" or officer rounds through the unit; these walks led to interactions with inmates. As officers circulated through the unit on intermittently scheduled rounds, they were expected to speak with inmates. The range walk also helped inmates who did not wish to be observed physically walking up to officers for a chat; they could talk with COs about an issue when they came around to their cell without appearing to be an informant or spending "too much" time with a CO. Several former officers recalled how range walks changed patterns of interaction at Stony Mountain:

> *There is more communication for a variety of reasons. COIIs have caseloads, so they have to talk to inmates and inmates have to talk to them, although maybe not that often. At Stony Mountain, we have more units now where inmates are confined to their range. With dynamic supervision, staff end up doing more range walks every half hour, forty-five minutes, so inmates have no choice but to socialize with their staff, right?* (Staff, SMI)

> *The system is now designed in a way that we are talking to them. As a correctional officer II, I was in charge of a caseload of eight or nine guys. But at the time, having a security mentality, I did not know enough about parole to contribute much to the case management team. But when I look back at it now, being forced to get to know the guys, knowing their names, knowing what they are doing on the unit, and knowing their case information is invaluable. But it is also important to share what you know with the parole officer. And I also didn't realize how important the eyes of the correctional officers are to program staff, because let's face it, you can have a guy in a program, he might be wonderful, polite, the whole bit. Does what he is asked of, no concerns. But at night, when he is interacting with the correctional staff, he is completely different! That is good information to have. I never realized it at the time, but for correctional officers, knowing the inmate and sharing, that is important.* (Staff, SMI)

> I: *The living unit officers* [security/counselling position used in the mid-1970s to early 1980s] *used to have some casework responsibilities, not much. COIIs now have responsibility for monthly summaries and limited input for other reports. For instance, if an inmate is going for a private family visit, the original one is done by the parole officer and then any subsequent ones the COII does. We hold weekly case conferences, the unit does, and the manager of the unit and the parole officers discuss their cases. The COIIs that are on are expected to be in there as well, discussing their cases.*
> W: *So you think that is a good thing for the officers?*
> I: *Yes. It helps to ensure that staff actually know their inmates, or at least some of them, and ensures that they have interaction with these*

inmates. Inmates also have incentives to talk with staff and will ask their particular officer for things. It definitely makes them mingle. (Staff, SMI)

It was the intent even in 1973 to move us to a greater dynamic intervention process, because, at least, that way we know, or we're supposed to know, what the hell's going on. Do we know more about what's going on or are we just being told a great deal more that has no foundation? I would say, overall, we know more about what's going on because inmates are more willing to talk to officers. Yes, there's still a benefit in it for them, because talking to their COIIs might help them get parole. But so long as you have a basis for dialogue, or even just get some good security information, so what? (Staff, SMI)

DS was resisted by correctional staff when the first direct supervision correctional institutions were built in Canada in the 1970s. The change in roles for COs has meant that even traditionally minded COs have had to try to adopt this style of inmate management. Several COs or former COs commented on how case management requirements were forcing them to adapt:

W: So the case management actually gives you something to talk about with an inmate?

I: It gives you a purpose of bringing out an inmate to talk to him. The older staff didn't want to do that. It wasn't their job; they were guards when they were hired. You know, if your fist didn't fit through the bar, you got to go to the second floor. If you were over 250 pounds, you went to the basement because it's a tough area, where the segregation guys are. We flip-flop it now; staff have to work different areas. Staff are expected to do their rounds, to have a rapport. We train staff in interpersonal skills. We train staff in case management. We have direct supervision areas where staff are required to be in there and deal and manage inmates accordingly. (Staff, HCC)

I: Every officer has from three to maybe five inmates on their caseload at one time.

W: Officers not interested can work in static posts?

I: Unfortunately, it is not a matter of interest; this is the way it is, if you are working within the units. If you have daily interaction with the inmates, you will have casework to do with them. (Staff, HCC)

We cannot assume, however, that all COs embrace and actively engage in their casework role. One manager observed that resistance still existed, and cited a need for improvement:

People fought this talking to inmates for so long. "It's not my job" sort of thing. We still could do better. (Staff, MI)

Inmates also noted the change required by the case management role. Because COIIs had some documentation responsibilities, some reluctant inmates were compelled to talk to staff. One lifer encouraged his peers to take advantage of the casework relationship:

The biggest change is that, and in itself, is the system where you have no choice but to deal with staff. Some of the old-timers are still not into that and say "No, they're pigs, we don't talk to them." They come to me, so I can solve the problem. But I don't do it for them. I say, "Listen, if you want this to work, if you want to fix this, we go together." So I build that bridge, and once that bridge is built, it's easy to bring people to that centre line. So we go together to talk to that officer. (Lifer, MI)

Some inmates viewed the case management role as a subterfuge for COs to get information. This Stony Mountain inmate remained wary of COs and their questions:

When I came here before, my brother was doing ten years here and he told me, "The guards here, they try and act like they wanna help you and be your friend, but don't trust them, man." So I don't really talk to them. The only time I come out and talk to them is if they are my case manager [a COII]. That's it. They ask me questions, how things are going. (Sentenced inmate and ex-gang member, SMI)

Some federal staff felt that they had not observed as much change as there should be, given the objectives of dynamic security. Several said that regardless of policy, purposeful communication would only occur with staff who favoured that particular style of inmate management:

To an extent, there is more interaction in dealing with the daily routines and the functions. Staff know an inmate's first name; back then, you knew their number. But it was like the troubled kid in the class – in the old days, you definitely knew who was who, and you observed, and you saw. There is more potential for interaction now, but that depends on the officer doing his job. (Staff, SMI)

They perceived that some of their colleagues went to great lengths to avoid contact with inmates. They believed that some officers had to be motivated to perform direct supervision, or required much closer supervision by managers to ensure it occurred. One staff felt that building an institutional culture of communication was necessary to promote interaction:

W: Do more staff talk to inmates now?
I: A lot do and a lot don't. I see it more as a style thing. Some don't change. Some are like, "Get the hell out of my office" to the inmates, so I don't see a lot of difference. Some are good. Some don't bother. I don't think there is a lot of supervision. There needs to be some accountability, some follow-up. Every jail I've seen has a culture of their own. That culture will affect whether or not that inmate–staff chatter goes on or not. When the inmates are talking to the staff, they talk to all the staff, not just their parole officers. (Staff, SMI)

Prison Design

The institutions in this study varied considerably in their ability to physically accommodate direct supervision goals. Stony Mountain and Matsqui had older designs, and SMI in particular had large units or ranges with eighty to ninety inmates. Matsqui had smaller units or ranges but limited ability to monitor inmates. Fort Saskatchewan, by contrast, had been built on the dynamic supervision model, with a staff kiosk right inside a forty-eight-bed unit with no glass separating inmates from staff. Despite initial resistance to dynamic security at Fort Saskatchewan when that new facility opened in the late 1980s, DS became popular with inmates and staff. This staff recalled how personnel there finally adapted to the new design:

> When it first opened, both inmates and staff didn't care for how open it was. Eventually, most got used to it. Now it's a pretty mellow place, nicer place to work in a lot of ways, and people are used to standing at the kiosk [staff station on the unit], but some old-timers miss the old Fort. (Staff, FSCC)

Staff and inmate perceptions at Headingley Correctional Centre were of particular interest, because the institution housed inmates in both old- and new-style prison buildings. HCC attempted to implement the direct supervision approach in the mid-1990s in the old, linear-style units and experienced considerable opposition from COs (Hughes, 1996). The original physical plant, built in 1931, was totally inappropriate for direct supervision. The old units were built using the indirect supervision day room concept, where inmates would come out of their cells to an adjoining common "day" area. They were still separated from staff by bars while in the common room. Officers would walk along the bars and talk through them to inmates when they made their rounds. Staff stations were off the unit, and if an officer was not in the unit, cameras had to suffice for monitoring. When the living unit system came in, the conflict between administration and staff led to an erosion of operational control. This staff–administration struggle was observed by Justice Ted Hughes, in his independent inquiry, to be a key factor contributing to the brutal Headingley prison riot in 1996 (Hughes, 1996).

The Manitoba provincial government responded to the riot by constructing a ninety-six-bed high-security building, completed in 2000. Ironically, it used "softer" (in some respects) direct supervision architecture, with five units of varying sizes. One might expect that given its recent history, HCC would have had little success in another attempt to implement DS, but in fact, inmates and staff in this study tended to be among the most ardent supporters of this approach. This is even more surprising when one considers that most inmates I interviewed at HCC were ex-federal inmates with significant prior criminal histories (housed by the province because of remand status), with limited access to programs except for the domestic violence unit.

These Headingley correctional staff viewed the physical proximity required by the new, smaller open units as a powerful factor influencing CO–inmate interaction:

There is a certain "us and them" between the inmates and the staff. Keeping the same staff on a unit makes a big difference, though. The "us and them" lessens because inmates have to adapt to the staff because they are back every bloody day. (Staff, HCC)

There are a lot of guards who hate inmates; there are inmates who hate guards. But in a place like this, it is wide open; the guards are right there, so everybody's got to get along, otherwise its chaos. (Remand inmate, FSCC)

It was a change for us, having direct supervision, being in with the inmates. The old system, we just had to walk through the range; they were on one side of the bars and we were on the other side. It was very scary when we started approximately five or six years ago. You would be in there and constantly watching your back, thinking, "My God, there is thirty inmates in here. What if they want to jump us, take us hostage?" There was some bitterness at the beginning, because we all feared for our safety. It was hard on the inmates, too, at first, because if you talk to an officer, you are automatically a rat – you can't do that, it is just unheard of. But as time went on, even the inmates liked it. It took about a year before people got to like it. (Staff, HCC)

Physical design can limit interaction. Headingley is actually two jails. The main facility is an eighty- to ninety-year-old linear-style building with tiers, bars, and day rooms and a more traditional style of interaction between COs and inmates (which is to say, quite restricted). One staff member described how the mood was much more relaxed in the new direct supervision–style building, where officers worked right in the units:

W: *The physical plant in the old units is such that you can't really talk to an inmate without everyone being aware?*
I: *That is just it – it is quite obvious and awkward. We are talking through bars at each other. The smaller direct supervision units have an office and the inmates do come in to talk. They might say to you, "I really got to make a phone call. This is happening and that is happening." And I*

think there is now more consideration by staff towards what they need than there ever was before. Because before it was, "You got to make a call, but I'll get to you when I can." You know, they need certain hygiene products, and it's, "Well, you know, I just made a round. I will be back in a half an hour." And you really didn't go out of your way to go the extra mile. Now it seems like, between them and us, we are working together a lot better than we ever did before. And I think the fear level has gone down. I mean, it is always here, but the tension isn't as thick as it used to be. You being right in there sort of keeps tension out. Even if inmates are scared of other inmates, they see an officer there and now they feel safer. So now, they will come out of their cells. They will interact. They will watch TV together. They will do things knowing that there isn't going to be anybody that is going to jump them. (Staff, HCC)

This HCC staff observed the difference in atmosphere between the linear building and DS units, and how it had the potential to improve CO–inmate relations:

You definitely cannot have the same relationship with inmates on the old cell block as you can in the direct supervision units. When you do a round in the day room, with the bars between you and them, they don't much want to talk with you. They might yell some insult at you from the back of the range, but you can't really see who did it. That never happens on the new units. There is some limited choice, so some of the old-school inmates might go to the old cell block. Most seem to like the DS units. (Staff, HCC)

Inmates felt greater safety in the DS units. Two staff reported that the visibility of inmates to COs, and the greater presence of COs in the unit, reduced worries:

W: Inmates feel safer in direct supervision?
I: The inmates themselves have learned to adapt, and I think, to a certain degree, they feel more secure in the prison system now than they ever did before, as far as their safety and everything else. The officers are on the floor or sitting in a nearby office, not off-unit. (Staff, HCC)

I don't want to get taken out of here [DS unit]. *Don't take me out of here early. I ain't going back to the main* [building] *or something, you know. I'm saying, this is a lot better than the main. I was there, too. They kinda threaten you with the main here, you know. Like, they always hold it over your head. Like, "You're going back to the main." Here, it's laid back, like, you have that interaction with the guards.* (Sentenced inmate, HCC)

The situation in Matsqui and Stony Mountain, which are older federal penitentiaries, was different partly due to the size of the facilities and inmate housing units. I literally felt the physical difference when I was on a ninety-person tier at Stony Mountain compared to the smaller DS units at Headingley and Fort Saskatchewan. At Stony Mountain, there was considerable distance from one end of the tier to the other, and the officer kiosk, although on the range, was quite a distance from the inmates. One Stony Mountain staff commented on the limited architectural change in their physical plant and how that negatively influenced communication patterns:

> I: *The physical layout hasn't changed at all – a bit odd that they haven't built to keep up with the times. Cells are really tiny. Doors are ancient.*
> W: *But there have been renovations?*
> I: *The renovations here eliminated the dome* [a central area everyone walked through in the old-style radial prisons]; *it's just an empty shell now. All the units are managed by the end of the wing. That was a major construction. It roomed out nicer offices. The officers have better facilities. The kiosk is nicer. At the front of the unit, where the officers are, it's kind of a no man's land, those areas. Part of the inmate code is that they don't go into this no man's land, don't really go formally out of their way to talk to staff. Yeah, they talk on their terms; it's when the officers do range walks. As an inmate, you wouldn't go to the kiosk and chit-chat for too long. Only if you have something serious, or if you were a unit cleaner.* (Staff, SMI)

Matsqui offered a very awkward design for direct supervision or dynamic security: the officer staff station was at a nexus of four 26-bed units, with a similar design on all three floors. Thus staff had about 100 inmates per floor to contend with, similar to Stony Mountain. Unless they had 360-degree vision, officers could only monitor one unit or group of

25 inmates of the 100 at once. They had to rely on their peripheral vision or cameras to catch activity in other places.

The free movement in Matsqui was valued by the inmates, but the flow of inmates from one unit to the next further limited the ability of staff to engage in dynamic security. Because of the large number of inmates at Matsqui constantly coming and going, when assaults or other negative events occurred it was difficult to know which inmates might have been involved. Staff at Matsqui identified the physical configuration of their units as a problem in controlling inmate misconduct. About six months after my interviews, Matsqui began restricting inmate movement to contend with this issue. This staff observed that too many inmates were being assaulted in the stairwells between floors or in other "blind" spots that COs or institutional cameras were unable to monitor:

> *Our physical set-up is a problem. The units are too large, and our staff have difficulty monitoring every place at once. Our free inmate movement has been at the root of some of the violence and other problems we have experienced lately. We would be much better off with smaller, dynamic security units.* (Staff, MI)

One might try to explain the perception that the DS units at FSCC and HCC were more favourable environments to differences between federal and provincial inmates. That is, perhaps provincial remand inmates were easier to manage because most of them were less serious offenders than federal inmates, who historically serve longer sentences for more serious, violent crimes. Yet one has to consider that in Alberta and Manitoba, many ex-federal inmates were serving more of their overall custody in provincial correctional centres on remand – indeed, high remand rates persist in both those provinces (Statistics Canada, 2015). Most of the federally experienced inmates I interviewed at FSCC and HCC (both provincial centres) had long criminal records, frequently for violence (see Table 2.1).

Institutional design clearly made a difference to my respondents, and I observed the differences myself when visiting these facilities. Stony Mountain and Matsqui are saddled with outdated designs that would be prohibitively expensive to overhaul. Usually it is cheaper to build new, state-of-the-art units, like Headingley did, than to attempt to renovate existing facilities. The Headingley DS units seem to be a nice balance of small, self-contained units that can deliver unit-based programs, manage difficult inmates, or protect inmates at risk.

There are costs associated with running smaller housing areas in a correctional facility, but there are also ways to construct units so that they require fewer staff – for example, by providing adequate back-up and continuous camera monitoring. Large units holding many inmates create a difficult dynamic. To establish relations with inmates, staff must always battle the more impersonal nature of these heavily populated settings.

Technology

Technology has an impact on the criminal justice workplace in terms of how people relate to one another as well as how they approach and perform their jobs (Aas, 2004). How technology is used in corrections ties into policy and CO job functions in security and casework. Changes wrought by new technology have affected the CO role. Metal detectors, drug-detecting ion scanners, X-ray scanners, and cellphone detectors are all new features in most federal and some provincial institutions. In terms of inmate relations, likely the biggest effect of technology is that staff can now familiarize themselves about inmates through computers at their work posts. Video cameras that place staff as well as inmates under constant surveillance are also influencing staff behaviour. Staff reported that video cameras and on-site computers were having a significant impact on day-to-day behaviour:

> Technology has helped in two ways. First, video cameras have their limit-ations, but they have reduced inmate opportunities to assault each other. Secondly, the computer system we have now allows most staff access to documents and information about inmates. This makes them less mysteri-ous, makes staff more familiar with them. Familiarity reduces social dis-tance. Staff know a lot more, are encouraged to know a lot more about the inmates on the ranges, and that translates into more humane treatment, more participation in their lives. (Staff, SMI)

> W: You were trying to do some case management [provincial, Manitoba] with COs by the mid-1990s?

I: Yeah, but first we didn't have computers, then we had a computer but everything was hand-logged. There was no templates. There was no nice Excel forms. Even then, we had a guy who worked here twenty years, you told him to be a case manager and turn on a computer and holy cow! It was French to him. There was no way he wanted to touch that. That has changed – everyone pretty much has to be computer literate. (Staff, HCC)

When we started, everything was pretty much pencil and paper. Now we pretty much log on to the computers as soon as we come in – check e-mails, what is going to take place today, what happened last week? You get a good feel of what space the inmates may be in because there is the daily log, every inmate's running record [on the computer]. *So you can read up on how John might have been feeling yesterday versus three days ago and things like that.* (Staff, HCC)

There are some downsides to technology. Accountability requirements have increased the amount of routine work that has to be done, and daily records are part of that. Staff were concerned that for all the data systems in place, corrections automation still lagged and far too many records were not accessible. This Stony Mountain staff indicated that too much information was still solely on paper:

For our reports, we need to know, did they get their legal call, did they get their shower, did they get their fax, did they get this? If I was a good computer programmer, I could work myself out of a job in a lot of ways. We have to pull this information from different areas. Our reports could be done that way, extracting different sections like risk assessment, institutional checks – you know, pulling those into new reports and asking for updates, that kind of thing. So technology's not being used to its full advantage. It's so tedious; you have to force yourself to concentrate on paperwork. (Staff, SMI)

Conclusion

The CO primary frame has changed over the past twenty-five years and has been influenced by policy, architecture, and technology. Modest case management duties, including small caseloads and minimal documentation, have required even the most reticent officers to engage in conversation with inmates. Range walks in the federal service have provided further impetus for interaction. Prison architecture that requires officers to be present on the units has been an additional inducement for inmates and COs to interact. Smaller direct supervision units such as those found at Headingley hold the most potential to encourage communication between inmates and staff. Finally, technology in the form of computers, coupled with the need for case management information, is providing staff with inmate background information and a further basis for conversation. Like Lombardo (1989), Liebling (2004), and Crewe (2011), I found that policy and role changes impacted the day-to-day frame of inmate–CO relations. Taking on more case management functions gave both staff and inmates reason to communicate.

Technology has long been associated with providing more security for correctional institutions and safety for COs (Griffiths and Murdoch, 2014). Radios, metal detectors, ion scanners for drugs, and cameras on units are usually associated with static security, a form of supervision that tends to distance COs from inmates. However, I found that technology (in the form of automated databases) served to promote dialogue between inmates and staff. Contrary to the "disengagement" hypothesis put forth by Aas (2004), however, the use of technology helped increase, not decrease interaction between criminal justice agents and offenders. This may be because of the lack of physical contact between COs and inmates and the social distance created by the old relationships. Physical distance may contribute to less personal relations. Probation and parole officers gather a lot of information and know a lot about their clients, but they only meet physically once a week at most, usually less, and conduct much of their casework duties in front of a computer (Griffiths & Murdoch, 2014).

From a policy perspective, there are many benefits to ensuring that COs' job responsibilities are structured around activities that require inmate interaction and time on the unit, or time spent in other physical spaces occupied by inmates. Continued CO involvement in case management and access to inmate background information through technology appear to be worthwhile practices. While it is undoubtedly true that COs vary in communication style, emphasizing the value of interaction and physical time on the unit should be part of CO training. Of course, this would be in conjunction with specific training on best practices using procedural justice in working with inmates.

8

Boundary Violations by Correctional Officers

Frame keying or breaking occurs when one of the participants in an interaction breaks the normative rules set around that situation, or both do. Adjustment happens when frame rules are broken and then reset to allow new parameters to govern interaction (Goffman, 1974). Frame breaking can be intentional and comprise behaviour where everyone is aware of what is occurring. For example, creating comedy requires anyone hearing a joke to realize it is an attempt at humour, even when the joker is describing or acting out behaviour that is normally considered inappropriate. Simulations like acting and the theatre present behaviour that is out of the ordinary and depend on an audience both to suspend disbelief and to understand the situation is make-believe. Some examples of frame breaking, then, are harmless and even creative. In contrast, rude or aggressively aberrant out-of-frame behaviour can be jarring and create anxiety (Goffman, 1974). Beyond a certain point, however, adjustments to social scripts are no longer a keying around the edges of interpretation; rather, they represent an actual change. For example, salacious and derogatory comments about women were once acceptable but now constitute sexual harassment. That frame has been adjusted, and negative comments are no longer acceptable in mixed company.

This chapter assesses three critical issues affecting COs that have either emerged or been ongoing in corrections over the past twenty-five years. These issues and related problems can be placed under the typologies of "correctional officer deviance" recently outlined by Jeffrey Ian Ross (2013). Deviant behaviours by COs are clear acts of frame breaking. In other words,

COs who violate the norms or observe their violation are well aware that they are keying or breaking accepted frames of interaction and behaviour. There are other areas, though, where it is not so clear whether frames are only being adjusted around the edges, whether the boundaries are only being pushed. Areas of concern identified by Ross include general inter-personal boundary violations with inmates, abuse of authority, discrimination, violence, excessive force and forms of resistance, and even sexual harassment by male COs against female officers (Ross, 2013). I am concerned about these behaviours insofar as they challenge the formal framing of legitimate relations discussed in previous chapters – that is, fair and impartial treatment of inmates and mutual support and respect among peers. What are the perceived gains from these behaviours, and what are the costs, if any?

An emergent issue is that of interpersonal boundaries between COs and inmates. So far, I have shown that the frames severely restricting interaction and more cordial relations between COs and inmates have been mostly shattered and replaced, but what about the fringes that remain around the frame of social distance? At what point do COs or inmates overstep the bounds of appropriate relations (Marquart, Barnhill, & Balshaw-Biddle, 2001)? In addition, an enduring concern since the 1970s in Canada has been the use of force by COs on inmates (Marin, 2013). The illicit assault of inmates by staff constitutes a grim smashing of the correctional frame. How has this changed or remained the same over the years? A third discernible crack in the correctional frame has been the presence of female officers in male prisons (which began in a big way in the 1980s). The introduction of female officers in male correctional institutions has remained controversial in Western countries (Crewe, 2006; Newbold, 2005; Trammell, Raby, Anderson, Hampton, & Stickney, 2014). How have female COs been received in Canada, and what norms have shaped the framing of female COs' relations with staff and inmates in the world of the prison?

Boundaries between Staff and Inmates

Work-related relationships are bounded by norms prohibiting too much personal information disclosure, overly familiar relations, and romantic or physical intimacy. Boundary violations in working relationships are a particular concern where there is a power imbalance (e.g., supervisor–

subordinate). In the human services, examples of power relations include psychiatrist–patient, social worker–client, and CO–inmate. There is a fairly extensive literature on boundary violations in the fields of psychiatry and social work (O'Leary, Tsui, & Ruch, 2013), but little in corrections (for an example, see Marquart et al., 2001). Canadian inquiries have unearthed serious staff behavioural violations such as corruption and sexual exploitation of female inmates by male staff going back to the nineteenth century (Brown, 1849). But there has been little in the way of systematic research concerning staff–inmate boundary violations; correctional organizations appear content to dismiss staff or negotiate resignations over improper conduct, relying on the "bad apple" theory of staff misconduct – that is, malfeasance is not systemic, but can be explained by a small number of weak staff (Ross, 2013).

The dynamics of CO–inmate relations have always placed pressure on COs to use discretion and not enforce every rule. Sykes's (1958) theory of the "corruption of authority" continues to resonate, with its assertion that staff are always outnumbered and so must rule by a tacit consent, and hence are pressured to accommodate inmates. Staff adjustments can result in compromise when the inmates are depended on too much to maintain order on a unit. The classic training exercise, "anatomy of a set-up," revolves around a CO who is manipulated by inmates; they help him manage other inmates so that he can show his superiors he is in control of the unit, but then they use this informal assistance to leverage favours, extorting the officer to bring in more and more serious contraband into the prison.

Boundary violations are important to reconsider in light of the changes in inmate–staff communication and the new, more open frames around inmate communication. The norms around social distance have weakened on both sides. This has created opportunities for staff to exert a pro-social influence and model positive behaviour. But it can be hypothesized that reducing the social distance between inmates and staff has led to them spending more time chatting informally, and participating together in recreational activities, and that this has heightened the possibility that staff will "lose the balance" between appropriate and inappropriate conduct with inmates. Pessimistically, it certainly creates more opportunities for inmates to manipulate staff.

Staff and Inmates on Boundary Violations

Interviewees (especially senior staff) indicated that boundary violation had indeed become more of a problem because of more inmate communication, particularly for new staff. They were concerned that small disclosures by COs (i.e., discussion of personal information) would lead to more serious violations. This senior manager at Stony Mountain saw boundaries as an old problem that had become more difficult with more inmate/staff talking:

> *Boundaries are an existing old problem. Part of it is staff learning to realize where they are and catching on. Some people don't catch on, right? For example, there is a relatively new woman staff who talks to me and complains that inmates are all hitting her up for dates. You know what, this woman never stops talking. She is down range, rambling on. One day, the staff are walking down range, and she is singing the Disney Mickey Mouse song, spelling her name. It is little things like that that just prompts them to start and push the boundaries with her. Her ex-husband's car was just stolen, and she found out about it an hour later. An inmate on the range comes down and tells her, "We got your car." You just get some people who cannot catch on, or it takes them a long time, and that creates problems. Others are a little bit more the other way – they will not say anything or help inmates with little things. You have to be professional, and you have to kind of be mellow, in-between, to work it out. And that can take a bit of doing for some people.*
> (Staff, SMI)

> *You have to know your boundaries. We have been trained in things like "anatomy of the set-up." What is really crossing the line? I guess someone could argue giving an inmate a smoke technically is contraband, but is it that big a deal? I think there are deal makers and deal breakers. For example, anytime it involves any sort of intimacy or sexual relations with an inmate, there is no room for debate. Bringing in drugs, no room for debate. You always have to be aware of those things. Asking yourself, "What is the motive here?" because in a way, we are trained not to trust these guys, right? So whenever they say something, you don't want to just take it at face value. But at the same time, I think that comes with experience and getting to know them as they get to know you. Experience helps you make the judgment calls.* (Staff, SMI)

W: What about personal information?

I: That is touchy. We are in an environment where, I think, sometimes, people forget that as much as we are observing them and taking in information, they are doing the exact same thing. So if all of a sudden, you and I are at the kiosk and someone is talking about, "How is that new motorbike you got?" The next thing you know, the inmate is saying, "So, hey, what kind of bike did you get and where did you get it from?" And really, it doesn't take much. I think an inmate can find out a lot of information on staff if we are not aware of it. I think it goes back to, remember where you work. You can't hide everything, though. Most of the guys in my program will know that I am married. I don't tell them, but they know I am from Winnipeg. I don't tell them where I grew up, but I guess if someone wanted to take a proactive approach, you know, typing up my name, Google it, they could find out. So some of the small stuff, who cares? (Staff, SMI)

While boundary violations were not necessarily a new problem, most respondents saw the increased communication between inmates and staff as contributing to more inappropriate familiarity. These Fort Saskatchewan and Headingley staff viewed boundary issues as a real potential downside to more CO–inmate talk:

From my perspective, more communication can be a bad thing. I think there should be a line between staff and inmates. The staff should keep a professional distance from inmates, then we don't have staff bringing in drugs; we don't have staff doing things for inmates; we don't get staff doing things with inmates they shouldn't be doing. New staff can go one way or the other – they get really strict, overly strict, or they try to be too friendly to compensate for maybe not being as comfortable working in a correctional institution. Young people have problems with that line. (Staff, FSCC)

You make your personal choices of what you think is suitable and what is not suitable to share with these inmates. I have seen a lot more officers coming in that actually know the inmates from the outside. For whatever reason, a lot of gang inmates know a lot of these new officers from the street. We have had a fair amount of officers suspended or fired because of drugs coming into the institution. That seems to be happening a little more often than it used to. And it involves staff who have gone over the line. Sometimes women who get involved with gang inmates, sometimes just guys making an extra buck. (Staff, HCC)

There always has to be a barrier between you and the inmate. You have to remember to be fair and do your job. Your job comes first; you cannot take a personal interest in an inmate. To me, that is never going to be effective. (Staff, FSCC)

I think personal boundaries have definitely become more of an issue than back ten years ago. Because we all knew, for whatever reason, that you just don't share some things. I think staff can forget where we are and the reason why we are here. People should not get on a personal level and [should] discourage questions like, "How is your wife? How is your family?" Like, "How old are your children?" Like, "What do you do on your days off?" I like to keep conversation towards business, which is like, "How are you today? I'm fine today. Do you need to make a phone call, and are you feeling suicidal?" Things to do with my job in the institution. Some of the officers don't understand because they are new, and you have to give them the benefit of the doubt. You try to share your experiences to help them out. (Staff, HCC)

Newer staff were identified as having the most problems managing boundaries. Inexperienced staff were thought to be vulnerable to manipulation, even though they were arguably better oriented and trained. This senior Headingley staff member believed that many new staff lacked the necessary aptitude for inmate communication:

Now every officer in here has to have a counselling ability. You know, we send them to training classes for that, but as far as dealing with the inmates, the communication brings them a little closer, makes them a little more familiar. But they have to watch out – inmates will more or less tell the staff what they want to hear. Newer staff, they have no idea, and these inmates will play them, because these inmates have been in the system for years and years and they love to watch these new kids kind of squirm. (Staff, HCC)

This same person saw new staff as being susceptible to going over the line on self-disclosure, to the point where even inmates might object!

> W: *Are boundaries difficult for newer staff?*
> I: *It's human nature. If you and I sit here for the next three or four hours over a couple of days, you and I are going to find stuff about each other that maybe we didn't want to give out. We will really get to know each other and get a little more familiar with each other. So inmates, over time, can get personal information from the officers if they keep at it. And officers will actually give it up, thinking that they are going to be helping a lot of these inmates.*
> W: *But the boundary issues existed even back in the 1980s. Wouldn't you have some staff who might go over board?*
> I: *Yes, but not as many in those days. It's a bigger problem today. Even some of the inmates go, "I don't want to get all that personal with you, Mr. CO. I got to get along with you, 'cause I'm here and you're here." When the inmates start complaining, you know that's a problem!* (Staff, HCC)

The other issue with boundaries was that relationships might become too close to allow COs to effectively administer their authority. According to one staff member, the line between friend and CO was too easily crossed:

> And it is harder in a disciplinary process when you have a friendly rela-tionship. When a supervisor comes in and says, "Okay, I want you to take this guy down to the hole, or down the block, or to segregation," they have a harder time with it because they went over that line. I think there must be some boundaries between inmates and correctional officers. (Staff, HCC)

This was consistent with what inmates told me. They mentioned how uncomfortable some staff made them with some of the things they shared. Staff and inmates both recounted situations where COs would begin with familiar, harmless interactions, and then engage in more inappropriate exchanges that resulted in unethical or illegal relationships, such as intimate ones or those involving the illicit sharing of confidential information or the smuggling of contraband.

This remand inmate had observed problems with some of the female officers. Becoming compromised can happen quickly:

Then there is also females, because we work with females. Sometimes they get involved in relationships with inmates. It starts off just intimate, but then eventually it's, "Hey, bring me some weed." Because it's no big deal – it's just weed, right? They tell them it's weed, but they're exchanging it for something else that's in there, and they keep bringing it in. Other officers don't know. They keep it pretty hush-hush. But people are going to find out about it, and then that person is going to get busted. Eventually, just because of word of mouth. (Remand inmate, HCC)

This lifer was not as big a believer as others might be in the power of communication. He wanted his interactions with COs kept professional and did not want intimate details of a CO's personal life.

I like an officer who just does his job. Some of them want to talk about their personal problems or complain about their wife. I don't want to hear it. (Lifer, MI)

Boundary violations were not seen as irresolvable, however. The general consensus was that better training and, eventually, experience would help staff learn how to maintain professional working relationships with co-workers and inmates. These two officers saw most staff eventually learning the parameters of appropriate dialogue:

You see the young people get fooled sometimes, but the ones who stick with it figure it out. Most new staff get burned, and they figure it out. (Female staff, FSCC)

Some, but not all, of our new staff have difficulty understanding boundaries, but most learn how to deal with it. (Staff, SMI)

Over the past twenty-five years the increase in CO–inmate communication has changed the rules in their interactive frame, and the rules are certainly different from those in the old inmate and CO subcultures, which emphasized social distance (Figure 8.1). Balancing interaction with inmates with the maintenance of appropriate social distance was difficult for COs. Some interaction was needed to establish legitimacy, engage in casework, and gather enough information about unit goings-on to enable effective offender management. But in establishing close relationships, COs ran the risk of compromising themselves. Framing relations with inmates had certainly become more nuanced, and what constituted frame breaking was not always clear. Regardless, COs need to exercise caution in disclosing too much personal information (e.g., marital problems), or seeing themselves as an inmate friend or advocate, and they must refrain from complaining about other staff or management. Consistent with the literature, this was a bigger problem for newer staff than for those with experience (Worley & Worley, 2011).

FIGURE 8.1
Frame breaking and the female CO frame

Frame breaking and adjustment	
Outside boundaries in inmate–CO interaction	**CO misconduct: Inmates**
Mismanagement of Social Distance • Disclosure of too much personal information • Inmate friend/advocate instead of professional relationship • Complain about other correctional officers and management Exceed Boundaries into Illicit Behaviour • Intimate relationship • Sexual relations • Bringing in contraband/drugs	• Verbally abusive behaviour • Not providing services on the unit such as giving towels, bedding • Providing potentially compromising information to other inmates • Being overly aggressive in restraint situations • Pressure for sexual services • Coming to work impaired by drugs or alcohol • Bringing in contraband/drugs • Assault

Female CO frames	
Female COs–inmates	**Female COs–male COs**
• Maternal/empathetic (easier to talk to) • Vulnerable (chivalrous) • Sex object (good to look at each day) • Positive prison influence (reminds inmates how to behave in front of women) No gender – as a correctional officer – competent or not	• Not physically or mentally tough enough to work in prison • Vulnerable (need to be protected) • Sex object (fair game to tease about sex or pursue) No gender – as a correctional officer – competent or not

From an organizational and policy perspective, training for new COs needs to address the maintenance of constructive interactions and the pitfalls of trying too hard to establish cordial relations with inmates. Correctional organizations would do well to consult the social work and psychiatry worlds, where the maintenance of boundaries has been studied for a number of years. At the same time, training needs to emphasize that COs should not shy away from inmate interaction; if handled correctly, the gains are sizable.

Use of Force and Misconduct

Earlier it was argued that dynamic security, greater interaction with inmates, changes in correctional policy, and new technology had helped bring about a decline in some of the more negative aspects of the CO code, such as punitive attitudes towards inmates. This analysis is extended here to assess how CO misconduct has been influenced from the outside by the federal Correctional Investigator, provincial ombudsmen, legislative changes, court decisions, and national policy directives, as well as by internal changes such as the use of video camera technology. Appropriate behaviour for COs in more difficult situations is governed by the rule of law and the duty to act fairly: force can only be used after other means of gaining inmate compliance have been exhausted, and even then, only when an inmate must be moved (e.g., admission from court, required transfer from prison, sent to segregation) or when a staff or inmate's personal safety is in jeopardy (Hannah-Moffat & Klassen, 2013). Embedded in the CO frame are rules around interaction with regard to when it is or is not appropriate to use force.

The old CO code's strongest rule is to not "write up" or report a fellow staff member for misconduct; this is analogous to the inmate code's "no ratting" rule (Farkas, 1997). It is a concern, of course, when staff who abuse inmates psychologically are protected by their peers, but it is a serious issue when staff physically assault inmates and are not held to account. Certainly, COs are in an excellent position to covertly man-handle offenders in custody. COs hold power over inmates and can isolate them and outnumber them if they wish. They can find private places within a correctional institution to victimize inmates, or they can sequester prisoners on night shift when everyone else is locked up.

Supervisors cannot always be present, and indeed some may even approve of such unauthorized activity to help informally maintain order. Senior inmates, gang members, or physically imposing inmates have sometimes been used to discipline other inmates. The word of an inmate against a CO does not carry much weight. As long as other COs do not inform on their delinquent peers, it is very possible for them to escape sanctions for misbehaviour. This may become even more prevalent when such activity becomes part of the prison culture (Crouch & Marquart, 1980; Jackson, 2002; MacGuigan, 1977; Marin, 2013; Marquart, 2001; Marquart & Roebuck, 1985).

Court Decisions and Legislation

Over the past thirty-five years, a number of laws, court decisions, and inquiries have addressed the issue of discipline in Canadian correctional facilities and mandated staff to follow the rule of law within correctional institutions. The MacGuigan Report of 1977, the *Martineau v. Matsqui* decision of the Supreme Court of 1980, the Corrections and Conditional Release Act (CCRA) of 1992, and the Arbour Inquiry of 1996 have attempted to shape staff behaviour in Canadian prisons.[1] *Martineau v. Matsqui* was a pivotal Supreme Court case; it ruled that federal corrections (this decision flowed down to provincial corrections) must follow the rule of law and take seriously the "duty to act fairly." This means advising inmates of the nature of any charges or allegations against them and not arbitrarily detaining them in segregation. Prior to this decision, COs might place troublesome inmates in lock-up without a formal charge being written or the inmate being informed of what specifically the problem was. The Corrections and Conditional Release Act codified the rule of law and the duty to act fairly. The Arbour Inquiry, called after a riot at the Kingston Prison for Women, was especially damning for COs, insofar as it revealed a cover-up of physical abuse by CSC staff. Most embarrassingly for the CSC, this covert misbehaviour occurred almost fifteen years after the *Martineau* decision and after the enactment of the CCRA.

The Marin Report of 2013, prepared by the Ontario Ombudsman, suggested that COs still abuse their authority. The ombudsman found that COs were still colluding and lying to avoid detection in cases of inmate assaults. Mary Ann Farkas's (1997) key CO work principle – never inform on a colleague – was still strong among provincial COs in Ontario. The ombudsman found that effective oversight policies required strong managers to make sure they were followed. Videotapes of CO–inmate confrontations and CCTV on housing units were useful for detecting and discouraging abuse, but more areas needed monitoring to prevent COs from exploiting "blind spots" where it was possible to avoid monitoring.

Technology and Misconduct

Legislation may well have influenced COs in their use of force, but the introduction of video cameras in correctional institutions may have had an even greater impact on CO behaviour. Research has shown that awareness of being watched influences human behaviour, generally making people more rule-compliant (for related research, see Bateson, Nettle, & Roberts, 2006; Chartrand & Bargh, 1999; Munger & Harris, 1989). This has been one rationale for the use of video cameras on police cars, and the placement of body-worn video (BWV) on police officers (Farrar & Ariel, 2013). These mechanisms capture the activities of individuals who encounter police, but they also track police behaviour. Recording devices can serve as order maintenance or crime-fighting tools: video can encourage compliance with police authority or capture clear evidence of individual offending. It is logical to assume that knowing that their behaviour is being recorded will also discourage rude, inappropriate, or illegal behaviour by police (Harris, 2010). Preliminary results are encouraging: US studies by Tony Farrar and Barak Ariel (2013) in California and by Allyson Roy (2014) in Arizona found that officers who used the BWV were involved in fewer incidents involving use of force and that the number of citizen complaints went down.

Have video cameras detected and discouraged abusive behaviour or the unauthorized or excessive use of force by COs? Indirectly, they may have, but video cameras are only as effective as the areas they survey. The Marin Report, which investigated inmate assaults in Ontario, found that COs in that province had begun systematically beating difficult inmates in areas not monitored by cameras. Some COs were found out by investigators when videotapes of areas adjacent to inmate assaults captured images of officers washing clothing covered in blood and getting fresh clothing for an injured inmate. One of the report's recommendations, not surprisingly, was to install more video cameras in Ontario's correctional institutions.

Staff and Inmates on CO Misconduct

To understand prison life in Canada today, it is important to appraise the darker side of inmate–staff relations. What do inmates and staff say about levels of misconduct on the job? I consider staff assaults first; then I evaluate other forms of malfeasance and unprofessional conduct.

Inmates and staff confirmed that CO culture was more physically aggressive in the 1970s and 1980s. Some COs would "tune up"[2] inmates considered behaviour problems on the units by assaulting them. The most common method reported involved removing an inmate from his cell on the night shift (when only a few staff and perhaps one manager were on duty) and giving him a beating.

This staff person never worked as a CO but became familiar with CO deviance when he first started with the CSC:

> *Violence against inmates was still going on in the 1980s, for sure. I was working in Drumheller when they had 3:00 a.m. tune-ups. When I first heard of these, I was like, "You guys do that?" So at 3:00 a.m., they get some inmate up and beat him with a bar. And that was acceptable. But that's ended, to my knowledge.* (Staff, MI)

This younger CO was very aware of the limits placed on becoming physical with inmates. Prison lore at Headingley asserted that violence against inmates had at one time been organized and administered by a specific band of COs:

> *You get told, as a new officer, about how things have changed at Headingley. You can't really get away with beating up inmates, and most of the new staff aren't really interested in that, anyway. There were lots of stories when I started about the early 1980s and how things were managed. A group of officers called "the Dirty Dozen" were a macho bunch that were supposed*

to have taken care of problem inmates. That just doesn't go anymore.
(Staff, HCC)

The consensus among inmates and COs was that physical assaults
carried out by staff now rarely occurred, although they had not been eliminated completely. This frame breaking still occurs. Surprisingly, staff did
not ascribe this change to better training or an improvement in COs' inmate
management skills. One factor influencing the perceived decline in physical
abuse was the type of staff being recruited. Two supervisors (former COs)
indicated that many new staff were not as aggressive and were unwilling
to resort to violence to address problem inmates unless absolutely
necessary:

When I started in 1989, you had to be willing to be aggressive with inmates.
You didn't turn around and walk away or back off, because then you were
weak. That's changed. It's funny, though, when I became a keeper [super-
visor], the staff that I had difficulty with were the ones that wouldn't back
off. They ended up creating problems. They'd get into an inmate's face and,
next thing you know, fists are flying, and then I have to write a report, and
I have to send somebody to the hospital. Our newer staff are less likely to
get into fights. (Staff, SMI)

There is not as much rough stuff as before. But years ago, you couldn't let an
inmate challenge you in front of a group; you had to mix it up. Our new staff
will just walk away. They think differently than the old staff. (Staff, FSCC)

Overwhelmingly, however, correctional staff indicated that accountability measures had had the strongest impact on reducing the illicit use
of force by staff. Two Stony Mountain staff summarized the consensus –
legislation had made a difference:

The first few years I was in the service, we were under the old Penitentiary
Act. Things changed, but seemed to change quickly after the CCRA came
in. So there has been a real transformation on how we saw the job and
what we were expected to do, what we could do, and what we could get
away with, from the time of the old Penitentiary Act. I didn't agree with

it, but things in the penitentiary were different thirty years ago. Inmate and staff did not have conversations; there was a lot of activity outside of the law. And a lot of things were done inside the penitentiary – that wall of silence, inmates not talking; the staff was the same way. If you witnessed something or if you were involved with something, it was a "do not talk" sort of thing. If you spoke, there was a fear of parking-lot justice from your colleagues. And I'm sure there were other forms of revenge outside of the property. At the same time, there was comradeships formed, the honour around workers. It was about survival; you needed to survive. You didn't want to get stabbed, beaten up; it was a very angry, violent environment. Every time you walked into an open area, you depended on someone to back you up. Justice took the form of people accidentally falling down the stairs, accidentally falling off their bunk, or bumping into a wall – those things would occur. And I mean specifically under the old system. What happened changed over time. You started to see a decline in the battle and wall between staff and inmates in the eighties. There was violence in prisons. There were still problems. But there was more accountability.
(Staff, MI)

The CCRA made a change for us in accountability, sure, but it was coming one way or another. You could see just working there that inmate beatings were not being tolerated by management. Things were changing.
(Staff, SMI)

Policies (arising from legislation) coupled with technology played a large part in the reduction in staff violence. There are now video cameras throughout most institutions that put officers on display in the event that they are tempted to assault inmates. Staff felt that in situations where physical coercion was still required, policies requiring the video-taping of potentially explosive events, such as cell extractions, made a difference, as colleagues acted differently when they knew they were being observed.

These senior officers at Stony Mountain viewed cameras and strict policies as factors constraining the abuse of inmates by staff:

I think that, overall, the situation has improved quite a bit. There was a time when I was in the system that you just didn't want to cross an officer, because if you did, there were ways of dealing with that. There were no video cameras in those days [laughs]. *So in that regard, things have become far more professional.* (Staff, SMI)

When I first started, we had no such thing as an IERT [institutional emergency response team]. *If somebody has to come out of his cell, he was coming out of his cell, didn't matter. If you had to send ten COs in there, it didn't matter. He was coming out. You had inmates getting handcuffed, officers getting handcuffed together, and things like that, because you just had absolute chaos. Now we film everything. There is no room. There is a process, a chain of events that must take place, and the first one is obviously negotiation. And then you go down the line from there. So nowadays, that would never happen. Is that better? I would say so, because that way nobody gets hurt.* (Staff, SMI)

This staff person dated his experience back to stories of corporal punishment when he began, and to rumours of staff-on-inmate assaults. He attributed the likely decline in such assaults to the advent of videotape, stricter policies, and more vigorous investigations of alleged assaults:

It's only been forty years or thereabouts since they were actually whipping people here, you know. Not in my time, but back in the sixties, a former colleague would tell me about that – corporal punishment was a part of corrections, at least in the early sixties. The anecdotal stories you hear of prisoners getting assaulted by guards were probably quite valid. I think, nowadays, there's very little of that. Probably because they have to videotape every cell extraction, document carefully all interactions, and inmates have access to the Correctional Investigator. They have all sorts of redress agreements and opportunities. I think the life for convicts in here is a lot more secure, and they don't have to worry about anything being visited upon them by staff. (Staff, SMI)

There were limits to the efficacy of cameras, however, for COs could learn where they had been placed in the institution and where they had not been. One officer recalled inmate beatings in elevators in her early years that were eerily similar to those reported recently in Ontario (Marin,

2013). She reported that COs had figured out that no videotaping was occurring on elevators, so they targeted inmates there:

> *Don't get me back on the elevator rides. When I started in BC, inmates were still getting beaten up. That's where the cameras came in. They put them on the units, which cut down on the abuse there. But then officers realized there were no cameras on the elevators. So inmates used to get taken for "elevator rides" and get beaten up. That wasn't even that long ago [1990s]. Then they put cameras in the elevators.* (Staff, MI)

Oversight policies that were intended to increase COs' adherence to more professional aspects of the CO frame still required aggressive follow-up by management. For example, as these former COs indicate, managers now need to rigorously investigate inmate complaints or alleged failures to follow policy during cell extractions, or other situations where use of force was required:

> *There's no room for cowboys anymore. If you think you'll be the keeper [supervisor] that lets correctional officers go down there and kick some ass, it's just not gonna happen because you're gonna have to explain that. It's gonna be your job. Staff won't allow you to do it. There was a time where a keeper in Stony Mountain was pretty much next to God; now, that's not quite the case. Even the union will hold you accountable. I think, for the most part, that those changes are all a positive thing. The downside is, you know, that some of the guys liked having the power. You could just go up to an inmate and tell them to go and do it. They listened to you and went and did it, you know, no questions, 'cause they knew what the alternative was. But those days are gone.* (Staff, SMI)

> *More inmate rights are the largest change that I have seen in the prison system. Huge. Even in the 1990s, inmates did not have many rights in the BC provincial system where I started. When I first started, you could do anything, and no one would question it. One of the things we used to do as living unit officers, for no reason, we could lock someone up for twenty-three hours. You wouldn't need paperwork. But now, you need permission and forms, and you don't have the right to do that.* (Staff, MI)

Respondents indicated that these changes affected how managers and supervisors viewed their jobs and responsibilities, and likely also influenced the CO culture. Two former federal COs from Matsqui and Stony Mountain even felt that this had weakened the COs' supposedly blind eye to malfeasance by their colleagues:

> *The officers probably have a stronger code than the inmates, even though theirs is becoming loosely defined also. In the past, there were the days of "stand together," the "blue flu," to get what they wanted. And even then, I'm not sure the code was truly there, but I think so.* (Staff, MI)

> *I feel the correctional officer code has changed. They still stand together, but they do not have anywhere near the strength in numbers or the strength in solidarity that they had twenty-plus years ago.* (Staff, SMI)

Correctional staff reported conflicting feelings about the increase in accountability measures. They reiterated that they did not believe in physically abusing inmates, but they also felt that their jobs were now more difficult because of bureaucratic requirements. Investigations could be stressful. Implementation of the rule of law had introduced more onerous staff requirements in order to maintain discipline, such as more detailed reports, stricter attention to process rules, and videotaping of potential incidents. Inmates now have much easier access to external agencies such as the Ombudsman (for provincial corrections) and the Correctional Investigator (in the federal system). Some staff, like this CO from Fort Saskatchewan, expressed resentment over how these agencies were advocating on behalf of inmates:

> *The human rights, they bring lawyers in and everything, so now discipline is sure less and less. You charge or violate inmates in the system, but in the end you are doing all the paperwork and you are getting questioned. Did you actually see that? Did this actually happen? Did they really say that? So I think that is probably the most frustrating thing around here.* (Staff, FSCC)

Two Headingley staff felt that things had "gone too far." They viewed accountability measures as ultimately creating a culture where too many inmates were challenging them on small things, making day-to-day life more troublesome:

> One of the biggest changes is inmate discipline. We go through a whole process now where we have our own prosecutor that deals with incidents internally. Inmates have a lot more access to their lawyers, access to external agencies. They didn't have this when I first started. A guy gets caught with a little bit of contraband; well, instead of going down and doing nine days in punitive seg, he brings in his lawyer. They contact the ombudsman because he figures he is being harassed. I think we spend far too much time dealing with minor stuff. (Staff, HCC)

> W: Do you have to videotape cell extractions or similar situations?
> I: Yes. This is something I like in one way and don't like in another. It can vindicate us of any allegations of excessive force, which is good. But I don't like the way it is forced on us by seemingly outside agencies – you know, "Prove you didn't beat the guy." I resent the way we are looked as the guilty one as soon as there is a complaint. We are much more strictly evaluated in terms of how we follow procedure. Unfortunately, a lot of these guys only respect the rule of force. I do not advocate a brutal system by any means, but there is the odd guy where the only real way you can keep him in line is that he has to know that you will kick his ass if he gets out of line. When they know you can't, they will push it as far as they can. (Staff, HCC)

A few inmates and staff preferred the old, informal methods of resolving differences. Staff in their fifties or older were more likely to feel that the old ways had maintained better discipline, so long as measures did not become excessive. Even some inmates longed for the "old days" when inmate–staff disputes were resolved one-on-one and nothing was written down. Their recollections romanticized old conflicts as noble one-on-one battles resulting in mutual respect and less conflict between COs and inmates. The following two respondents – an officer, and an ex-biker gang inmate from Headingley – appeared to have an "ideal type" view of CO–prisoner conflict:

> When I started it was literally, if the supervisors trusted you, everything was verbal, no written reports. "Hey, did you drag that guy down to block

nine and backhand him one?" "Yep." "Why?" "Well, he was going to block nine because he had been in a fight on the block, and when we got down there in front of all the other inmates and staff, he calls the officer a cock-sucker or something. And yeah, he got backhanded right in the mouth." Okay. It wasn't excessive; it wasn't uncalled for, whatever, you know, if the supervisors had confidence in the staff that it was reasonable and they trusted them to be reasonable. A lot of times, there wasn't even a paper trail. A lot of times, even the inmate knew when he had crossed the line. Nobody would like to get a backhander in the mouth, but yeah, the inmate knows he had that one coming. (Staff, HCC)

Correctional officers now have a whole different mentality than the old system. I don't believe it is a better way of doin' it. Are they more professional? Yeah, for the most part. You don't have the fist-to-fist battles, you don't have the good ol' days, but I don't know if it's a good thing or a bad thing. You used to settle your differences, and you went your own way, and it was over. Nowadays, it's reports and you gotta deal with this guy, and you gotta deal with that guy, and this guy knows this and this and this. It's, "Holy mackerel, we're flooded in paper work here." How many trees are you killing out there? (Remand inmate and ex-biker gang member, HCC)

One ex-gang inmate had a less than idyllic recollection of conflict in the 1980s. His memories were more consistent with those of most respondents. Rather extreme measures, like a meat hook, would be used to "socialize" inmates:

Some changes have been for the better and some for the worse. But in general, it has changed, yeah. Hell, at one time back in the 1970s, we use to get hung on a meat hook here at Headingley and beat. That don't happen no more, so that is a good change, you know. The inmates called it "the meat hook," and they handcuffed you up there and they would kick away an old milk stool from underneath your feet. And then you admitted to what you did, or you told what was going on. If you didn't talk, they would work you over. Now some guys never got as far as the hook, but a lot of us did. (Remand inmate and ex-gang member, HCC)

Covert violence by staff was not viewed as a serious problem by inmates. That said, correctional staff can be overly aggressive in resolving situations. Sudden, violent altercations can arise when, for example, an inmate on charge is being taken to segregation, or when staff are performing a cell extraction (removing a reluctant inmate from his or her cell). Once in control of the inmate (e.g., once the handcuffs are on), officers sometimes used excessive force to discourage more resistance or to take revenge if the inmate had hit them while they were being extracted from their unit or cell. These types of assaults take place in what Anthony Bottoms (1999) and others have described as the "rubbing points" of institutional life, places or situations where movement is required. Unnecessary or overzealous use of force has been noted as a growing problem by the federal Correctional Investigator, Howard Sapers (2014), and the Ontario Ombudsman, André Marin (2013), found revenge to be a motivator for some of the inmate beatings he investigated. This Matsqui inmate was outraged when he observed correctional staff losing their cool while chasing a drunk inmate:

> I've been in Matsqui for three years now, and there wouldn't be much violence against staff if they wouldn't provoke. There was one fellow in the yard, he was drunk; they detected the smell of alcohol. They wanted to lock him up or take him to seg, and he started running, and they had to chase him for a good thirty minutes. And we're having a good laugh at all this. But when they catch this poor kid, they have him on the ground, and they're sticking their thumbs in his eyes. They have his face in the dirt. Another officer comes and drops his knee on his face. And I said, "If I ever see that again, I'll call the police myself." And the officer's, like, "Get out of here. It's none of your business." "You just made it my business," I told him. So I took it up with management. There was another officer that was here – now he's in Mission penitentiary because he was provoking inmates, literally causing fights between staff and inmates. (Lifer, MI)

Likewise, this staff person felt that COs sometimes were unnecessarily rough in situations where little force was actually needed to gain control of an inmate:

> Secret assaults seem to have stopped, for the most part. But the way that they take an inmate down, sometimes that bothers me. Yeah, control them,

but when you have six guys, one on each limb, is that necessary? But when I ask that question, I become "con lover." Some of the COs seem fearful. But I've worked construction and believe me, that's more dangerous than working here. We had a military base in Kelowna close, so we had ex-military go to work at Kent [maximum security federal institution] as guards. And they're like, "That's it ... you call this dangerous?" (Staff, MI)

This Matsqui inmate also pointed out that inmates managing mental health problems should be given a bit more latitude by COs. He singled out emergency response teams, which appeared to rush in without any consideration of the sort of prisoner they were dealing with:

It happens, but not as much as it used to. I think the public should expect good behaviour from the guards. Nobody "has it coming to them." A correctional officer is supposed to be a professional; he is supposed to be a mature individual who is trained. Sometimes these emergency response teams are excessive. They rush in and if a guy is being a jerk, maybe he is being a jerk because he has mental issues. The guards should realize that and not go off the deep end doing their job. (Sentenced inmate, MI)

COs can gain credibility for themselves through procedurally just behaviours such as showing inmates respect, listening, and being fair and consistent, but they can just as easily delegitimize their status through negative behaviour. Poor communication, excessive aggression in carrying out CO duties, and outright misconduct weighed heavily on inmates' minds. Things thought amusing by COs were taken very seriously by inmates. For example, joking about sex offender status can risk injury to inmates and COs. These two inmates found COs far too casual when it came to this critical area:

Sometimes COs are just not very professional or smart about how they deal with inmates. An officer walked by a lifer who was sitting in a group. For a joke, the CO says to him in front of the others, "By the way, your transfer to Mountain Institution [prison for sex offenders] has been approved." The lifer is stunned, shaking his head trying to think of something to say back. So I went to the officer and I said, "Mr. ———, I don't know what you think

*you were doing, but what you did to inmate —— was wrong." I pointed out
that the lifer was sitting with guys who have reputations for stabbing people
and punching them out. They aren't sure it's a joke. Anyway, the officer did
the right thing and told him he was joking, in front of the same group of
inmates. But someone could have got hurt.* (Lifer, MI)

*There's one guard, his name's ——. He's a correctional officer, but pure
criminal. He's like, "Yo man, when do you get out? I'm looking for a computer, man. Laptops especially. Can you get me one?" Or he tells people,
"That guy's a skinner. That guy's in for rape." Like, what the fuck you tellin'
me for or other inmates? Or he says to an inmate who had his jaw wired
shut, "Don't make me break your jaw and wire it shut like it was before."
Like, what the fuck are you doing? You're supposed to be professional here.*
(Remand inmate, HCC)

Sex offence convictions are not the only status that can imperil an
inmate. Information about gang status can create a dire situation for some
inmates, as this Stony Mountain prisoner relates:

*I've had some bad experiences. Sometimes staff will lie about you. In one
provincial jail, I was labelled as an Indian Posse [IP] member, then put in
a Manitoba Warriors [MW] unit [IP and MW are prison gangs]. They
are mortal enemies. They placed bets on who was gonna come outta that,
could have cared less about me. Inmates know what's happening, but they
can't say anything. They can't do nothing about it. Because it's our word
against theirs. Still, there's some good officers here.* (Sentenced inmate and
ex-gang member, SMI)

Correctional Officers and the Rule of Law

In summary, serious covert violence by staff appears to have declined, and
this is likely attributable to accountability measures implemented by correctional administrations, either proactively or in response to court decisions, legislation, or pressure from external investigative agencies.
Technology has also exerted a significant influence through surveillance
cameras and other recording devices. While this is positive news, other
forms of CO misconduct still exist.

As suggested in Chapter 5, acts of misconduct or failure to act in a just manner seemed to undermine COs' ability to obtain legitimacy among inmates. Furthermore, serious frame breaking can create unrest and seriously impair CO legitimacy: in turn, this can reduce inmate and CO safety. A number of instances of serious frame breaking are listed in Figure 8.1. Being verbally abusive, withholding basic services, providing compromising information about other inmates, and being overly aggressive in restraint situations all reflect poorly on COs and weaken their credibility and influence. Illegal acts such as pressuring inmates for sexual services, coming to work impaired by drugs or alcohol, and engaging in assault were looked down upon by inmates. While COs may find it frustrating to always have to respect the rights of sometimes disrespectful or uncooperative inmates, the findings here support policy that emphasizes vigorous investigation of inmate complaints.

The use of video cameras in prison settings has reduced CO malfeasance, for people do behave differently when they think they are being watched. However, the findings reported here and federal and provincial watchdogs indicate that COs can determine where camera sight lines are, or ferret out where there are no cameras, and managers can be complicit in beatings or less than demanding in their investigations. While extensive use of video cameras and their strategic placement is endorsed, Michael White (2014) has summarized police research that suggests that the use of body video cameras is probably a stronger method for discouraging misbehaviour by both correctional staff and inmates. Correctional organizations would do well to at least track the research results of police-related BVC projects, as they show promise for reducing illicit behaviour by law enforcement.

Female Correctional Officer Frame

So far this chapter has examined the breaks and adjustments in interpersonal frames that centre on inmate–staff relations. A related change to consider is just *who* is now doing the communicating from the CO side: over the past twenty-five years, female COs have increased their presence in male prisons. Male–female differences may well affect CO relationships with inmates. I had not originally intended to examine the introduction of female COs in Canada's correctional institutions; however, most of my initial interview subjects brought it up as a significant change in prison life over the past twenty-five years, calling my attention to it.

Arguments for and against female COs in male inmate facilities are generally driven by gender-based notions of female behaviour (Britton, 2003; Crewe, 2006; Crouch, 1985; Szockyj, 1989). A common stereotype is that only men have the aggressive nature, physical strength, and courage to control and manage other men, while women are too timid, too weak, or too compassionate to work effectively with male offenders. In rebuttal, there are many gender-based qualities favouring women's presence in correctional institutions. Their existence helps achieve a more representative workforce. The mere presence of women is thought to have a calming effect on the male world of adult correctional institutions. In the 1980s, Ben Crouch (1985) in the United States and Elizabeth Szockyj (1989) in Canada found that women officers were thought to be strong communicators, easy to talk to, and better at empathizing with inmates. Considering these arguments, one might conclude that female COs would be less punitive and more pro-rehabilitation in orientation, and indeed, some investigators have found this (Bruhn, 2013; Hemmens, Stohr, Schoeler, & Miller, 2002).

But studies have also found that female COs are not always more likely to favour programs. The literature on female COs is equivocal regarding their job satisfaction, custodial orientation, and interest in rehabilitation. Steven Walters and David Lagace (1999), found that female COs in Canadian federal penitentiaries were no more likely than male peers to support rehabilitation but that they were less likely to have a custodial orientation; also, they report higher job satisfaction. In experimental, scenario-based studies on aggression, American investigators Mary Ann Farkas (2000) and Denise Jenne and Robert Kersting (1996) found that female COs react as aggressively as males or even more aggressively! Similarities in aggression may be due to overcompensation by female officers, their socialization as COs, or the recruitment of more aggressive women to CO positions (see Chesney-Lind & Pollock, 1995; Jenne & Kersting, 1996).

Canadian studies of federal and provincial institutions conducted by Margaret Cadwaladr (1993), David Lagace (1994), and Elizabeth Szockyj (1989) have found that female COs faced significant resistance from male

COs when they were actively recruited in the 1980s and 1990s; this was consistent with studies by Elaine Crawley (2004) in Britain and Ben Crouch (1985) in the United States. Corrections scholars have argued that male COs resist women because women's gendered view of how to do the CO job may well threaten their own perspective and self-identity, which is tied up in traditional notions of masculinity (Crawley, 2004; Martin & Jurik, 1996). In his Canadian study, James Gruber (1998) found this "sexual spillover" hypothesis to be salient in explaining resistance to women in other male-dominated workplaces with physical requirements such as firefighting, policing, and the military; McDonald (2012) found similar evidence in her review of sexual harassment policies. The sexual spillover hypothesis suggests that where one gender physically dominates a work-place, that particular sexual identity will influence how the job is supposed to be performed. Because men have tended to dominate the CO position, their view is likely to be the most prominent: that the CO job is a highly dangerous one in which masculine traits of aggression and physical tough-ness are paramount. This male-centric view of the CO job is challenged by female COs who can perform effectively despite being physically smaller and whose perspective is not tied directly to masculine values.

Researchers have found that beyond just being resisted or resented by their male colleagues, female COs were harassed, personally and sexually, when they entered the world of the prison (Cadwaladr, 1993; Lagace, 1994; Szockyj, 1989). The frequency and severity of this harassment varied by individual officer. Federal and provincial organizations have introduced policies, procedures, training, and grievance mechanisms to deal with workplace sexual harassment (McDonald, 2012). In a nationwide survey, Gruber (1998) found that Canadian women were more likely to report sexual harassment in workplaces where they were few in number and had more frequent contact with men. Promisingly, this effect was attenuated by active policies and complaint systems against harassment. Later studies have also found that proactive efforts can reduce the incidence of sexual harassment (McDonald, 2012). Sexual harassment policies have apparently had some effect.

Lynn Zimmer (1986) and, more recently, Ben Crewe (2006) have found that male inmates relate to female COs in different ways, some gender-based, some not. Inmates have been found to hold gender-based views of women ranging from highly sexualized (female officers are desirable, and perhaps are working in prison to get admired or have sex) to maternal (they are good to talk to, nurturing) and even chivalrous (they are vulnerable and worthy of respect). However, many inmates (up to one-third in Crewe's study) viewed female COs simply as COs, and judged them on their competence.

In the following section, my respondents reflect on how female COs have affected the framing of behaviour for both CO–CO and CO–inmate relations. How have perceptions of female COs changed over the past twenty-five years in Canada? Are they more accepted by inmates and staff? Have other correctional trends, such as dynamic security, affected their place in adult correctional institutions? If they have faced resistance, how has that been affected by workplace policies, such as those relating to sexual harassment? Do the perceptions of inmates and staff jibe with or refute the various gender-based depictions of female officers? Are behaviours related to procedural justice influenced at all by gender?

Staff and Inmates on Female COs

Female officers interviewed for this study reported that co-workers directed strong opposition at them when they first entered Canadian correctional institutions in the late 1970s and 1980s. Consistent with the literature, the responses of their male colleagues ranged from unpleasantness to outright hostility. Women who persevered seemed to be mentally tough and fairly thick-skinned; they also liked their work. Some respondents observed that even by the late 1980s, it was easier for women to be accepted on the job. They also felt that by the 1990s, sexual harassment policies were having a deterrent effect on potential abusers. Also by the 1990s, the attitudes of many young men coming into the job had changed. These young men had grown up watching their mothers, aunts, and older sisters working full-time, some of them in non-traditional roles in trades and law enforcement. Sexist attitudes persisted, but they seemed to be held by a minority. Female respondents from Fort Saskatchewan and Matsqui and male staff from Headingley all reported that it was older COs, not the younger ones, who still held resistant attitudes towards the presence of female COs in male prisons:

> I: *I'll tell you, Mike, in those days, when we started in corrections, women had*
> *six months of terrible harassment. The male officers tried to get rid*

of us. So a lot quit, but I was one of the few, one of a handful that stayed. And this one time, we went to the legion for a drink, and this one officer was kind of drunk, and he says to me, "How can you handle all of this?" I says, "In one ear out the other." I needed a job, and I kind of liked corrections. And I will tell you, Mike, to this day, there are some officers here that still give us a rough time. Right today, right in here. Because we got some of them that have been here since I started, maybe even a few years before me, and they don't like women in corrections.

W: *What about younger staff?*

I: *They are fine. Once all the older staff goes, it is mainly supervisors. Then it will all die. But some keep it going because they won't change. With the young people coming up, it is a piece of cake because they're trained different today, not like they were trained thirty years ago. In the early nineties, mid-nineties, you could see the young staff coming, and it's all different. The other thing was sexual harassment. That policy made a big difference. So that if you even said the word "harassment," they backed off, and they still do. I mean big-time. Now, I have never written anybody up, no. But I have spoken to a few male staff. And then it is settled.* (Female staff, FSCC)

I: *When I started in the late 1980s, there weren't that many women, so you had to prove yourself. Nowadays there are more women, but they still have to prove themselves. They still think about, "What if something happens and I need you to be my back-up." I have seen some women staff that have not worked out that well. I have seen some male staff that have not worked out that well. You know, I have had men staff come to me and say, "I'd rather work with you than so and so," because he knows that I am reliable in a tough situation.*

W: *Did you get resistance from some of your colleagues when you started?*

I: *Actually, I found that the transition into this job was so easy. I was treated very well when I started. That was kind of surprising because I was a woman. There was something about me that they liked. I have seen the way they have treated some of the women they did not like. I remember another girl that started – she probably started four or five months after me – and they did not like her right from the start. She is no longer in corrections. I think the difference was that I came in and asked them to teach me, show me what to do. "How do I do this," you know? And she came in and said, "I already know what I'm doing. You don't need to show me anything." There is a difference.* (Female staff, FSCC)

I started in the provincial system in BC. When I began, it was at the point where women officers were getting to be more common. About five years before, it was uncommon. When I left, it was up to about 50 percent in the provincial system. The problem for women when I was there was the old staff. It wasn't the inmates or the new staff; it was the old staff. There are probably some that are still there. (Female staff, MI)

I: The first few months were hard. People wouldn't show you what to do; they resented us being there. There were a few nice people here – there were a few young people and women who had just come out of university, or most of them have had the experience. And those were the people I was attracted to, and basically, we would laugh at the stuff happening. Because I moved out here [British Columbia], *I had to pay my way here, so I was kind of stuck here.*

W: Has the position for female officers changed?

I: I think it has become accepted that women will be doing this job. But when I started in 1987, it was not easy. They didn't even have uniforms for women. There were men's uniforms. So eventually, somebody realized that there was a lot of women and started making clothes. Or even the toilet situation, which was awful [no separate toilets for women]. *It was terrible. I think it's not in your face, as it was before, the hostility, the jokes, things that were done. And the word "harassment" was not really used in corrections. So in that respect, it has changed; now women can go forward and say, "This is happening to me."*

W: How did the inmates accept you?

I: Actually, I never had a problem with the inmates. I worked in PC [protective custody], *and I worked with a girl there who was a very nice person. We had a new inmate, and we said to him, "You're in here now," and he said, "Thank you, lady. I really appreciate it. You've really changed this place." And we said, "Well, thank you."* (Female staff, MI)

I: Attitudes have changed, and a lot of that is due to the harassment policy. When we didn't have a harassment policy, we had only 10 to 15 percent females; now we have 50 to 60 percent. Male staff have to learn to watch what they say; you have to realize you are not just working with the guys. Around a female staff, you can't say certain words or use certain expressions. It's been a learning thing for everyone since I started, because it has definitely changed. I never had a problem working with women, but it took a while to understand how to work with them.

W: *Do some of the older officers have problems with the increase* [in female staff]?

I: *There is no doubt in my mind that some of the older staff don't want females here. Some people, just in their hearts, believe that women should not be in a man's prison. But we got a lot of young staff here, and a lot of these young staff are used to working with females in other jobs and other capacities or gone to school with them, so they do not see it as intimidating as it was to the older generation.* (Male staff, HCC)

Things seem to have changed in a favourable way for female COs in Canada. Overall, the respondents supported their presence in male prisons. Sexual harassment policies had had a big impact, according to both female and male respondents. The breaking and reshaping of the female CO frame seems to have been driven by changes in the attitudes of the male staff being hired by the 1990s, a rising proportion of women on the job (at least in the provincial system), and the implementation of sexual harassment policies.

Most inmates were quite enthusiastic about having female COs on their unit. Many of the reasons they favoured women were gender-based: they were perceived as being easier to talk to, more caring, and better communicators. Some inmates argued that it was vital to have women on shift, because otherwise their peers would not have a chance to remember how to act in front of a woman. Sexist rationales were also provided – for example, having female COs was good because you got to look at attractive women. These gender-based portrayals are not unique to Canadian inmates, as noted earlier (Crawley, 2004; Crewe, 2006; Zimmer, 1986):

Yeah, now there's lots of female officers, and it's a good thing. You're locked in jail – who wouldn't want to see a female every now and then, right? You don't want to look at the guys and get used to them. I know a couple female guards that are pretty decent with attitude. When you incorporate women into the mix, then they soften the environment. An inmate's attitude changes as soon as a woman's around. It complements the other male inmates, you know what I mean? A prison with all males, guards, and inmates, that's a whole different place to do time. (Sentenced inmate and ex-gang member, SMI)

This Stony Mountain lifer perceived female COs as necessary to help inmates learn proper social interaction and maintain social skills from the community:

Women officers in prison is a good thing. You need that variety. You have a lot of guys who are getting back out once their sentence is up. They have to learn how to react with people, including women. If you have been in jail for twenty years and all you see is men, when you get out, you are screwed. You will never be able to properly interact with a woman. I think it is setting them up for a fall. So I think the introduction of women is a plus. Women officers are a little bit more open-minded than most men. They are willing to ask questions; they are willing to probe a little bit. I think it is a good thing, just for the fact of keeping the interaction between the different sexes open. I believe it would be hard to fall back into normal life on the outside without them. (Lifer, SMI)

According to this long-time Stony Mountain inmate and former gang member, the introduction of women had improved life in that facility:

I think more women guards is great. Ten, fifteen years ago, there was, like, all kinds of porno magazines, porno pictures hanging on the wall. For me, I was never into stuff like that, because a real woman wouldn't expose herself like that. Then women guards came along and just got rid of that. I really liked that. But I look forward to seeing the women guards. They make the day of a lot of inmates. It's nice to see women day after day, especially in a place like this. (Sentenced inmate and ex-gang member, SMI)

This Matsqui inmate felt that a female CO was more effective at communicating with him than a male, and believed that her counsel had saved him from a serious mistake:

There are more females. I don't really judge the gender. But women working in corrections is a good thing. I'll just flip back to a lesson of life I learned when I was in a PC joint in Ontario. It was a mix of drug/alcohol guys like me and sex offenders. Bad mix. I talked to way more staff than inmates there, because I didn't want to meet with a sex offender, period. I was even thinking of doing a number on one of those skinners. It was a female correctional officer who explained to me that if I beat this guy up, this heinous sex crime guy, if I didn't kill him, then his next victim will be in worse shape. So, I didn't understand that might happen. But I understand they're more compassionate. Men will want to talk with female officers. Who did most people go to when things started at home? Mom! Right? It's a little different, but still ... (Lifer, MI)

This Matsqui inmate recalled that his privacy had been more limited when women were first introduced in the 1980s. But he believed that, overall, they had a very positive effect on his behaviour:

I remember how intimidated I was when women first started in men's prison. Geez, you were afraid to use the washroom because a woman might be looking. All of a sudden, you have a woman and you're sitting on the can. You got to worry about women poking their head out the window, and you're naked in your cell. But I love women; I'm happy to have them in the jail. I still can't treat them like other guards. It's still, "Yes ma'am, no ma'am." I go out of my way not be rude in front of them. I go out of my way not swear in front of them. I go out of my way to be dressed properly in front of them. I go out of my way to be polite. So they affect some people. I'm not sure about the generation after my generation – they think it's okay to hit women. (Sentenced inmate, MI)

There were limitations to the perceived efficacy of female COs, however. They were not viewed as universally better COs. Whether white, brown, old, young, male, or female, a good CO was a good CO. To establish legitimacy among inmates, a woman still needed to know and act through the correctional frame in a manner consistent with procedural justice. Women might be more empathetic and better listeners (good PJ traits), but they still needed to know their jobs, make good decisions, demonstrate respect and courtesy, keep their commitments, and avoid punitive attitudes and behaviours. Some females did not meet that standard, just as some male COs did not. These two Manitoba inmates generally liked female officers, but noted there were still a few of them who were not respected:

> *Ya, there really is a lot of female guards here. Some are okay to talk to, too, eh? They gotta have the respect though, guards male or female.* (Remand inmate, HCC)

> I: *I think more female correctional officers is a good thing. Easier on the eyes, you know. Back in the day, there wasn't many females. Nowadays, they're everywhere at Headingley. It's always the females playing the cards with us, so that's a good thing, eh?*
> W: *Do you notice any difference in their ability to do the job?*
> I: *I think the females actually bring the stress level down, to be honest. You're playing cards with them; you're talking to them. Some treat you with a bit more respect, you know. Some women are just wicked retards. But some make you feel human instead of just a con.* (Sentenced inmate, HCC)

This senior prison gang member believed that some inmates still viewed female officers as sex objects, but he himself tried to view and judge them on their abilities as COs:

> *I don't see more women correctional officers as a bad thing. Some eye candy, you know. Some guys wonder why a gorgeous-looking broad would be all of a sudden working here – a fucking cock tease or what? To me, it is whatever – it is her career, it is her profession, what she chooses to do. I don't see nothing wrong with it. You can become friends with the guards, or you can see them as an enemy.* (Sentenced inmate and senior gang member, SMI)

Female officers were not liked by all inmates. A minority of older inmates, like these two ex-biker gang Headingley prisoners, seemed to long for the days when male institutions were an all-boys club:

> *I'm not a male chauvinist pig, so I don't have a problem with the women. I think, though, that they should realize that you're in a men's prison, so don't*

come in here trying to push women's issues. Like, no sunshine girls [bathing suit pin-ups], *and no, you know, no this magazine, no that magazine, no that, this, and that. If you don't like it, don't work in a men's prison. Go to a woman's prison then.* (Remand inmate and ex-biker gang member, HCC)

The female officers have never been a good thing in a man's prison. Inmates now have to walk to the shower completely dressed; you can't even go in your boxer shorts or you get charged. If I was a male officer, I wouldn't feel that safe having a bunch of women come up to settle a thing, you know what I mean? If I was a guard working in a jail, I don't think I would really want a fifty-five-year-old woman, badly out of shape, coming to back me in a jail fight. (Remand inmate and ex-gang member, HCC).

Staff generally took a positive view of female COs. They appreciated that having men *and* women in a workplace can generate a more positive atmosphere. Women on the job can mean men avoiding foul language and dressing better for the job, and a more communal feeling among all staff. The respondents viewed women as quite capable in most physical situations. Some were seen as more effective than others, but this variation in competence was also found among male COs.

A minority of staff, however, like these officers from Headingley, were concerned that some female officers were not up to managing serious situations, such as a large disturbance involving a lot of inmates becoming violent. Headingley stands out among the institutions in this study as having 50 percent women on its CO shifts, which is much higher than in the other facilities:

Most of the women here, in fact, are as capable under most circumstances as anybody else. I think they have gone overboard because there are cases now where we have so many on we can't even do some of our routine strip searches and stuff. They don't want to put a quota on, but it is hard to organize routine searches when you have 50 percent female officers on a shift. (Staff, HCC)[3]

I think females bring a different dynamic to the jail. Females generally are more empathetic, more nurturing than maybe a male officer. Some inmates would rather talk to a female staff and cry with them rather than cry with us 'cause of that nurturing, caring effect. It depends on the female, though. I don't want to say this without being rude or anything, but some females get very intimidated and very scared. (Staff, HCC)

There were no women when I started; it was a men's-only club. Now there is a lot of women being hired. Some women belong here; some women don't. Some guys belong here and some guys don't. In here, you are either a "protector" or you are a "protected." If I think you are a protected, then I have to be watching you as well as watching these inmates. I have a hard time with that. If you are not going to help me out in any kind of situation, then I don't want you here. I tell you, though, I got a lot of girls in here that would be in there in a scrap before guys will. But then there are some that are a little too timid to handle situations that do come up in here. When situations arise, I need to be able to count on all my staff, not only for my safety but also for inmate safety. (Staff, HCC)

This former CO from Matsqui heard his fellow officers talk a lot about opposing women COs when they started, but their own behaviour was affected in a positive way:

I remember very well when I was a living unit officer, male officers would say, "There is no way I'd work with a woman in a maximum security institution; that's just not going to happen." They said they would boycott coming to work. Well, you know what, when women came in, a lot of my peers who were threatening to be mean and nasty, they were starting to put on a clean shirt, they were shaving before they came to work, they even put on a little bit of cologne. What it really comes down to is that 99 percent of situations are defused by talking to offenders. Women work differently and are usually better at talking to offenders. I think their presence affects male staff and inmates. I think most will agree that it's complementary to have male and female officers. (Staff, MI)

Female Officers in Male Prisons

Women originally were perceived as a break in the inmate–CO frame; however, the results presented here indicate that the presence of female COs represents more of an adjustment to the frame (see Figure 8.1). Overall, inmate behaviour has modified as a result of their presence: they are more communicative with female officers, and there is less social distance in many interactions. For better or worse, many inmates perceive women officers as vulnerable, and this brings out their chivalrous behaviours, though this is sometimes more condescending than respectful. Most of the inmates I interviewed saw female COs as improving the prison atmosphere and as helping them greatly to remember how to behave in front of women. Less favourably, some inmates viewed women as sex objects, and a minority viewed them as totally inappropriate for the CO role. To be respected and perceived as strong by inmates, female COs needed to be seen as competent and effective within the CO frame. For inmates, it was important for female COs to behave in procedurally just ways, which included showing respect and being knowledgeable, fair, courteous, and empathetic.

Likewise, female officers earned respect from other COs by fulfilling the primary features of the CO frame: being strong/managing fear, managing inmates effectively, keeping the correct social distance, and knowing the routines of the job. Somewhat unfairly, women faced a greater onus to prove themselves to be physically/mentally tough (to be a protector, not a protected). Some older officers still might sexually harass their female colleagues, and there were still a minority of inmates and COs (again older) who resented the intrusion of women into the prison. It is possible that at Headingley, the higher proportion of female COs (50 percent) affected perceptions of them among both staff and inmates. Estimates provided to me indicate that at Stony Mountain and Matsqui, 15 to 18 percent of COs were women, and at Fort Saskatchewan, 30 percent.

From a policy perspective, the issue of sexual harassment is an important component of training modules that promote a respectful workplace. Such modules encompass not only gender issues but also race, sexuality, and disability. Future researchers could test the "sexual spillover" hypothesis by comparing masculine attitudes at correctional centres with different proportions of female COs. Does having more women in a workplace affect the gendered nature of the correctional environment? Manitoba, with 50 percent female officers in provincial institutions such as Headingley, compared to 15 percent in federal penitentiaries such as Stony Mountain, offers a strong potential study site.

9

The Effect of Programs

The preceding chapters have focused largely on the offender's initial adjustment to prison, inmate–inmate relations, and legitimacy in CO–inmate relations. All of these are critical in shaping an offender's behaviour and overall perception of custody. This chapter shifts the analysis somewhat to appraise inmate and staff views on the legitimacy of programs and how institutional behaviour is framed. Of particular interest is the introduction of cognitive-behavioural (CBT) programs over the past twenty-five years and a debate about them that has arisen recently; some observers question the utility of CBT programs for inmates and contend that vocational training would lead to more lucrative employment upon release and a concurrent drop in recidivism (Review Panel, 2007).

Canada is generally recognized as a progressive nation that offers many well-designed offender programs. American Frank Cullen, well known as an advocate for rehabilitation, has lauded Canadian scholars and correctional treatment programmers as world leaders in the science of offender treatment (Cullen, 2005). As discussed in Chapter 1, however, the programs themselves have been questioned by many, with some scholars raising doubts about their effectiveness. This chapter considers programs from a broader perspective. I asked inmates and correctional staff to assess the impact of the treatment regimes introduced over the past twenty-five years. How do staff and inmates frame relations around programs? Do they view those programs as a valuable and legitimate part of the institutional regime? And do inmates and staff prefer behavioural programs to vocational ones?

Framing Programs

Program efficacy is most frequently evaluated by measuring recidivism. But not all observers view preventing reoffence as a program's *raison d'être*. Maintaining order and reducing illicit activity within prison are also potential by-products of treatment. Recall that in his prison behaviour model, Anthony Bottoms (1999) hypothesized that program availability and quality would impact overall inmate perceptions of prison legitimacy, along with other tangibles such as opportunities for meaningful work and access to recreation, visits, and leisure time. Likewise, conservative academics such as David Farabee (2005), Charles Logan and Gerald Gaes (1993), and more liberal scholars such as Sheila French and Paul Gendreau (2006) see order maintenance or a reduction in violence in prisons as crucial outcomes for programming (Gendreau & Keyes, 2001). Farabee (2005, 78) dismissed the use of treatment because of a lack of strong evidence of program efficacy in reducing recidivism, and then built on earlier arguments by Logan and Gaes to advocate that programs be used as "institutional management tools" rather than instruments of behavioural change. Gendreau and Keyes (2001) also promoted programs as a means to reduce prison misconduct, citing evidence from a survey of institutional managers who viewed more treatment and programs as the best means of reducing inmate misbehaviour. In fact, empirical studies have generally supported the notion that program participation reduces institutional misconduct: inmates who are involved in treatment get into less trouble (French & Gendreau, 2006; Steiner & Wooldredge, 2008).

If programs have benefits, should offenders be taking behaviourally oriented treatment programs such as CBT, or should they be more involved in applied programs such as basic education and vocational training? The Federal Corrections Blue Ribbon Panel (Review Panel, 2007) came out strongly in support of academic/vocational programming (rather than behavioural programming), a controversial position and one that was almost oppositional to the CSC's development and implementation of more sophisticated programs over the past twenty-five years. Of course, there has always been some disagreement over how best to involve inmates in programming. Social historians Michel Foucault (1977) and David Rothman (1980) argued that organizations have always viewed the provision of work routines, not counselling, as the key to socializing inmates.

It was thought that most inmates were bereft of a work ethic, so they were to learn in prison how to get up in the morning and be at a job at least five days a week. This socialization ideal took another step in the way of reform in the late nineteenth century with the introduction of the reformatory, a prison intended to provide education and vocational training in skilled trades such as carpentry, mechanics, and welding (for a review, see Pisciotta, 1996). This training notion has an intuitive appeal, given that many inmates have limited education and thin work histories.

The arguments in favour of vocational training in prisons are not new, and include the following. Vocational programs are attractive to inmates, most of whom come from working-class backgrounds. For example, offenders with blue-collar origins have more potential to work with their hands, which is likely better for them than undertaking academic learning involving reading and writing. Moreover, vocational programs can provide inmates with a good living upon release, allowing them to transition to a pro-social lifestyle and even providing an incentive to stay away from crime. Studies provide some empirical support for the efficacy of academic/ vocational training, although this approach has not been proven more successful than behavioural programs (for reviews, see MacKenzie & Hickman, 2006; Wilson, Gallagher, & MacKenzie, 2000). CBT programs do not have the same intuitive appeal as vocational training: anger management and relapse prevention courses are intended to change behaviour but do not provide the inmate a means to find a job with a reasonable salary. Steering inmates towards skilled employment has a common-sense appeal to the public. On the other hand, as discussed in Chapter 1, behavioural programs are intended to help inmates make better decisions and engage in more pro-social behaviour (Andrews & Bonta, 2010; MacKenzie & Hickman, 2006). An offender is unlikely to keep a job if he cannot get along with others, control his temper, or manage his addiction.

While much has been written about rehabilitation and programming in corrections by scholars, practitioners, and community activists, the inmates themselves are rarely consulted. Convict criminologists, ex-offenders who usually have gone on to obtain academic credentials after imprisonment, have written in a fairly guarded manner about the potential benefits of programs. Emphasizing his former convict status, criminologist Greg Newbold (2003) viewed the state as having a responsibility to provide programs in prison, but did not agree that pressure should be put on inmates to take them. Offender agency (individual choice) needed to be acknowledged; in other words, the inmates themselves could best determine when and where they would change their behaviour, and it was up to them to decide whether or not a particular program might help them. Treatment should be truly voluntary and not tied to parole eligibility, which is a subtle form of coercion.

Taking the personal choice notion one step further, Lior Gideon (2010) provocatively concluded that individual motivation was key to success, not the type of program or its quality or integrity. She believed that the importance of programs was grossly exaggerated in the literature. Applying Albert Bandura's (1977) personal efficacy theory to a group of drug-addicted offenders, she found that the offender's interest in changing was the essential factor in achieving outcomes of reduced drug use and pro-social behaviour. Once offenders achieved "sincere motivation," they found that refraining from drugs and adopting a pro-social lifestyle was straightforward and not difficult and that they required little assistance from others. For example, problems in obtaining a good-paying job are often cited as a barrier for parolees, who drift back into criminal activities and enterprises to get money; however, the "sincerely motivated" in Gideon's study found that they could obtain employment regardless of barriers because they "really wanted to."

Inmate Program Frames

In Canada's legal system, remand inmates cannot be required to participate in treatment because they are innocent until proven guilty. However, pre-trial detainees are often given the option of involving themselves in programs. Indeed, because of the proliferation of remands in Canada, the two provincial institutions in this study, Headingley and Fort Saskatchewan, have been converted into multi-purpose facilities housing both sentenced and (mostly) remand offenders. Sentenced inmates faced stronger pressures to make decisions about involvement in treatment. When sentenced inmates enter an institution, programs are pitched to them as pathways to early release (i.e., a correctional plan must be developed and programs undertaken to obtain an early release). Offenders who do not have problems or do not wish to take treatment can decline, but doing so may limit their chances at parole. Inmates who take a program must manage interactions with staff and other inmates inside and outside the treatment setting, and this can pose its own challenges.

In my inmate interviews, I found that most saw value in programs and that many, like these respondents from Matsqui and Fort Saskatchewan, were enthusiastic about past successes:

> *I completed this cooking course, and I got a certificate from Molson College, for my culinary arts, foundation level one. And I graduated from it five months later, and something I took advantage of. I put it on my résumé, and when I got replies to job inquiries, that was noted in two of the three letters, my culinary arts certificate.* (Sentenced inmate, MI)

> *I couldn't turn on a computer but learned all that inside. You should look at me go now!* (Remand inmate, FSCC)

The respondents endorsed cognitive behavioural and other intensive programs. Those with a history of addiction especially believed that taking programs and courses (perhaps even more than once) was a necessary part of a lifelong battle with substance abuse. Support for behavioural programs was frequently for "other" inmates, but it was undeniably there. This long-time inmate serving remand time at Fort Saskatchewan was especially enthusiastic about CBT:

> *The cog skills is good, but we don't have that here. They should – they have it at the Pen [federal penitentiary], but not here. They should have that here because it really works. That kept me out of trouble for a couple years, actually.* (Remand inmate, FSCC)

Key for inmates was the notion that individuals had to be ready, and that only they could decide to change. According to these two inmates, when it came to program success, individual agency mattered:

> *Programs are important. If you want to change, the programs are there and they work. But I'm only seeing that now, you know. If you want to change, they're there. For the Pen, they're important because you*

get paid for them. So you will make yourself drag your ass, go to a program.
(Sentenced inmate, HCC)

Programs are important. Our teachers are excellent. But you have to be ready for them. Because you're not going to learn until you shut up and listen, until it's over. It goes through my head every day, I'm in a substance abuse class, high end, which is six months – a long time. I now understand that you need a lot of time. (Lifer, MI)

Some inmates presented as careful consumers of institutional treatment. They criticized CBT programs that were poorly conceptualized or run:

The general idea of programs is good. The content of the programs I took leaves a lot to be desired. I partake in two programs that were on my correctional plan, and I've found that they overlapped. Stages of change, decision of balance, long-term consequences, whatever. A lot of them have the same content with a different title, and that different title may constitute 20 percent of new materials, and in that regard I think there has to be a lot more emphasis on improving these programs and making them world-class. Work needs to be done, but overall I think it's a good idea. (Sentenced inmate, MI)

So there was support among inmates for programs. Furthermore, many inmates – especially remand inmates or inmates in split remand/sentenced facilities like Headingley and Fort Saskatchewan – were disturbed about the lack of programs or the wait times for them. Because of the high number of remands, shorter programs were being offered, and thus provincial inmates arguably were not getting the same quality of programs as previously, when more provincial inmates were serving longer sentences. Also, getting into programs, even voluntarily, was difficult for remand offenders, for they were not as high a priority as provincial sentenced offenders. These two ex-gang inmates and another Headingley remand prisoner all voiced displeasure over the limited program offerings in provincial jails:

There is not enough to do here. Not enough time off the units, too long to wait for programs or even a job. (Remand inmate and ex-gang member, HCC)

During my stay here in Headingley, I would like to do some programming, but since I'm not sentenced, I am not a priority for the programming, and I'm gonna be here for, you know, overall more than six months, and so I do have the time to actually do it. (Remand inmate, HCC)

So far, I've done parenting and anger management, but I'd like to do more, but they only offer them every four, five, or six months. One was a week, and one was two weeks. (Remand inmate and ex-gang member, HCC)

Remand inmates were generally not well served by programs. The lack of programs reflected the general lack of activities for pre-trial cases: they spent most of their time confined to their units, which was an appalling waste of time.

Inmates on Vocational versus Behavioural Programming

Inmates tended to be supportive of vocational programming. This appeared related to the working-class background of many offenders. Most respondents did not come from families where higher educational levels were achieved, but many had relatives or friends with skilled trades backgrounds, and some inmates had this training or experience themselves. Overall, there was more support for educational/vocational programs than for behavioural programs like CBT.

While I tended to focus on vocational training in the interviews, educational upgrading (K–12) was viewed as important by my respondents. Inmates with high school and trades training, or who had a fair work history, tended to observe that their less skilled peers required stronger basic skills to get good jobs and stay out of trouble. These two inmates believed that many of their peers desperately needed to get at least high school and to be able to read and write to simply deal better with life, never mind getting a high-paying job:

You look at a lot of inmates, and they don't have any job skills or even know how to get a job. So I think some of the programs they have here are going to help. Like how to write a résumé, how to get a job. Half the guys here were selling crack their whole life; they don't even know what a job is. You need to be able to read and write to be able to get a job. Have some basic computer skills. Get them to a grade ten level or something, some basic computer skills, a way to get a job. If you go to the pen, you have more time, but at least the provincial system gives them the basic education and some computer skills. (Remand inmate, FSCC)

I don't think a lot of the programs are doing any good. Okay, let's look at it this way. Let's say bring a young kid in here today – you teach him to be a better criminal, that's one thing you teach him. Why would you not teach him something he can use when he leaves here? I don't care whether it's cooking, carpentry, small engines, metal shops. Bring back the old days where we used to work. Ninety percent of these kids that come in here can't cook an egg. Give 'em cooking classes, whatever! These mental health programs and everything, what good do those programs do 'em on the street? Does it get 'em a job? No, he's got no skills. You teach him about drugs, and you teach him about this, and you teach him about that. Does he listen when he leaves here? No. (Remand inmate and ex-biker gang member, HCC)

These three inmates believed that the big advantage of vocational training was that it allowed one to make a living attractive enough to serve as a viable alternative to stealing or drug dealing:

A lot of these guys, they're never going to be able to go out there and get a job. They grew up in poverty, mom on welfare, dad drinking. They don't know how to work. I think employment programs have to be big for guys to stay out. (Sentenced inmate and former gang member, SMI)

I think the better thing for prisons would be trades, to learn actual trades. You get out, you can become a carpenter, welder, or a painter, or a skilled trade like a plumber, mechanic, or autobody man. Something where you can have a decent job when you get out. (Sentenced inmate, SMI)

Guys get out of jail and what do they know? To sell drugs. So what are they going to do? Sell drugs. If you get out of jail and you got your first year welding, well, I am going to go welding right away. Boom, I got a job, or set them up with a job. (Remand inmate, FSCC)

Older inmates recalled a time when more vocational programs were available for offenders, and felt that this emphasis should return. Inmates did not seem to be against behavioural programs per se, but in terms of priority they viewed applied training as more essential. These British Columbia and Manitoba inmates perceived that more trades training had been offered in the past, and that the shift from them had not been for the better:

> *I think the programs are fine, if the guy is motivated. They should have trades back, where they could go back and find meaningful employment, where they can make a relatively decent wage, they can support themselves, and they can have some self-esteem. Then they're not thinking about getting high. They're not going to kick in your house or mine to support their drug habit.* (Lifer, MI)

> *Someone is going to tell you, "Well, we have been through the trades and it doesn't work, either." No, it may not work at the time, but you know what? I got an apprentice of mechanics that I used for a while from Stony Mountain penitentiary. So if it wasn't there, I would have never been able to fall back on it. I also got the start of an apprenticeship in carpentry in Stony Mountain penitentiary. As for anger management and those types of programs, yeah, eventually people may apply them, too, but just back them off a little. Not make them the be all to end all, because they aren't. We have got to get trades back into the jails again.* (Remand inmate and ex-gang member, HCC)

Aboriginal Cultural Programming

Indigenous cultural programming has come a long way in the past twenty-five years, but was falling short as far as most Aboriginal inmates were concerned. There was strong support for cultural programs, but respondents did not feel that enough was being offered, especially in the provincial systems:

> *I would like to see more about Native cultures. Interpretations about our culture and towards yourself. We should get more Native spiritual services in here and Elders addressing this problem. We need an Elder here to*

help – not just once a month, we need an Elder that's here every day. To help the population here, because there is a lot of Native people here, young kids, seventeen, eighteen, are here, and I see them walking around and they're lost. You can see it in their hygiene, in their emotions, in their feelings, also their facial features – you can see. A good program that I have been in here is the sharing circle. (Remand inmate, FSCC)

I'd like to take a fuckin', maybe, anger management, I guess. I don't know, whatever types of programs there are, I'd take. I like to be busy. Aboriginal culture would be good, too. (Remand inmate and gang member, HCC)

One big one would be cultural, say for Aboriginal, right? Out here, there is not a big population, but Mission [nearby federal penitentiary], 30 percent of the population is Aboriginal. So I would think that teaching them how to make, like, ... different beaded necklaces, or drums, or stuff like that, would be beneficial, help them find out where they come from, what they're used for, and then, not even for themselves for profit, but donate themselves to community, trying to help Native communities, and young people and stuff, give them these things. (Inmate, MI)

Inmates involved in the Ni-Miikana Aboriginal cultural unit at SMI spoke highly of the program. The unit held about forty inmates when my interviews were done, and conducted cultural ceremonies such as sweet-grass burning, pipe ceremonies, sweats, and sharing circles, and supported Aboriginal hobbies and crafts such as blanket making and traditional drumming. To get in, inmates had to apply and indicate an interest in participating in Indigenous cultural ceremonies. Inmates commented favourably on this program. Ni-Miikana had an admission process and was not easy to get into. It also demanded effort by inmates, if they wished to stay. This lifer viewed this program unit as a safe place with high expectations:

For the most part, Ni-Miikana is a safer range. The guys resort to talking about things first, before things happen, before they drop their gloves. But it is also the kind of range where staff expectation of inmates is really high. So if you are not following the rules, you get moved off, simple as that. There is turnover on that range. There are mandatory drug tests once a month,

guaranteed. That is over and above the national one that is random. They
have to sign a paper saying that you will stay drug free. (Lifer, SMI)

Inmates I interviewed from the Ni-Miikana unit spoke favourably about
the program and its integration of an Indigenous approach with institutional life. Inmates were allowed to reside in the unit without worrying
about gangs, and some of the social distance between inmates – a barrier
to making friendships – appeared to diminish. These two program members spoke highly of the unit and its atmosphere:

It's my first time being in a unit like that, after like thirty years of doing
time. It's given me more insight and stopped a revolving door for me. I've
taken a look at what's going on in other units, with all the gang activity.
Ni-Miikana is just a more spiritual way of life, respecting each other,
doing things for each other. I never thought that this would ever happen
in any prison, man, but it's really helping a lot of guys. Young guys that
want to stay out of gangs, they have no way but this way. (Sentenced
inmate, SMI)

At Ni-Miikana, we pretty much like watch over one another, and I think
the guards like working there, too, because it's more relaxed and it's not so
intense. (Sentenced inmate, SMI)

The Ni-Miikana unit holds some potential for providing Aboriginal
inmates with more programming. The use of treatment units warrants
more study. For instance, the Ni-Miikana unit was not tainted by being
called protective custody or a "transition" unit, but it still managed to
provide a safe place to do time – a valuable service within an institution.
According to these two Stony Mountain inmates, even sex offenders – a
heavily stigmatized group – had been integrated into the program unit:

We have inmates with bad beefs like sexual assault, but I think that everyone
makes mistakes. (Sentenced inmate, SMI)

I know they sneak the odd skinner in here. But I am not going to make an
issue of it. It's a unit where you can do your time quietly. I'm not into Native
culture at all. I'm just doing it to be on that unit. It's a relaxed unit, right?

I'm a city boy, you know? I grew up in a city all my life; I'm urbanized. I do go to a ceremony every once in a while, support the guys. (Sentenced inmate and ex-gang member, SMI)

Inmate Program Frames

Programs do not work as well when they are run in an institutional setting, compared to when they are offered in the community (Andrews et al., 1990). Treatment regimes within a correctional institution face challenges. Unlike programs run in the community, they must work around prison routines, rules, and regulations. Also, the ongoing problems of lockdowns, absences of participants for reasons unrelated to the program (new charges, discipline, transfer), and even the baggage of conflicts within the institution affect participation. Programs in the community, by contrast, operate on a regular schedule, and there are fewer factors in the external environment that can impede their operations. Offenders mix with participants who are strangers and who live in other parts of the city or town, which increases the assurance that what is said in the group will be kept confidential. Furthermore, because other participants such as addicts or anger-challenged individuals in the community may not be involved with the criminal justice system, offenders are exposed to individuals with different perspectives and backgrounds.

Institutional programs do not offer the same diversity as community ones. Inmates take treatment with other offenders, whom they usually encounter again after the program finishes that day. Furthermore, many inmates who are not taking programs cause problems for those who do by stigmatizing them. The primary inmate frame structures relations around achieving respect, and this relies heavily on an impression of strength and toughness. So the first rule of the inmate program frame requires an inmate to assert that he will change only when he wants to change. Programs will not help unless an inmate agrees to be helped; he must remain in control of this process. Taking this one step further, an inmate who really wants to change will not really need programs. For some offenders, programs are an admission of weakness.

So an inmate who decides to participate in a program faces intense scrutiny by other offenders that may affect his status. An inmate who engages seriously in a program is potentially acknowledging a personal weakness, admitting a deficiency to his peers, and accepting stigma, with the consequent loss of respect. He is ascribed a status analogous to John Irwin's (1970) "gleaners" – inmates who actively try to improve themselves in prison, at the expense of their status among the inmate population.

The program frame that guided inmates in their interactions with staff directed them to demonstrate keen interest in a program, at least enough to gain admission to it (Figure 9.1). And once in the program, an offender had to convince the program manager that he had performed adequately

FIGURE 9.1
Behavioural program frames

Inmates	
Other inmates	**Correctional staff**

• Do not take program
   o Change when I want to change
   o Do not want to change
• Take program, but be dismissive of program involvement
   o Taking because bored
   o Taking to get institutional benefit
• *The above might be feigned, or true*
	• Express interest, enthusiasm for program
	   o Indicate participation for personal growth
	   o Participate enthusiastically
	   o Participate sufficiently to complete
	   o Trust other inmate participants in group
	• *The above might be feigned, or true*

Correctional staff	
Inmates	**Other staff**
• Encourage as method for change • Encourage as something to do • View as indicator of interest in improvement/rehabilitation • View as possible manipulation by inmate	• Be positive, but cautious about programs as a method for inmates to change • Be positive about programs as a method to keep inmates occupied • Even helping one inmate out of ten is worthwhile • Do not view programs as helpful, just a part of the job • Above frames vary from staff to staff, but most adhere to the first, second, and third points; the fourth point is held by a minority
Frame break **(Inmate frame: Other inmates)** • Be positive about program involvement • Acknowledge personal need, contest stigma, or ignore other inmates	

to continue in the program, in order to eventually graduate. Having completed the program, the inmate gains points towards security reduction or early release. Of course, this frame may be sincere and not feigned. Inmates may well be honest in their representations to staff; they may very well intend to benefit from behavioural programs.

Conversely, the inmate program frame requires them to present a less sincere, dismissive face to their peers. Interaction likely will focus on how futile programs are and how the inmate controls his own destiny and can change when he decides. Other inmates may be told that an inmate has chosen to participate in a program for a variety of reasons: boredom, the female facilitator is attractive, or participation is a ruse to earn a lower security rating or deceive correctional staff. Thus, the legitimacy of programs generally is downplayed to other inmates.

An inmate attending an institutional program presents a positive face when applying his inmate–correctional staff frame, while showing a more restrained, cynical face when working within the primary inmate-to-inmate frame. Offenders, of course, often juggle frames when dealing with inmate and staff actors, and this duality seems to require quite active impression management. Can frame breaking occur in such situations? Yes and no. When an offender adopts two distinct frames to relate to different others (inmate or staff), no specific frame is broken. Motivation for programs, however, may result in keying or frame breaking. Crewe, Warr, Bennett, and Smith (2013) report that some inmates found a treatment group and their program room to be one of the few areas in a correctional institution where they felt they could be open with other offenders. Many of my respondents expressed positive feelings towards treatment and reported that they were working hard at their programs. This lifer was able to manage relations with others despite going outside the norm, by finding a supportive group:

> It takes a while sometimes, but when you get a good group, you can share, let things out. We had a good bunch of guys in my last drug treatment program; you could trust them. (Lifer, MI)

Another Matsqui lifer managed by not caring what other inmates thought about his program involvement. He was prepared to "break frame" and resist stigma from his peers when he went to church or spoke about religion on his unit:

> *I don't have much in common with other inmates here; I don't think like them anymore. Church is the most important thing to me now. I don't give a shit what others think.* (Lifer, MI)

Inmates reported there were limits to program benefits because of the prison setting. Despite the relative weakness of the inmate subculture, the primary inmate frame still held sufficient force to make program participation a delicate matter. For example, the subcultural emphasis on masculine values and the frame of "being strong" discouraged some offenders from applying many of the skills they had learned in behavioural treatment: aggression or appearing tough was still valued by many over diplomacy in resolving conflicts. These two inmates reported little opportunity on the unit to apply "lessons learned" from their daily sessions:

> *But the thing I want to bring up, Michael, is you could have the best programming in the institution, but once you leave the classroom, you're back into a negative environment. You will not survive in prison practising the skills you've learned in the classroom. For example, violence prevention program, it is all about preventing violence. Somebody calls you a name, okay, usually you would be violent, but now that I know these skills, I'm not going to be violent. But now I am back in the prison population, if someone calls me a goof, I'm going to choose not to practise violence. But I'm probably going to get beat up by someone else, because I didn't do anything about it or because I didn't fight the other person. It's counter-productive sometimes, because you're teaching someone something that they cannot utilize in the inmate population. You need a supportive environment, a lack of negative influences around you; I think that those two factors alone can be very conducive to your maintaining the skills that you've learned. You can't do it here – or you can, but you risk injury if you take it too far.* (Inmate, MI)

> *When the staff who run the program can conduct it correctly, the people can understand what's going on. Then they use it. It helps. It benefits – it*

does. But the problem is, then you get locked back on the range where people who don't want to take the program, who don't care, are sitting, doing nothing, collecting institutional welfare [$15 every two weeks]. How is it going to benefit you when you've been thrown back into situations like that? Then when you go back to the program the next day, you have to rebuild everything all over again. More programs should be run for the same people on the same range, or at least where they want to take programs. When you are with criminals, guys that don't really care whether they're in or out or just out there, just pulling bullcrap, how are you going to succeed? How are you going to benefit? (Sentenced inmate, SMI)

The lack of privacy in an institution also was a detriment. Group programs rely on interaction and sharing, but in an institution, it is a challenge to develop this sort of trust in peers. Individuals who take a program in the community have a better chance of having their participation kept confidential, for they are usually geographically dispersed from one another. Not so in the prison, where everyone knows if you are taking a program and may even know what you shared in group that day. This inmate found that the frame requiring caution and social distance from inmate peers worked against program efficacy, for it impeded personal disclosure and active participation:

I think some of them [programs] have to use more private one-on-one counselling. In a group program, say you want to ask a question, but you don't want the other guys to laugh at you, right. So you say nothing. But it's tough, there are thousands of inmates across Canada you know; you can't go one-on-one each time. But it would be better, because then you can really let go. (Remand inmate, HCC)

Finally, even thinking in a more pro-social manner can be difficult on some units, where many inmates want to talk about past and future crimes. As Shadd Maruna (2001) concluded, offenders who wish to change their behaviour engage more actively in "change talk" – that is, how they are going to change for the better – and spend less time talking about their crimes or less constructive activities such as drug use. It is tough for inmates to think, talk, and act in ways that reflect or promote personal change when they are surrounded by others who are less interested in modifying their behaviour. This federal inmate heard a lot of crime talk, much of it repetitive.

> *And some people just get off sitting around telling stories all day. Unfortunately, I've heard them all; honestly, I can say I've heard every one. And I don't mean stretching the truth, not to insult people, but I'm like, "You know how many times I've heard that story."* (Sentenced inmate and former gang member, SMI)

This Headingley inmate did not need a recidivism meta-analysis to deduce that a community-based program might work better for him. He saw residing in the community and away from other offenders as crucial to making his program more effective:

> *They'd* [programs] *be helpful, but not in this kind of setting, not in jail. There's a lot of criminal-minded people that talk all the time, they talk at you, and it makes it hard to take stuff serious. It works better in the community. I've been at AFM on the street. It was really good, way better than the program in jail. I didn't have the other inmates and jail problems in my head.* (Remand inmate and ex-gang member, HCC)

The Correctional Staff Program Frame

Like inmates, correctional staff had ambivalent attitudes towards treatment, but overall there was support for offering institutionally based programs. Placing opinions on a continuum, at the positive end, many staff held strongly favourable opinions towards treatment for inmates, while at the other, more pessimistic end, a small number believed that programs were a waste of time. Some staff felt that programs had little effect but were preferable to having inmates sitting on their unit doing nothing. It is significant that a number of staff identified the provision of programs as a pivotal change in corrections in Canada over the past twenty-five years, and that along with staff–inmate communication, they perceived that treatment had contributed to a much better custodial environment.

Most staff were not concerned about the inmates' level of motivation. CSC program facilitators tended to believe the most strongly that programs were important. They were familiar with the national statistics about their programs, took pride in studies supporting their own effectiveness as facilitators, and took the long view of treatment: that it takes time to change behaviour. Even if they could not help many, they held to the belief that perhaps the next time an offender came in, he or she might benefit from their program. For all respondents, confidence in programs was eroded by the large number of inmates they had seen return to prison. They understood the notion of a negative reporting system (i.e., they only see the inmates who return to prison, not those who succeed) but felt that they still saw too many reoffend. Like inmates, staff believed that offenders who really wanted the programs to work would benefit from them, but that others were there just for something to do or to get an earlier release.

Correctional staff respondents, whether they were programmers, case managers, supervisors, or COs, recognized that not all offenders were motivated and realized that even the motivated might falter after release. Staff viewed programs as a fundamental responsibility of the corrections system, which was to provide inmates with an opportunity to change. They acknowledged that even they were not sure about the benefits of some programs. Correctional staff dealt with this ambivalence by adopting a program frame. Program frames had staff acting and communicating mostly on the belief that offenders have an interest in treatment.

For case managers and treatment program facilitators especially, the program frame led to a positive but cautious belief in treatment efficacy. Regardless, they weighted their representations to their inmate caseloads to the potential benefits of programs. The program frame they presented to other staff gave a much more cautious view about chances for successful behaviour change, and in some cases they were downright pessimistic. Realizing that reoffence rates were high, staff respondents appeared to maintain feelings of self-efficacy by downgrading their own expectations of success and by elevating the possibility of potential long-term impact. Within the correctional staff program frame, the success of one individual was much better than no success at all. Also, one never knew how far in the future a program might prove to have actually been a pivotal event or turning point on an inmate's journey to a law-abiding life.

Thus, correctional staff, much like inmates, needed to work actively to manage two frames, one governing interactions with inmates, the other interactions with their co-workers. These two Headingley staff were wary of programs initially but eventually saw some value, although they were generally pessimistic about the possible treatment outcomes:

> *Get the guy interested or at least looking at something, and maybe he will pursue it, maybe not. All I ever reasonably expected to accomplish with the programs I was involved with was to hopefully get a guy a whiff of the coffee before he goes. Then later on the street, he thinks, "Maybe I should check into AFM [Addictions Foundation of Manitoba] and find out whether this is what is getting me screwed up all the time."* (Staff, HCC)

> *When they first offered programs, correctional officers (including me) took the view that inmates were taking them for the sole reason of conning staff and getting out early. But as time goes on, you realize that programs are not bad because a lot of guys actually do want to change, make a difference, and stay out of the system. Some guys use the program solely for the purpose of thinking it looks good for their lawyers, it looks good for their instructors and the caseworkers, and plus maybe it will give them some good time off. But you can't judge everybody; every individual deserves a break. You know what, we are all about change, and everybody is capable of making some kind of change if they really want to. So you always have to think positive.* (Staff, HCC)

The quality of programs was a huge issue for staff. They felt that adequate resources had to be invested in programs. In cases where program modules were not updated, where there was no therapeutic integrity, they questioned why a program should be run at all:

> *I think that programs within prisons need to be available but not forced. If you are going to do programs, do a proper job of it. I was involved in program delivery for a while, and I eventually just told them to jam it because it became nothing but a bullshit production of statistics. The program I was involved with was about drug and alcohol use. They sent*

us on training courses through AFM, and we had good materials to work with. We had some prep time to screen out applicants and to get our equipment in order and everything else. Then they started whittling away at it, and pretty soon you didn't have the prep days, you didn't have two people involved in delivering a program; it was down to one. Whatever videos you had were suddenly copies; the books and written materials became copies. Then one day, they became not even good copies. (Staff, HCC)

This Matsqui staff felt that quality control was important for programs to be effective:

Cognitive skills, breaking barriers, was the one good program, in my opinion, that we ran in the BC provincial [correctional] system. Here in the federal system, you have quality control, where they look at tapes [of instructors]. In the province, it wasn't monitored as closely. But that's part of our model, and it's a good thing or else some instructors get lazy. (Staff, MI)

The program frame required a wide lens in terms of staff assumptions regarding what worked for offenders. I did not find their beliefs to be homogenous. Correctional staff varied when it came to recommending which types of programming to emphasize. Most appreciated that inmates needed to address personal issues such as anger, criminal thinking, and substance abuse. But there was not even consensus on which model worked best for behavioural programs. For example, this Headingley staff saw value in domestic violence and anger management cognitive-based courses, but another staff at Matsqui wondered how long better thinking would last once an inmate had been released and again confronted the pressures of life outside the prison:

The domestic violence program appears to make some of them think a bit before they act. They talk differently about women by the end of the program. Some of it gets through. The anger management program is actually fairly decent for some of the guys; they seem to get a grip on how to recognize an issue before it becomes a major issue. (Staff, HCC)

Everything had to be cognitively based. To change the way they think. I disagree with that theory. You can tell people how to think, but when I'm mad, I'm not thinking so good. If I'm drunk, I'm not thinking good. But it's nice to believe that you can be thinking ahead of that. The approach that I like is used in the violent offender program and the sex offender program at Pacific. They're six-month programs that are emotionally based. They go back to all the stuff when you were a kid – they look at all the stuff in your life, not just as an inmate. (Staff, MI)

Most staff felt that vocational programs had declined in importance, and like most inmates, they felt strongly that this was a negative development. They believed that vocational programs needed to be re-emphasized, because most inmates came from blue-collar backgrounds. These three long-time staff had found over the years that most inmates had little aptitude for formal academic education, but they believed that most offenders could be taught a trade:

One of the biggest changes I have seen is the decline in trades training. It used to be better, programs perfectly suited for many of our First Nations inmates, like home construction. They would build a home in a big industrial area, in a warehouse. They would frame it out. A bit smaller, right, of course, but frame it out, insulate it, wire it ... Then those guys go back home, and they can do these things. They don't have a ticket per se, but that doesn't matter; they know how, how to do the basics to get a job in construction. (Staff, SMI)

Vocational ones for sure; 90 percent of our clientele are labourers or people who work in that part of the world. (Staff, FSCC)

When I started in Drumheller, vocational programs were huge. We had guys doing apprenticeships, huge, huge program. I like it; I don't know if that's the answer. Some will work places and get skills. Without that, it's a matter of luck. I much prefer that they do vocational skills, than having them as a unit cleaner that takes fifteen minutes in the morning and fifteen minutes in the afternoon. I think productive use of their time is essential. (Staff, MI)

These two staff believed that opportunities for good-paying jobs upon release were likely to increase the chances of successful community reintegration:

> *We had a bricklaying vocational programmer, was just excellent. You take a look in the paper every day, they are looking for guys who know how to carry cement and build stuff. We had an autobody shop. I mean, you take a look at most autobody shops, and you take a look at the people who work in the back there, and a lot of that clientele here is where they started.* (Staff, FSCC)

> *We need more vocational training. When a guy gets out of jail, what is going to be the most benefit to him: living skills or get out and go for a job because you did some sort of training for it? I think it totally negligent to not have it. They'd love to learn some kind of trade, like autobody.* (Staff, MI)

There may be no clear answer as to whether CBT and other counselling approaches are more important than job training. Trying to provide both, perhaps even daytime and evening programs, is an appealing option. However, just finding resources to provide the basics was a concern for this respondent:

> *Do you wanna give them vocational or educational programming, or do you wanna give them behavioural-based training? Is it the chicken or the egg? You give a guy a new skill, he can do body work and that, but he's got a raging personal history where you know the abuse and everything has never been resolved. He's not gonna be a very productive member of society because it's just a matter of time before he hits the bottle or the needle. Eventually, it's gonna spiral out of control. Then, on the other side, you give a guy drug counselling, deal with all his unresolved issues. But then they hit the street, and they don't know how to do anything because they've been in prison for ten years. Well, good luck finding a job, so now what? I think there's value for both, but there may only be money for one or the other.* (Staff, SMI)

The Impact of High Remand Rates

The rise of CBT programs and decline of vocational programs (and their possible revival) have been noteworthy developments over the past twenty-five years. The other key operational challenge over time for programming has been the remand problem, especially in provincial systems, because so many more inmates are pre-trial detainees than was the case thirty years ago. Put simply, there are fewer sentenced inmates to involve in longer-term programs, and too many remand inmates who are not required to take programs, and even for those who might, their time in custody is too short or, at best, uncertain.

Provincial institutions and federal penitentiaries differ in their ability to provide programs. Federal corrections has always had the advantage of bigger budgets, economies of scale (because they are bigger), and a national system; but most importantly, they hold inmates longer, which allows more opportunity to engage offenders in programs. That said, the Alberta and Manitoba correctional systems involved in this study have long offered programs in their institutions. Fort Saskatchewan and Headingley have both been viewed as the flagship facilities in their provinces, and new programs are often piloted in these places. Programs have had to be scaled back in both places, however, because of the dramatic increase in remand inmates housed by provincial correctional systems. Statistics Canada shows that provincial rates of remand ran at about 50 percent at the time of this study (Kong & Peters, 2008), but were even higher on the prairies: at Fort Saskatchewan and Headingley, between 70 and 80 percent of inmates were being held on pre-trial detention. The remand rate has gone down nationally, but in 2014 it still exceeded 60 percent in Alberta and Manitoba (confirmed by provincial head offices). This means that fewer than half the inmates in most provincial institutions have any onus placed on them to take treatment; remand inmates are exempt from programs, for they are considered not guilty. Some remands volunteer to take programs anyway, but to accommodate them, provincial systems must run programs for shorter periods of time. Even then, remand inmates may be moved at any time, released on bail, sent back to court, or transferred to another correctional facility for another reason. This makes running programs for remand inmates extremely difficult.

This provincial staff and a remand inmate viewed the provision of programs to pre-trial cases as a serious problem:

Less than 20 percent of our inmates are serving inmates. They can't have any long programs, so a lot of the programs have been cut back. They do the very, very basics of it. They can't do more programming; there is so much controlled movement, they can't. (Staff, FSCC)

It's bullshit. It's really hard to get in. I'll give you an example: small engine repair, I think they got twelve people in there, that's a three-week program. Right, and that's basically all they got. And if you want to get into school, like, they have the lower, medium, and upper academics. The lower, I don't know, maybe has fifteen people in it, that's out of the whole joint. That's all the spots. People want to get in there but they can't. (Remand inmate, FSCC)

Also, the remand problem has sometimes indirectly affected the federal system's ability to provide programs. In the past, criminal cases took longer to get through the courts, so when inmates got enhanced credit for time served on remand ("two for one" for each day served), average federal terms became shorter. Thus, an inmate with a six-year sentence who had served two years on remand would get forty-eight months' credit (i.e., two times twenty-four months), leaving only two years to serve in a federal penitentiary. These shorter federal custody periods placed great pressure on staff to develop correctional plans more quickly, get inmates into programs, and prepare release applications for the parole board's review. Two institutional parole staff expressed great frustration when it came to getting inmates processed through the system in a timely manner:

I think there seems to be a general misunderstanding that we can give these programs whenever. It's not a sausage factory; it's totally misguided. What has happened is, in the past eight years or so, we have all these correctional plans where we give these guys all these programs. But we can't offer all these programs, because we don't have enough guys trained. And we don't have the money, and then we have these inmates serving shorter sentences. So now we have the log jam of people, and they ask why can't they get parole. Well, because you have to take high-intensity programs, and none of these programs can be done in a reasonable amount of time. (Staff, MI)

The biggest complaint about programs is that every guy coming through intake has a correctional plan of what needs to be done, but we can't do all of it. At times, the list is overwhelming and programs are costly, they take a lot of time and effort. The drawback with these short sentences is that guys are not getting the programs in the timely manner that they should. (Staff, SMI)

Conclusion

Different program or self-improvement schemes have existed since prisons emerged in a big way in the nineteenth century. Provincial and federal institutions offer case management and programming for all inmates, but this is limited for remanded inmates. One of the most significant changes over the past twenty-five years has been the increased use of CBT programs. The impact of these more sophisticated programs, however, has been attenuated by the increase in remand inmates. Shorter or uncertain provincial sentences have resulted, and also shorter sentences for federal inmates because of pre-trial credit, and these two phenomena have resulted in less opportunity for more intense programs for both federal and provincial inmates.

Inmates face a certain amount of personal reproach and group stigma from being involved in treatment and often adopt differing program frames for staff and inmates: they must pretend to other inmates that they are not truly interested in taking a program even while trying to give the impression to their case managers that they are highly motivated. The potential benefit of programs is weakened by the primary inmate frame – more specifically, the need to retain respect and appear tough back on the unit discourages inmates from applying lessons learned from programs such as anger management. Offenders generally supported programs emphasizing behavioural change, but their inmate frame maxim was "I'll change when I want to change." There seemed to be an exception to this in treatment units such as Ni-Miikana at Stony Mountain, where the environment supported efforts at personal change.

The correctional program frame for staff was a guarded frame. Staff believed in the CBT model but did not have high expectations when it came to program efficacy. They stressed the importance of therapeutic integrity and of programs being properly resourced.

Because so many offenders come from working-class backgrounds, inmates were more supportive of academic/vocational programs, especially trades training. The utility of those programs appealed to inmates, who linked the likelihood of more lucrative employment to this approach. Staff and inmates strongly concurred that there should be greater emphasis on vocational programs. However, staff cautioned that offenders who could not maintain relationships with others, or manage anger or addictions, were unlikely to keep a job for long. Behavioural programs were still important for successful release into the community.

Aboriginal inmates desired more Indigenous programming. Access to Elders and to pipe ceremonies and sweats has arguably improved over the past twenty-five years, but complaints about limited access to spiritual ceremonies and lack of respect for culture were common among inmates. Indigenous programming was reported to be stronger in the federal system. Again, the Ni-Miikana unit at Stony Mountain showed some promise in providing Indigenous programming and a positive milieu for inmates motivated to change.

From a policy perspective, the high remand rate currently experienced by inmates is likely the biggest obstacle to effective programming in Canada. Too many inmates are sitting on remand for long periods of time; too few sentenced inmates are receiving programming. Remand inmates typically attend short, cursory programs, if any. For practice to improve, the remand rate needs to go down. The recent passage of Bill C-25, ostensibly intended to discourage sitting on remand for "two for one," has had little impact thus far. Shorter times to trial, as I have advocated elsewhere (Weinrath, 2009a), are much more likely to result in reduced remand populations.

Behavioural programs have improved over the past twenty-five years, but long, intense programs with high therapeutic integrity are more often found in federal institutions, which are better-resourced. Provincial authorities must balance the short time periods that inmates are in custody with available programs. Headingley and Fort Saskatchewan did not receive enough long-serving inmates for them to run very many intensive long-term programs. For inmates, more provincial time in sentenced as opposed to remand status would provide better opportunities to participate in helpful programs.

10

The Rise of Prison Gangs

Prison gangs have had a significant impact on Canadian correctional institutions in recent years. This chapter examines their activities and how they have affected inmates' lives as well as the work of correctional staff. Data from the study's sample of offenders and correctional staff from four Western Canadian correctional institutions is enriched by a purposefully selected sub-group of six current prison gang members, three associates,[1] and five ex-gang members. Most gang members interviewed were affiliated with Aboriginal street gangs, but I also interviewed two former outlaw motorcycle gang members. This chapter examines gang recruitment, life in a prison gang, and how inmates leave prison gangs, as well as the impact of gangs on other inmates and on institutional life. Prison gang frames within the gang, external to the gang, and towards staff are developed. Also, frames that are reciprocally forged in response to prison gang behaviour by other inmates and by staff are delineated.

The challenges posed by prison gangs include their aggressiveness, their involvement in contraband, and their intimidation of other inmates (DeLisi et al., 2004; Gaes et al., 2002; Griffin & Hepburn, 2006; Zaitzow & Houston, 1999). Brian Grant and Rick Ruddell (2011) reported from CSC that the presence of gangs in federal institutions has been growing, and Aboriginal gangs in particular have a large presence in western Canada (Grekul & LaBoucane-Benson, 2008; Weinrath et al., 1999). Recent federal and provincial studies, however, suggest that the gang problem is growing in provinces other than the prairies (Grant & Ruddell, 2011; Marin, 2013;

Ruddell & Gottschall, 2011). In a published review, the CSC found African and Caribbean immigrant Canadian gangs in eastern Canada, and that traditional organized crime gangs were a rising problem. The Ontario Ombudsman, André Marin (2013), has commented on the growing problems that prison gangs are posing to that province's correctional system.

Framing Prison Gangs

Not surprisingly, my respondents indicated that inmates framed their interactions differently when it came to gang members. Beyond the primary inmate frame, gang members adopted their own cues to guide communication and behaviour among one another, as well as between themselves and non-gang members and staff. Prison gang members tended to occupy the more predatory end of the continuum in the primary inmate frame: they acted strong and tough, demanded respect, reacted violently to perceived slights, and intimidated other inmates where they could. Control of drugs and other contraband was maintained through violence or the threat of violence. Within the prairie institutions examined in this study, conflicts with other gangs fuelled a certain amount of violence. Overall, then, the activities and behaviours of prison gangs in this study were similar to those observed in the United States.

Old-Style Prison Gangs, Present-Day Gangs, and the New Recruitment

In the 1980s, biker gangs held considerable sway within prairie prisons. For example, respondents reported that Los Bravos and the Grim Reapers were prominent in Stony Mountain during that decade. Their recruitment methods were similar to those practised when recruiting on the street. At that time, it was a privilege to be asked to be a "striker" or associate (probationer) of a biker gang. Traditional biker gangs were highly selective in their recruitment strategies and admitted members only after long periods of assessment to ensure they were competent and trustworthy. This limited "full-patch" admissions to just a few each year. This staff member recalled that at Stony Mountain in the 1980s, the two biggest Winnipeg biker gangs, the Grim Reapers and Los Bravos, wielded considerable influence although they usually only had small numbers in the institution:

They didn't have large numbers, but in the 1980s the biker gangs ran the place. We used to joke that when the Grim Reapers were all in segregation, the Los Bravos ran the institution, and vice versa. They had a lot of influence, we used to negotiate over whether or not some PC [protective custody] cases could come back into population. They could get the other inmates to guarantee the safety of people coming back. (Staff, SMI)

In the late 1980s and early 1990s, the Indian Posse was the first large Aboriginal prison gang; they later became a Manitoba street gang. They first formed as a self-protection group at Stony Mountain, in much the same way as outlined by Salvador Buentello, Robert Fong, and Ronald Vogel (1991) in their study of Texas prison gangs. The Indian Posse evolved from a self-protection group into a predatory group, began victimizing other inmates, and moved to control the drug trade inside Stony Mountain. After being released, its members continued their activities as a street gang in Winnipeg. Since then, many smaller prison gangs have come and gone. The Manitoba Warriors and Native Syndicate have been the two largest gangs since the late 1990s. Both began in the community and have continued to operate within prisons as their members have been incarcerated. By the time of this study, the Indian Posse prison gang had shrunk in size and influence: it had only twenty-seven members at Stony Mountain, and it had been isolated from other inmates in a separate unit after inflicting too much violence against other inmates:

Yeah, the Posse were a jailhouse gang, formed twenty years back or so. We've had others, but they were one of the only gangs to keep it up on the street, unfortunately. They're not doing too good right now. They just can't get along with any of the other inmates so we had to separate them. (Staff, SMI)

The Posse were isolated in a separate unit at Headingley as well. The violence between that prison gang and others meant that they could not be placed in the general population. This gang associate related the likely outcome of a meeting between the Indian Posse and a group like the Manitoba Warriors:

All Slobs get punched out here. Slobs would be like IP [Indian Posse gang] members, you know, Posse. All Slobs get punched out here. Why do you think they have their own little range? The ex-Deuce members, they're all in PC [protective custody].[2] They come down here [Manitoba Warriors units], we'd punch them right out. (Remand inmate and gang associate, HCC)

Prison gangs in Alberta and Manitoba correctional institutions differed from the old biker gangs and traditional organized crime gangs in that the emphasis was less on careful screening and more on aggressive recruitment to grow large memberships. The strategy was straight-forward. Once a large complement of prison gang members had been amassed, these superior forces were used to strategically outnumber, intimidate, and (if need be) assault other inmates. Potential gang members were offered "safety" in a curious way – they were warned about the high probability of victimization if they did not align with the gang. Initiation rites underscored the importance of toughness and the use of violence. New recruits faced a violent paddling when first initiated (a "beat-in"). Paddling was used for occasions like admission to the gang, but also on birthdays and at time of release. Hyper-masculine values are emphasized in prisons, but gangs had taken it to an extreme level, as Comack (2008) in Canada and Jewkes (2005) in Britain have observed. These two gang affiliates described their initiation with pride and reported that it was a means to establish status and a respected identity within the prison:

A solid inmate is respected in prison. Like me. I joined because I wanted to be somebody inside. When I got my initiation, I took it like a man. My initiation was two guys holding me down, and they pull your pants down and they spank the shit out of you with a big fuckin' rubber slipper. You gotta man up, and if you fuckin' cry, you get it. Last time I was in, I had to do a few things for the guys in here. What I mean by a few things was dealing with a couple guys that needed to be dealt with. I never got caught for that. (Remand inmate and gang associate, HCC)

First time in jail you'll get the spanks; if you're getting out, you'll get the spanks; or if it's your birthday, you'll get the spanks. The whole range will just all be just holding you, and if you're turning nineteen, nineteen spanks from everyone. This guy will come up to you and give you nineteen spanks [inaudible]. *Next guy, nineteen spanks. It's just wrong. But you gotta be quiet and take that.* (Remand inmate and gang member, HCC)

Gangs used to define themselves along racial lines. More recently, though, the Aboriginal prison gangs in Headingley, Stony Mountain, and Fort Saskatchewan have become multi-racial, taking in whites, African Canadians, Asians, and new Canadians from the Middle East. Respondents reported that it was more important for members to be "solid" than to be of the same race. These prison gangs have become true "equal opportunity" organizations. Two of the respondents – a senior gang inmate, and a staff person at Stony Mountain – had seen a shift towards non-Indigenous recruits. It was more important for members to be dependable and for their numbers to be great enough to win a conflict:

Yeah, we have taken in guys from other gangs, not always Indian. You gotta have guys you can count on. Sometimes it's just business. (Senior gang inmate, SMI)

The Warriors take all kinds now ... So do the others. It's all about the numbers. If you are going to outman other gangs, you can't be too picky. (Staff, SMI)

In Manitoba, smaller prison gangs sometimes formed within the prison, or recruited members while inside. By the time of my study, however, a strategy of absorbing smaller gangs had been launched by larger ones like the Indian Posse, Manitoba Warriors, and Native Syndicate. In what amounted to hostile takeovers, the smaller inmate gangs were told to disband and join the larger gang. Those who joined were required to be loyal to the larger gang's hierarchy; in return, they reaped the benefits of membership, such as status, protection from other inmates, and profit from the underground economy. These gang takeovers were violent if necessary. This former gang member had seen inmates who refused to switch allegiances either threatened with a beating or actually assaulted:

If you come in and you are a big-time drug dealer, you are going to have heavy pressure to join. They want your connections. Lots of people join gangs because, otherwise, it is a pretty miserable life if you don't. Guys just join because they don't want to get beat. (Remand inmate and ex-gang member, HCC)

Non-gang inmates were contemptuous of gang members who presented themselves as tough, given that they relied on sheer numbers to intimidate others. Besides which, the gangs were so desperate for numbers that they would "take anyone," the inference being that many recruits were not especially tough or competent. This ex-gang member was highly negative about today's prison gang inmates:

They tell everyone, "You can't use if you're a gang member." That's bullshit. They're all crackheads. All those Stony gangs are trying to do is get numbers. They're letting in skinheads [racist white inmates], rats. They don't care, as long as they got numbers. (Remand inmate and ex-gang member, HCC)

This Stony Mountain inmate saw gangs as having a very negative effect on newly admitted prisoners and on inmate society generally:

This is the gang's breeding ground, right here in jail. That's the biggest thing for me, they pick on these little kids – they're scared for their lives. So they join and before you know it, they got a taste of it. Oh geez, I don't need to fight one-on-one, now I can fight ten-on-one. Then they start acting tough. All that's doing is just screwing our inmate society. (Sentenced inmate, SMI)

Taking a minority position, senior gang members contested the views of other inmates in the general population. High-ranking prison gang members (or ex-members) disputed the degree to which they actively recruited or how low their standards were for admission. Two Stony Mountain gang leaders and a Headingley ex-biker gang member reported that inmates actively sought them out and that recruits had to be worthy of membership. Indeed, screening could be onerous:

You gotta make sure you're picking the right ones and choosing the right ones, too. You don't want to make a mistake. The guy could be the biggest, toughest, ugliest guy, but you don't know what his history is like. So when you see somebody and you want him to join, you gotta ask the guy for some sort of paperwork before you say, "Yeah." (Sentenced inmate and gang member, SMI)

We're turning guys away. I get asked all the time by guys who want to join our gang, but you can't just take anyone. (Sentenced inmate and gang member, SMI)

I don't promote the club with anybody. I don't go around promoting it. All the years I've been in the club, I never sponsored anybody, never brought anybody in. If you want to come, you come on your own. I am not looking for new guys and recruits. They seem to think we come to jail to recruit new members, but that's not the truth. Not the biker clubs. (Remand inmate and ex-biker gang member, HCC)

At the time of this research, in British Columbia, the inmates at Matsqui were proud of their ability to restrict the influence of gangs, claiming that prairie transfers with gang ties were quickly told to end their activities. Gang members who did reside at Matsqui generally kept a low profile and did not recruit. Respondents indicated there was a different culture and attitude towards gang members outside the Prairies:

I was in the SHU in Prince Albert [Special Handling Unit for difficult inmates at Saskatchewan federal penitentiary] *in the early 1990s when the gangs came in. The Indian Posse, Manitoba Warriors. The Aryan*

Brotherhood formed, white guys trying to protect themselves. The Aryans are not big in Saskatchewan or Manitoba, but more in Alberta. You don't hear much about gangs in BC; we don't tolerate them out here. Gang members usually stay quiet. (Lifer, MI)

We've had guys from the Prairies who come here and drop their colours. There was four or five of them. They thought they were going to pull their stuff here and got told right away, "No, we won't have anything nothing to do with gangs in this institution." Yeah, we do have cliques, though, half a dozen guys who hang out together all the time, and sometimes they become problematic. But it's not that gang mentality that comes with it, you know, ganging up on people, violence all the time. (Sentenced inmate, MI)

Prison Gang Life

There were obvious benefits to being in a prison gang. Gang members reported feeling safe. Some members reported past abuse as children or youth, and being afraid of family members or those with whom they had had to live when they were younger. Consistent with the qualitative findings by Elizabth Comack (2008) and Joseph Waldram (1997), most Aboriginal prison gang members reported a great deal of traumatic violence in their lives, especially when younger, and they wished to minimize their risk of further victimization. Recruiting large numbers, swearing loyalty to one another, and intimidating the rest of the inmate population obviously helped achieve these goals. These two prison gang–affiliated offenders discussed their troubled backgrounds, and those of other gang members:

What some people don't realize is that the majority of guys are damaged and come from broken families. That didn't get love from home. And found their way to a gang, 'cause a gang gives them that love and they go out of their way for each other. You know what I mean? They form a family. For me at home, I didn't feel loved, I didn't feel cared about at home. I was sexually abused when I was just a little kid. The only time my family was there for me was when they bought me something. Since I've grown up and got some size on me and started to do crazy stuff, they started depending on me to deal with their problems. (Sentenced inmate and gang member, SMI)

I'm an associate, but I wouldn't leave the gang. I've got my big brother in the gang, but basically the whole gang is my family. All the time, since I was 18. It's probably been about two years, but I knew they were Warriors right from the day. When I was like fifteen or sixteen, I was just a dumb little kid, runnin' around, stealing cars and stuff. But they looked out for me. If I wasn't in the Warriors, I'd be stuck up in population, getting into fights. Here, everybody's all family, so there's nothing really much to worry about. (Remand inmate and gang associate, HCI)

Some prison gang inmates reported feeling safer in custody than on the street, because they could better control their immediate environment, access to their peers, and health care. This gang leader liked having his fellow members close by:

I feel safer in prison than I feel on the street. You know, on the street, someone will come up and shoot you, you can get run over by a car. Here, the chances are that a guy will stab you, but if you got gang members around you protecting you, it is more than likely not going to happen. (Sentenced inmate, SMI)

This prison gang member also felt safer being in a correctional institution with close physical support at the ready, and proximity to medical aid through institutional emergency response teams and health care nursing staff:

Last time I came to prison, I felt like I was coming home. Sometimes when you get out of jail, you don't want to get out. Out there, it's like, you gotta be more cautious. You've got your homies backing you up here. See, even on the street, what if one day you're walking by yourself and then you get dogged, where's your homies, man? They might not be around. So it's safer in here than it is out there. Besides, here, you get into a fight, someone stabs you out, whatever. But you can stay safe, 'cause there's medical right here. But on the street, it's like, you get into a fight with somebody, they either shoot you or stab you, how long is it going to take for them to respond, man? By the time they get to you, you're dead. So I feel a bit safer in here than I do out there. (Sentenced inmate and gang member, SMI)

But there was a price to pay for feeling safe. Gang life was hierarchical, deference to top members was key, and willingness to use violence was required. Gang members at the top of the group held the most influence and control. Inmates on the lower rungs had to follow orders, no matter how gruesome or trivial. This prison gang member gave up significant privacy, but saw it as a price to be paid if he was to remain in the gang:

In my gang, members go through your stuff. They have to read your mail first before you get it, so that's how it goes. (Remand inmate and gang member, HCC)

There were other downsides to prison gang life. Despite feeling safer and having support, conflicts with other gangs increased the chances that a gang member would be seriously assaulted when by themselves in the prison. Also, if one got into a fight with members of other gangs, weapons were more likely to be used, and this brought with it a greater risk of injury. Also, a gang might decline in numbers, leaving individual members suddenly highly vulnerable to violence from other gangs. Gang status could result in a member being reclassified as "incompatible," which meant being moved to an undesirable unit, or even worse, to protective custody. Gang life was a high-risk life. Regardless, this gang leader found the benefits well worth it:

But I'm not saying that I won't get jumped. I have been in other fights in other jails, gang members gang up on me, the tables are turned, and it's just me and five–six of them. They would have shanks, you know, but I did some training, and I know how to fight. I feel that prison made me more of a man real fast. I feel like more of a bad guy coming here, knowing everyone, being feared and respected by a lot of people. It makes you feel like the king because you got control over so many guys. You can say, "You ten guys, go do that over there for me." They will go do it without any questions; it's done. (Sentenced inmate and gang member, SMI)

The alternatives for prison gang members were simply not palatable. Gang members viewed other inmates derisively if they had no significant connections with inmates of status. The worst fate imaginable for a prison gang member was to be defined as a "nobody":

> *Like, I can see nobodies, these guys that, like, they call them "nobodies" if they're not with a gang, right? I can see that they might feel afraid because they don't know if they're going to get rolled on by somebody or if they said something wrong to somebody. You really gotta watch what you do, what you say, or where you walk, or where you go, or where you eat. You know what I mean? But as a gang member, you don't know when that day's going to pop off, when someone's going to roll on you, you know what I mean? But I'd rather be a gang member than a nobody.* (Sentenced inmate and gang member, SMI)

Leaving the Gang

Prison gangs are thought to amplify violence within institutions and to create more hardened inmates as a result of their socialization as gang members (Gaes et al., 2002). A gang truism is that once in, you cannot leave the gang, on pain of death. This was not true. Most inmates reported that they knew many prison gang members who had left the gang upon release, by either moving away or keeping a low profile and avoiding contact with other gang members in the community. Gangs with large memberships were unlikely to expend the energy to track non-essential or peripheral members. There are two caveats to this observation. First, it is more difficult for core or full-patch members with intimate knowledge of prison gang operations to leave, for this information could jeopardize the gang's ability to function if it was passed on to law enforcement. Second, even correctional administrators were not enthused about inmates leaving a gang while still in custody. This meant at worst a possible "deboarding," or "beat-out" – a gauntlet of prison gang members physically assaulting someone leaving, with sometimes lethal results.[3] Other options were transfer to another facility or placement in a protective custody unit or cell, but these moves placed tremendous pressure on the administration to protect the gang leavers. Within a correctional facility, the gang leaver could still be "got to," even in an isolation unit. So staff did not encourage inmates to leave prison gangs while they were still imprisoned.

> *Once they join, we discourage inmates from leaving a gang while they are inside the institutions. It means that they are targeted; it means protective custody. And we do our best, but there always is a chance that someone will get at them while they are in there. If they go to another facility, it is also always possible that knowledge of their leaving will follow them. In a prison, leaving the gang is not a great idea.* (Staff, SMI)

This Stony Mountain inmate had seen a number of inmates leave their gang once released. It seems they had joined a prison gang out of convenience or for the sake of benefits while in custody:

> *Guys join up when they're in and quit when they get out. I see a lot of it. They join a gang to feel protected, and they run their mouth off because they'll have a bunch of other guys to back their play. When they get out, they leave the gang or move away from the city.* (Sentenced inmate, SMI)

According to this full-patch gang member, one could be released from prison and disassociate oneself from day-to-day criminal activities, but one could not fully leave the gang:

> I: *Yeah, when I'm released, I want to go back to my family. But I worry about getting ordered to do something when I'm back on the street.*
> W: *Couldn't you just leave or ask to leave?*
> I: *No, I don't think about that. I'll be in it until I die, I guess. Other people leave; they just leave; they're like, "Leave me alone." When somebody leaves nowadays, they're gone; you don't hear from them anymore. If you're full patch, it works different. These guys are my family, but for the time being, I'm in jail, I'm gonna be gone for a long time. I got nobody. All I got is [gang name]. That's all I got now, man.* (Remand inmate and gang member, HCC)

Living with Prison Gangs

Consistent with much of the research literature, my study participants identified prison gangs as a large problem in two significant ways: such gangs promoted the use of violence and intimidation, and they used their street contacts to bring drugs and other contraband into prison. One can counter that these supposed "problems" of violence and drugs have always been present in prisons whether gangs are present or not – that there have always been inmate "heavies" or groups that intimidate others, as well as people willing to smuggle in drugs if there is a market for them. But prison gangs have created a different dynamic within the institution, compared to smaller groupings of troublesome inmates. Their sheer numbers and their willingness to use violence have made them a greater threat to others. They are more willing to use serious violence to collect drug, gambling, and other contraband-related debts: "pay up or else."

Many forms of institutional violence can be linked directly to gangs. Inmates who resist joining a gang are often assaulted, and beat-ins for new recruits can be brutal. A further layer of physical violence involves conflict between gangs over recruits and control of the drug trade. Also, violence – including lethal violence – may arise *within* gangs over status within the group or threats to leave one gang for another. Finally, gang members largely ignore key features of the inmate code that once promoted harmony among inmates, such as those relating to leaving conflicts from the community "on the street," fighting one-on-one, and doing your own time.

This Fort Saskatchewan inmate marvelled at how the gang dynamic had changed how inmates related to one another:

> I see more gangs related to violence. And the problems that come with gangs are just retarded. You get a few of them together, and all of a sudden, you can watch them change. It's too bad because you get the people alone and they are not bad guys. But I don't understand the whole gang mentality. If you get the wrong people together, you're going to have violence, right? They use jail as a big recruitment centre. (Remand inmate, FSCC)

The influence of prison gangs was pervasive. This Headingley inmate saw them indirectly controlling all contraband. For those smaller gangs bringing in contraband,

Each crew has their own business happening in there. Be it tobacco, drugs, canteen, even. But it's not just one person, one crew; it's everybody, as long as you got crew. The smaller gangs, if they survive – independent operators like me – we gotta pay some rent, you know. (Sentenced inmate, HCC)

This Stony Mountain inmate recalled days when the inmate code helped prisoners avoid violence, and discussed how that had changed:

In the old days, there was no murders, really, and if there was, it was acci-dental, or it was something very serious. Or it was very private between two people, you know. In the old days, you always considered prison neutral grounds. None of us wanted to be here, but we had to be here because of the nature of the way we lived, so it was considered neutral grounds. You didn't bring beefs in from the street. If you were trying to beef a guy from the street, guards told you leave it for the street, and it was left for the street. But nowadays, this is where they air everything. (Sentenced inmate and former gang member, SMI)

At Stony Mountain, transition units (TRUs) were used to house inmates who did not get along with others, or were "incompatible." Recall that the incompatible inmate is a recent phenomenon. Such inmates are not informants or sex offenders but have been marked for serious assault by others due to conflicts with other inmates, usually originating in events in the community. Generally, correctional organizations, both federal and provincial, have become more sensitive to the potential of serious violence between inmates. For example, at Fort Saskatchewan and Headingley, incompatibles might be initially housed separately, but staff attempted to mediate conflicts so that inmates might be housed together.

Some offender placements in the Stony Mountain TRU were what one could term traditional protective custody cases: sex offenders or informants, and inmates who could not pay drug or other debts to gangs. But in many other cases they were inmates not typically thought of as protective custody candidates. For example, a number of ex-gang members or members of smaller gangs went to the TRUs because they had been "squeezed out" of prison life by the larger gangs. In some cases, those who refused to join other gangs did have other options, such as a transfer to another institution or some form of protective custody. At Headingley, small gang casualties also ended up in a protective custody unit. Both groups were understandably bitter about their placement:

> *Yeah, they just gang up on you, no balls; they're nothin'. But I'm the one who ends up on the TRU.* (Sentenced inmate and ex-gang member, SMI)

> I: *I used to be a gang leader. That's why I'm in PC; my gang got small and the other gangs are out to get me. I used to lead the ——. We were at war with the ——. So we took the —— out of our name and called ourselves the ——. But the Manitoba Warriors took that name for a new chapter of their gang, and they recruited us. So most of my guys left to join this new chapter of the Manitoba Warriors. They wanted us, but my brother-in-law and me didn't go. That's why I'm in protective custody, because I didn't go along with them.*
> W: *So they took your name?*
> I: *They took our name. Couldn't do nothin' and didn't want to. It's not worth people gettin' hurt over a name. Over stuff.* (Remand inmate and ex-gang member, HCC)

Older offenders resented the impact of the gangs but also felt there were incompatibles whose problems did not relate to gang involvement. They believed that younger inmates were not making enough effort to resolve differences amicably with their peers. Even so, prison gangs were still identified as the biggest reason for segregation between inmates in institutions where their numbers were high.

Inmates were assigned to units in such a way that incompatibles did not come face to face with members of the general population. This had a clear deleterious impact on quality of prison life. But to be fair, not all limitations on inmate movement were attributable to prison gangs. In provincial correctional centres, the large number of remands housed by necessity in what had once been prisons for sentenced inmates necessitated limited time off unit as well as a certain amount of segregation between inmate groups. This inmate at Headingley commented on the dramatic change in prisoner movement there over the years:

> *I think the movement thing is a thing of the past because of all the separation, the gangs. They've changed. I did time at Stony in '91. I was in SMI, and at that time, when they called supper, they would let everyone out. We would have two hundred guys in the dining hall. Today, you eat on the range from trays. There's no more movement like that. Your range will go as one unit, but they got everybody separated ... You got your own canteen, you don't go to gym with anybody else, so you're not mingling with everybody like it used to be. Then, the whole prison would be, "Okay, it's recreation time," and everybody goes to the rec yard. There was no such thing, you know, as separations between this guy and that guy. If you couldn't cut it in jail, then you were getting buggered up. And today, it's, "Oh, this guy's after me and this guy's after me and this guy's after me," so they put separation in. It's like the whole jail is protective custody.* (Remand inmate and ex-gang member, HCC)

This lifer at Stony Mountain attributed the creation of TRUs (protective custody by another name) at least partly to prison gangs:

> *About 50 percent of that transitional unit population is due to the sex offenders and informants, but the rest is due to debts and people trying to get out of a gang. Gang initiations and gang dropout, they are not easy things to deal with, eh?* (Lifer, SMI)

It is significant that in 2008, among my four study sites, Matsqui had no remands, the smallest number of gang inmates, and the freest inmate movement during the day and evening. This lifer commented on the lack of prison gangs at Matsqui compared to other places he had served time:

> *We have more movement in Matsqui than you do in other places I did time at, like Drumheller and Stony. Partly because gangs aren't such a problem here. There are street gang members in Matsqui, but they don't organize or recruit.* (Lifer, MI)

Surprisingly, prison gangs have contributed to the integration of sex offenders into the general population, which is generally considered a laudable goal of correctional administration. Sex offenders are often isolated or placed in protective custody. Such is the power of prison gangs that they can protect sex offenders from other inmates. Prison gang members did not admit that they were tolerant of "skinners," however. Sex offenders who were gang members would deny the allegations against them despite their crimes being well publicized. This Headingley inmate was incensed over this practice and saw it as a serious violation of one of the fundamental tenets of what remained of the old convict code:

> *They protect skinners. There was a guy at Stony that had a skin beef on his record. He said, "Oh, I didn't do it." "What the fuck," I said, "you got it on paper, man. If you're charged with it, if you plead out to it, you probably did it." He's still accepted into that crew* [gang]. *Bullshit.* (Sentenced inmate, HCC)

Setting Prison Gang Frames

The precursors for prison gang membership (see Figure 10.1) were very similar to the motivating factors for street gang membership found in gang studies by Elijah Anderson (1999) and James Vigil (2003). Individuals reported gaining safety, status, and a sense of belonging when they joined a prison gang; similar motivations were reported by youth joining gangs in impoverished areas where there was limited support from traditional social institutions such as the family and schools. Still, the most direct route for prison gang membership was having been a gang member on the outside, or having family members who were gang members. Continuation of the gang role in custody is, of course, the most direct route to prison gang membership; having a family member in a gang also led to membership, even if it was just associate status. Others joined to feel protected (i.e., for safety in numbers). A willingness to be violent was a necessary precursor of gang membership.

Once admitted to a prison gang, members adopted the features of the conventional inmate frame and displayed the common inmate frame behaviours. They did, of course, tend to engage more regularly in predatory interactions. Behaviours more often observed in a prison gang frame towards other inmates included acting in an intimidating manner, reacting aggressively and quickly to any sign of disrespect, and limiting the space where other inmates were allowed to walk. Prison gang members were also expected to engage in business-like behaviour; they were expected to be vigilant in seeking out customers for drugs or contraband, and otherwise to look out for opportunities to make money, typically by exploiting other inmates. Around other prison gangs, a member had to ensure he always appeared strong – that he presented a tougher and more masculine front than other inmates. He had to show loyalty by deferring to leaders and following orders, such as to assault other inmates who might be members of rival gangs, or who were late on payments for drugs, suspected of being informants, or deemed disrespectful.

Finally, prison gang members framed behaviours very cautiously around correctional staff. Much like the inhabitants immersed in Donald Clemmer's (1940) classic inmate subculture, prison gang members emphasized social distance; they were also very mistrustful of COs, even pushing back against their authority and trying to intimidate them. I found that prison gangs represented the worst features of the inmate subculture – that their values, particularly their willingness to use violence, were analogous to the street gang values other researchers have found (Anderson, 1999; Mears et al., 2013).

Frame Breaking: Staying Out of Prison Gangs

Numbers vary, but in Manitoba, the data provided by correctional authorities indicated that gang members comprised 30 to 35 percent of the inmate population at Headingley; that included smaller gangs not active in the institution. Fort Saskatchewan's inmate population was only about 16 percent prison gangs; in Alberta, most of the troublesome gang members were housed at the Edmonton Remand Centre. At Matsqui, only 16 percent of inmates were identified as gang members, but they did not recruit, so these prisoners simply mixed with the general population, were inconspicuous, and made no discernible efforts to form prison gangs.

It is intuitively logical that 30 to 35 percent of inmates, at most, would belong to a prison gang, given that gangs need customers for their products (drugs and other contraband) and that some inmates will be not suitable for membership. Recruitment into gangs was often aggressive, and the expectation of joining was strong in these situations; an inmate recruited to a gang would enjoy significant rewards, whereas not joining would leave him open to threats and assaults. Yet some inmates did not join gangs. If frame breaking means operating outside of expected normative expectations, then refusing to join a prison gang despite the danger of saying no certainly meets the criteria (Figure 10.1).

My respondents who refused to join a gang described a variety of methods for avoiding gang life. A small number of inmates used the influence of their gang-involved relatives to protect themselves. Friendships and external networks helped this inmate avoid joining:

FIGURE 10.1
Prison gang frames

Precursors	
• Street gang membership	• Status-seeking
• Family member a gang member	• Willingness to be violent
• Safety	• Support, belonging

The frame		
PG frame: Other inmates	**PG frame: Other PGs**	**PG frame: Correctional staff**
• Intimidate	• Be strong (act tough)	• Maintain extreme social distance (don't talk unless necessary)
• Be ready to use violence	• Show loyalty	
• Respond aggressively to disrespect	• Defer to leaders	• Be very cautious
	• Obey orders	• Be very mistrustful
• Show little respect to others		• Intimidate/push
• Look for opportunities to trade in contraband		

Other inmates frame: PG	Correctional staff frame: PG
• Be cautious	• Be cautious
• Be respectful	• Do not trust, monitor carefully
• Watch where you walk	• Do not let them intimidate you
• Avoid contact (trouble)	• Be firm in enforcing rules
• Make contact (drugs, contraband)	• Make efforts to involve in programming
• Pay your debts	
• Manage social distance	

Frame break: Other inmates–PG members
• Do not join gang despite pressure to do so
o Use family/social networks to avoid joining
o Say no and avoid gang members
o Say no and fight if required, even if you take a beating
o Enter into protective custody arrangement

I was going through the fish tank in '96, and there was —— in the van going back to the pen. My cousin at the time was basically running the show in Stony for that crew, so he just said, "Look, it's okay. One of us in the family is in; that's good enough for being a member." He told them to leave me alone. In the system, I'm known for drugs, you know, in Stony. So I look at it like nobody's going to harass a supplier. Nobody wants a fucking dead supplier. (Sentenced inmate, HCC)

Some ex-gang members and many older inmates took a direct route to avoid membership – they said no and were not bothered by the prison gangs:

I was asked to join a gang before but I refused them. I don't have one tattoo on me! I was in the fish tank, intake at Stony. One guy asked me, I said, "No, no, no." He goes, "Well think about it." And then he gives me a couple of days, comes back with three guys. I said, "No, I'm still thinking about it, man." Comes back with five guys, in my cell, and I said to them, "I think I'm gonna pass, man. You know, I'm good." He goes, "But if you join, we got your back. Population's crazy." And I said, "No," and they left. But you know, I had no problems in pop [general population]. (Remand inmate, HCC)

A fair number of inmates reported enduring a few assaults until the gangs left them alone. In most cases, gang members simply gave up trying to recruit. The risks associated with taking the beatings were dire. But for these three inmates, it was worth it:

A lot of gangs wanted me to join their gang, and I refused. I said I can get into enough trouble on my own, I didn't need their help. They tried for about three months. Eventually, they just figured, "If he is not going to join us, then we will just jump him." And so they did. So I fought with them, and they finally gave up. But I try to go away from violence. I am in here for a violent crime, and it is not good, and I don't wish that on anybody. (Lifer, SMI)

I got jumped by five MW [Manitoba Warriors] because I wouldn't bring drugs in. I wouldn't bow down. I'm not gonna bow down. (Sentenced inmate and former gang member, SMI)

IP, Deuce, and MW all tried to recruit me; didn't matter that I was a white guy. But I stood tall and stayed on my own the whole time I was in there. So I got stabbed a few times in Stony. Kept it to myself, sewed myself up in my cell. I didn't even stitch some of them, just bandaged them, but this one I put in five stitches in myself. If you go to medical and you're in the federal system, with a stab wound, they got to segregate you, or move you, or lock the place down and ask a whole bunch of questions, so I kept it to myself. (Remand inmate, HCC)

The motivation not to join was associated with a spirit of independence and, perhaps surprisingly, a dislike of the constant pressure to be violent. Inmate values of being tough and standing up for yourself are violated, to a degree, by having to join a gang and become subservient in the hierarchy. These two refusers were highly vocal about not wanting to be ordered about in the gang hierarchy:

W: Why didn't you join?
I: I don't like to be told what to do. You get told, "Go in and take that guy's TV or stereo," or "Go take his dope," or "Go take his tobacco," or "Go punch him out." I'm nobody's bitch. I've seen the way that gangs are conducted and the way guys are treated. Cleaning other guys' cells, washing their laundry and folding it for them, making their beds, and just stupid shit, like, why would you want to be in a gang and be their little Molly Maid? (Remand inmate, HCC)

I didn't join because too many enemies, too much pressure. You gotta prove yourself, bro. You gotta punch out that guy and prove yourself, or you gotta give me your stuff. Say if I sold drugs or whatever, I'd have to give them the profit of my drugs. Why would I want to do that? (Remand inmate and ex-gang member, HCC)

Prison gang members use strength of numbers to overwhelm and intimidate other inmates. But gangs do not control all potentially violent inmates in an institution. One Matsqui lifer had served time previously at a prison with gangs, and he commanded enough backing among other life-sentenced inmates to retaliate if pushed to join:

This NS [Native Syndicate] guy was trying to tell me where to walk when I served time at Stony Mountain. One of the top Native Syndicate guys worked in the kitchen with me, so I went and talked to him. "If your guy wants problems, I'll give him problems. This guy doesn't want no problems," like, I said, "I don't want no problems. But if there is, I'm not afraid to," and I said, "If he wants to bring his friends, I'll bring my lifers, we're going to have a dance." So he straightened it out, and I was able to walk where ever I wanted. (Lifer, MI)

Finally, some inmates avoided enlistment by the unsavoury but necessary move to protective custody:

People were asking me when I first got here, "You're IP?," because of my tattoos and stuff. I was like, "No, man, I'm not a gang member," but pretty much everybody knew that I used to be. So I told them, "Man, I used to be, but I dropped out long time ago." Didn't help, wouldn't join, so now I'm on the TRU [transition unit, form of PC]. (Sentenced inmate and former gang member, SMI)

Despite the myths about the pervasive influence of gangs inside and outside prison, this inmate was unworried about his future safety. He had refused to join a gang and had gone into a TRU, but felt that if he kept quiet when he was released, he would be free of repercussions:

W: You refused to join another gang when your guys left. Now you are in PC. Are people going to bother you now when you're on the street?
I: No, I know a lot of gang members. If anybody asks, I'll just say I was in prison, not tell 'em much" (Remand inmate and ex-gang member, HCC)

Correctional Staff on Prison Gangs

Correctional staff generally concurred with inmates in their analysis of prison gangs. They viewed them as violent, difficult to control, and largely responsible for inmate separations, the increased number of incompatibles, and the more controlled movement often seen in prairie correctional institutions. Despite these problems, staff viewed the early years of prison gangs in the mid-1990s as much worse. They reported that drugs, extortion, and serious violence had been much more common in correctional institutions during that period. Segregation of gangs in separate units (the concentration method; see Chapter 1) in provincial centres had alleviated some problems, as had more focused efforts at gang control in federal institutions (Winterdyk & Ruddell, 2010).

This staff person viewed younger gang members as problematic. Some of the younger members trying to earn a reputation could pose problems:

> *Young guys, especially those in gangs, are much more hot-headed than the older guys. There is a lot more gang members here now, and a lot of them are just out to make their reputations. Some of the gangs are literally African Mafia type where they have come from war-torn and impoverished countries like Somalia, where they grew up not knowing if they were going to live or die from one day to the next.* (Staff, HCC)

This CO felt that the concentration method reduced some of the problems gangs could create, but ultimately gave them more indirect influence in limiting Headingley's ability to place inmates. Maintaining specific gang ranges was a burden:

> *W: Didn't gangs have more influence twelve or fifteen years ago, around the time of the [1996] riot?*
> *I: No, there is more influence of the gangs now because we have to keep them apart so much more. Different gangs can't get along. It can change from day to day, too. Maintaining separations with 700 inmates in a place [HCC] that is supposed to hold about 350 is hard enough, and then you throw in the gangs. On Monday morning, this group gets along with that group so you figure, "Okay, if I am stuck for space, I can mix them." The next thing you know, someone is gouging the other guy's eye out with a pen. "Oh," you say, "I guess these two groups don't get along anymore now."* (Staff, HCC)

Nonetheless, prison gangs were thought to have eroded the quality of inmate life because of the violence they meted out against other gangs, among themselves, and of course against other inmates. While a few staff pointed out that gang members were not the only troublesome inmates, the consensus was that prison gangs had diminished institutional life for other inmates:

> *The gangs don't cause all the violence. I think that gangs are more interested now in moving drugs, making money, having power, than they are in just being vile to each other.* (Staff, SMI)

> *I would argue that violence has increased, when you think of the rituals of gang membership, rites of passage to get into a gang, involve violence. It can be committed randomly on innocents. I'm confident that gangs increase violence by some factor. Posturing is necessary in gangs, to show you are tough and constantly prove it. When you're an independent, there's not quite so much of a demand to impress your associates.* (Staff, SMI)

Staff relations with prison gang members could be difficult. This staff person found that prison gang members generally were reluctant to talk to him and assumed a fairly restrained approach in relations.

> *The gang members can be very reluctant to talk. I have had them come to my office, but they just hang by the door, looking over their shoulder, reluctant to come in. It's difficult to work with some of them.* (Staff, SMI)

Prison gang members who liked to talk to staff could still be difficult. This CO at Fort Saskatchewan found that gang inmates were likely to push on rules and regulations:

> *Some of the gang members can be pushy, so you have to be firm with them. If you give an inch, they'll keep pushing.* (Staff, FSCC)

Some staff members appeared to feel that prison gang inmates were manageable. This younger CO believed that he could relate to at least some prison gang inmates:

> *Some of these gang guys are just lost. They don't have much of a family behind them except the gang. Being young myself, I don't find it hard to talk to them or get them interested in things.* (Staff, HCC)

There was some disagreement over the amount of violence within the gangs themselves. Intra-gang violence was very difficult to detect or officially record, because gang members are perhaps the least likely inmates to inform staff that they had been victimized. But conflict over one's position in the gang, and the inherently aggressive nature of certain gang members, could result in violence. This Headingley CO observed violence even on a unit designated for a specific gang:

> There is a lot of animosity within gangs. For instance, the Manitoba Warriors have their own unit downstairs. But things are happening all the time, and these guys are not getting along. They are beating each other up, so they are no longer focused on what I can do for my gang. I think there is more violence within their own gangs than anywhere else. (Staff, HCC)

Correctional Staff Setting Boundaries for Prison Gang Frames

Correctional staff had to make strong efforts to manage prison gang members (see Figure 10.1). Being cautious and paying close attention to gang members was an important frame to adhere to. Principles that guided staff behaviour included watching gang members carefully, firmly enforcing rules, and not letting gangs intimidate you. Despite all of this, staff viewed prison gang members as capable of benefiting from programs, and they viewed involving prison gangs in them as part of their responsibility:

> We have to monitor gang members, but we have a responsibility to try and rehabilitate all our inmates. So you have to work with gang members and establish a correctional plan. You can't just give up on them. Some will benefit. (Staff, SMI)

This Stony Mountain program officer felt that it was possible to involve gang members in programs and that this was a way to get them to interact and gain respect for other inmates:

> Different gang members are not supposed to mix. They are not supposed to eat together, take rec together, be on the same unit. But when I interview guys for my program, what I have personally found is when I am showing

a gang guy a list of who is in the program, nine times out of ten guys will say, "I don't have a problem with these other guys." So we have Indian Posse and Native Syndicate ending up in the program, and I am not saying they become best friends in there. But what is interesting is the barriers kind of come down a little bit. They start to work in a group. You see them going out for a smoke together. Is it all a façade? Maybe, but maybe they also can start to realize all this hype of us versus them isn't going anywhere. You can still work with these gang guys. (Staff, SMI)

Strategies for Dealing with Prison Gangs

The dispersal and concentration methods of prison gang management were outlined earlier. Dispersal methods separate gang members by placing them throughout the institution; concentration restricts them to one unit with limited movement. When asked how best to deal with gangs, inmates favoured the concentration method. Inmates overall endorsed segregating prison gang inmates in their own unit and not allowing them out into the general population. They felt that prison gang inmates could not be trusted to behave appropriately in population. They believed that containment provided other prisoners with the greatest safety and that there should be some penalty associated with being a gang member. Some went so far as to suggest a separate prison for gang members.

Alberta's provincial system allowed a smaller proportion of gang members at Fort Saskatchewan, and they were dispersed in the general population, which kept their influence small. Alberta Corrections concentrated most of the prison gang leaders and higher-risk members at the Edmonton Remand Centre. At Headingley, large gangs like the Manitoba Warriors were placed on a separate unit, while small gangs were dispersed in population. Stony Mountain likewise used a mixed approach, with the troublesome Indian Posse held in a separate unit, while the Native Syndicate and Manitoba Warriors were dispersed and allowed out in general population. About a year after my interviews, Stony Mountain resorted to the concentration method to separate the larger prison gangs, after a large gang-related conflict and disturbance. Finally, Matsqui had only a few gang members, who were not a problem, and hence administration did not follow any strategy for managing them.

This Fort Saskatchewan inmate thought that the system in Alberta – isolating inmates at the old Remand Centre – was effective. Keeping prison gang inmates out of general population was key:

> But if you can somehow take the gangs out of the system. Look at the system that they have in Alberta provincial. Keeping the serious gang guys at the Edmonton Remand Centre, that's mellowed things a bit here at the Fort. I think that idea with the new remand centre they are building, keep the gangs out of population, that will help. (Remand inmate, FSCC)

A few inmates believed that gangs were unstoppable by correctional authorities. These Stony Mountain and Headingley inmates believed that gangs would find a way to work around their restrictions and always find someone to victimize:

> Letting these gang members collect all in the same unit, that doesn't help either. The twenty-six gang members on the thirty-bed unit going to prey on the five or six other guys that are on that one unit. (Sentenced inmate and ex-gang member, SMI)

> Gangs will not be stopped. You can take half the guys from one of the blocks and move them up to Edmonton, to be with the Angels and Zig Zags, and they'll still run things here. Okay, this guy goes, then this guy will move up. (Remand inmate and gang associate, HCC)

Federal and provincial authorities have used involuntary transfers (wide dispersal) to manage troublesome inmates for many years. Inmates who are transferred have their social networks disrupted and are "sent a message" that their behaviour is unacceptable. Efforts at this strategy with prison gang members in western Canada have generally been considered a spectacular failure. Moreover, this strategy has been blamed for the spread of prison gangs from Manitoba to Saskatchewan and Alberta. In the late 1990s the CSC decided to transfer problematic prison gang inmates from Stony Mountain to other prairie institutions to reduce problems in Manitoba and to informally discourage these inmates from misbehaviour. It was acknowledged to Jana Grekul and Patti Laboucane-Benson (2008) in their interviews with staff that this initiative helped spread prison gangs to Saskatchewan and Alberta. Despite this abject policy failure, some federally experienced inmates felt that gang leaders should have been shipped to other institutions to sap the strength of prairie gangs – a selective use of the dispersal strategy. This Headingley prisoner suggested that prison gang leaders be sent to the Ontario, Quebec, and Atlantic CSC regions, where existing gangs were smaller in numbers and did not recruit, or recruited sparingly. They felt that prison gangs would not be tolerated by these inmate populations:

> *A lot of it has to do with the main players, the leaders. If they shipped a lot of the leaders to different jails, it would shut down a lot of gangs, man. Also, get some kind of inmate exchange with other jails. Out of region, like British Columbia, Ontario, and Quebec, they don't put up with gang member bullshit. They don't gangbang down there, man. They got old school mentality. It's easier to do time down there. Take a bunch of guys from down east, bring them here, that would change a lot of shit you know.* (Remand inmate and ex-gang member, HCC)

However, a staff member involved in the original prairie dispersal in the late 1990s did not favour such a move:

> *Look, once bitten. Transferring all those inmates out to Edmonton Max, Sask Pen, it all seemed like a great idea that had worked before, but failed miserably and spread the gangs around. Street gangs are growing in the east; all we need is some of the leaders out here to get sent to their institutions. We'll see how long BC keeps gangs out. If the east sent their guys here, then we'd get them connected to our gangs. Why would we want that?* (Staff, SMI)

Given the failure of the prairie gang leader dispersal strategy in the late 1990s, inmates are likely quite optimistic in assuming that a similar transfer policy would work. The extension of gang ties and networks across Canada is a potentially disastrous downside. Furthermore, with prison gangs becoming more of a problem in Ontario, this seems less and less likely to be a viable intervention.

Staff described concentration as one method of managing gangs, but they also provided an overview of its disadvantages. It was felt that putting gangs in separate units would see staff give up power – specifically, it would give "control" of the housing space to the gang, which would hold the power to approve who came onto the unit:

> *Sometimes you have to separate them, but I don't like it. When they have their own range, then we have to check with them when we put an inmate in; it's like they're in charge. We are supposed to be running the jail, not them.* (Staff, HCC)

Staff also observed that even when gangs were segregated into separate units in institutions like Headingley, there were ways for them to recruit other inmates or arrange assaults on them. They had observed that because most concentration programs have a reintegration feature, sometimes prison gang members would pretend to leave a gang to enable them to exit the separated unit and enter general population. Once there, the gang member could recruit further and even arrange assaults on other inmates:

> *They can be crafty. An inmate can come and claim that they no longer want to be a part of a gang for their own reasons. So our process is to then ask them, "Where do you think you would fit in?" They are given the opportunity to say, "Well, I'd like the third floor because it's a very mellow floor." So they get to go to that location. For the first week or two, they stay pretty calm, cool, and collected. Then all of a sudden, they're running that floor, and now they're recruiting, muscling, "playing the heavy" [intimidating] in here. So within a month, he is moved from general population and put back in his gang unit. So they have their ways of getting at people or getting things they want to do to solve issues.*
>
> *They also have a lot of associates, young guys who want to impress. So the older guys will tell them to pretend they are leaving the gang and ask to be on a certain unit. Once there, they may have to beat someone up because the gang doesn't like him. It's not as bad as it used to be, but they can still find ways to cause problems even when we isolate them.* (Staff, HCC)

How did prison gang inmates see themselves as best being managed? Not surprisingly, they rejected the leader dispersal strategy. Prison gang inmates did not feel that the dispersal strategy would work because other gang members would be promoted to leadership if anyone was transferred out. They felt that the best way to "manage" prison gangs was to let them deal with smaller issues with other inmates on their own, and meet and discuss larger issues. This approach has some possible benefits; however, Stony Mountain appeared to be trying this approach when a disturbance involving three gangs occurred, and then there is the matter of a deboarding ceremony (beat-out) in 2003 that resulted in the death of an inmate allegedly leaving a gang. Putting faith in the ability of prison gangs to frame relations with others without involving violence poses a large risk for corrections officials.

Conclusion

The emergence of prison gangs in prairie correctional institutions is one of the most substantive changes in Canadian prison life over the past twenty-five years. The American and (albeit limited) Canadian literature on prison gangs presents them as a negative feature of institutional life, associated with the drug trade, predation and bullying of other inmates, and increases in lethal violence. The findings presented here do not dispute this research. Gangs have hurt the quality of prison life for other inmates. The qualitative data here paint a grim picture of the anger and frustration brought on by prison gang activities. Moreover, the prison gang frame essentially places more restrictions and cautions on non-gang inmates' institutional life, a life that already offers limited choices. Some inmates are already prison gang members when they are incarcerated; other inmates join for status, safety, and physical rewards. Pressure for suitable candidates to join is severe, and even when the benefits are not enticing enough, the alternative of violence is stark. Eligible inmates require considerable courage and fortitude, and perhaps good luck, to avoid prison gangs or (if they refuse) to escape gang violence.

Staff put on a different face when interacting with prison gang members, being a bit more cautious in their dealings with them. Their perseverance in offering programs is laudable, and is not inconsistent with other research findings that show prison gang inmates will take programs and benefit from them (Di Placido, Simon, Witte, Gu, & Wong, 2006; but cf. Weinrath, Murchison, & Markesteyn, 2013).

From a policy perspective, careful classification and protection, where possible, of new admissions is important to limit the recruitment efforts of inmates. Support should be offered to inmates who wish to leave or who have been targeted by prison gangs for victimization. Many prison gang members lack education and skills (Nafekh, 2002), thus emphasis on their involvement in programs should continue. Evidence of effective prison gang interventions was not readily found in the literature, and I did not find any particular winning strategy in my research. Dispersal and concentration methods were applied in different ways by each prairie institution, with modifications made as the inmate population dynamics changed or as events required the restriction of prison gang member movement. Situational applications of strategies essentially were based on the level of problems: dispersal was used when possible because it allowed for freer movement and easier inmate placement. If problems in the population became severe (usually serious assaults), concentration methods were used and gangs were isolated in specific units. It should be observed that access to programs by prison gang members was severely limited when they were confined to one unit. So it is recommended that the dispersal method be used whenever possible, for it supports inmates in any potential efforts by them to change.

Conclusion

This book examines the past twenty-five years of institutional corrections in Canada, largely through the eyes of two main stakeholder groups: inmates and correctional staff (with an emphasis on correctional officers). Has there been progress in Canada's correctional institutions, or just more problems? Goffman's frame analysis (1974) has provided a useful perspective for understanding how individual inmates and COs transition into their roles and how their self-presentations and day-to-day interactions unfold. It also helps us grasp at least some of their motivations and the contexts in which those motivations might change. Support was found for the adoption of procedurally just behaviours by correctional staff. The respondents concurred that COs who applied procedural justice enhanced their legitimacy, which helped them gain greater compliance from inmates. While some clear progress can be seen in Canada's provincial and federal institutions, problems persist, some old and some new. These are discussed below, along with suggestions for policies that would improve prison life. The chapter closes with a discussion of the study's limitations and data validity and with suggestions for future research.

Inmate Frames and CO Frames

Inmate frames were constructed through respondent interviews. Transitions for inmates are influenced by their criminal past, alcohol and drug use, and gang and family backgrounds, but remain difficult regardless of past socialization and life experiences. The stigma of being incarcerated has not changed over the years and is still a shock for offenders, even those with long criminal histories. Managing the stigma of becoming (or becoming again) an inmate structures their guarded relations with other offenders and with COs; it also drives the need for respect and the building of frames of being strong and being smart (e.g., do not be a victim). Even after prisoners have moderately adjusted to institutional life, most of them form few meaningful friendships. The features of the old inmate code promoting solidarity are largely gone, although a certain measure of social distance from staff is still emphasized. Some inmates, especially gang inmates, seek to exploit others through intimidation, gambling, selling illicit drugs, or distributing contraband. Relations with staff also vary, although COs who engage in procedurally just behaviours are given more respect. In their relations with external others, inmates generally assume a pro-social face that is not always an honest frame. Some inmates value hearing about the outside from family or friends, but others often find this painful, to the point that many offenders limit or cut off contact with the outside. Inmates support correctional programs; they have a preference for vocational offerings but also see value in behavioural treatment. Unfortunately, what remains of the inmate code is still strong enough to discourage inmates from practising skills learned in treatment programs.

COs also go through a period of adjustment when they enter a prison and seek to gain respect from both their peers and the inmates. They learn to adopt a demeanour of strength and toughness, and they try to avoid showing fear. While social distance has diminished, COs still cannot be too friendly with inmates. Ways to gain respect from fellow staff include being competent, not embarrassing another officer in front of an inmate, and not informing on another officer or being too friendly with management. Effectiveness in managing inmates is also valued. Staff training has improved significantly over the years, and COs are generally better prepared than twenty-five years ago, when officers were hired "by the pound." To gain legitimacy with inmates, showing respect is most important; so is being courteous, empathetic, non-judgmental, and knowledgeable about institutional rules. Being physically on the unit is also valued. Avoiding unjust behaviours is perhaps even more important: disrespect, not listening, not caring about an inmate's race-related culture, and being punitive in enforcing rules were all identified as problematic by inmates. The largest change in staff–inmate relations was a shrinking of social distance, which allowed staff to engage in more proactive problem solving by gathering more information from inmates. New challenges and broken frames now exist in the areas of boundary maintenance and illicit behaviour by COs. More communication with inmates is not always for the better.

Progress

Efforts to develop correctional staff who interact with inmates and utilize a dynamic supervision style date from the early 1970s and now appear to have "arrived" in Canada. COs have come to accept the new expectations placed on them. Over the past twenty-five years, the building of more new-generation prisons, policy changes that have established a casework function for COs, and technology that allows COs to learn about their cases have all contributed considerably to changes in the CO role. The need for greater interaction between COs and inmates has helped erode the inmate code of conduct and partly collapsed the social distance between COs and inmates. Inmates report having few friendships, which suggests that the informal networks among inmates have been dissolving over the past twenty-five years. This lack of inmate camaraderie has created more potential for COs to establish relationships with inmates and to influence them informally. Achieving legitimacy is a tactic worth pursuing: both inmate and staff respondents supported CO behaviours such as fairness, consistency, listening, competence, and some level of empathy for the difficult position of inmates. Findings indicate that staff training and annual personnel evaluations need to emphasize Liebling's "tactics of talk" and the adoption of procedurally just behaviours. When properly used, increased dialogue between inmates and staff has contributed to better security. Correctional staff report getting information from inmates that allows them to prevent problems and deal with issues.

Stricter policies and more thorough investigations, as well as the use of video cameras, were reported to have reduced the incidence of physical assaults by COs to control inmates. While female COs experienced considerable resistance and harassment from their male colleagues when they first came on the scene in the 1980s, there has been improvement in this regard since the introduction and enforcement of sexual harassment policies in the 1990s, and because of the increasing presence of young males who grew up with working mothers.

Overall, inmate and correctional staff respondents favoured educational/vocational training over behavioural treatment, likely because of the working-class background of most offenders. Yet support for cognitive-behavioural treatment (and for programs generally) was still strong among inmate respondents, including (surprisingly) long-term inmates, offenders with long criminal histories, and prison gang members. Clearly, inmates were interested in making constructive use of their time in custody. On the staff side, most respondents strongly endorsed programs and saw treatment as a key responsibility of correctional systems. Some staff were cynical about program effectiveness, but theirs was a minority position. While there are academic critics of CBT and rehabilitative programming generally (Farabee, 2005), it has been fairly well documented that treatment can reduce recidivism, albeit not as much as hoped (MacKenzie & Hickman, 2006). Cognitive-based programs have been shown to have an impact even on prison gang members (Di Placido et al., 2006).

Two programs that were noticeable in their impact on their respective local institutions were the Ni-Miikana Pathways unit at Stony Mountain and the peer support program at Matsqui. The Ni-Miikana unit seemed to provide an opportunity for inmates to pursue Aboriginal culture, but even more than this, it provided a respite from the negative influences of other inmates in the institution. Avoiding negative others and "crime talk" was valued by these individuals. Likewise, the peer support group, while challenging of staff authority, offered inmates a mechanism for pursuing grievances and solving problems with staff and administration in an informal manner. The peer support group also seemed to provide at least a few inmates with friendship within the institution.

Problems

Despite the decline in the force of the inmate code, significant challenges persist within correctional institutions. Because of the large number of remands throughout the country, a great many inmates have few constructive opportunities to spend their time. Double and triple bunking, limited recreation and movement around the institution, and short programs or no programs at all are features of prison life I observed or heard about at length. Overall, provincial custody rates and remand populations have increased since the time of my interviews, indicating that the problem has worsened, if anything. To improve prison life in Canada, reducing the number of remands is an important first step.

The greater dialogue between inmates and COs has not resulted in as positive a change in relations as might be expected. COs should have assumed greater non-coercive influence over inmates, and we should have observed less institutional violence. Few inmates report close relationships, and there has been a general decline in inmate solidarity, yet at the same time, COs have underachieved at improving legitimacy. While progress was observed, too many COs still fall short in their approach to the job, eschewing procedurally just measures and instead either relying on coercion or engaging in disrespectful behaviour that costs them legitimacy. Understanding the value of procedural justice must be a priority for Canadian COs.

Greater interaction has its downsides. Both staff and inmates observed that increased dialogue between COs and inmates is not always managed well; especially for younger staff, proper boundaries are an issue at times. Better training and mentorship would enhance performance, and other fields, such as social work, may have helpful experience to offer corrections in this nuanced area of communication and interpersonal relations. Respondents reported less illicit violence by COs towards inmates, but government inquiries indicate that this behaviour has not disappeared. COs recently have been found to succumb to temptation and are able to find video camera "blind spots" where they can enact their version of street justice (Marin, 2013). This problem is not unique to correctional staff, of course. To discourage police misbehaviour, law enforcement agencies have experimented with body-worn video cameras, and the preliminary results of this are promising: citizen complaints are down in pilot studies. Respondents expressed a strong belief that cameras had discouraged a fair bit of misbehaviour, so it seems very likely that body-worn cameras would encourage proper CO conduct and greater inmate compliance.

It is difficult to ascertain the level of violence in correctional institutions, although the Correctional Investigator has indicated that inmate assaults and injuries are on the rise in federal penitentiaries (Sapers, 2014). An unfortunate corollary to the reported lack of solidarity and friendships among inmates is the increase in the number of inmates who are "incompatible" with others, to the point that serious violence ensues unless certain offenders are separated. The old convict code edict, "problems from outside are left on the street," is no longer respected – a very unfortunate shift in relations among inmates. Incompatibles have to contend with even more constrained movement within the institution, further eroding the quality of inmate life. Prison gangs are another negative change over the past twenty-five years in Canada's correctional institutions. These gangs are contributing to general violence and to the increase in incompatibles. Their intimidation of other inmates is also a concern. Prison gang involvement in programs is a laudable development that should be further encouraged; even so, concentration strategies may be necessary to limit assaults on inmates and other illicit activities.

On the Reliability and Validity of the Data

A content analysis of criminology and criminal justice journals by Heath Copes, Anastasia Brown, and Richard Tewksbury (2011) revealed that of 4,743 articles, only 175, or 3.69 percent, were qualitative, which points to a preference for quantitative methods in the field. Qualitative research has been praised for the richness of its data and for its descriptive strengths but is not considered strong in terms of its external validity (i.e., its generalizability to other settings) because of its lack of large, representative samples. The present study was pursued using a qualitative methodology because, frankly, I felt that a quantitative survey could not really get at the essence of prison life in the same way that interviews and site visits would. I contend that there are several features of this study that speak to the reliability and validity of the findings reported here.

This qualitative research involved interviews of thirty-seven inmate and twenty-four staff respondents, as well as some limited observation by myself at four western Canadian institutions. Multi-site studies are rare in qualitative correctional investigations, and the present sample is relatively large for this type of research. For example, Copes and his colleagues (2011) found that the average sample size for all qualitative studies published in criminology and criminal justice journals was 46.33, considerably lower than my total of 61 respondents. While there were some clear distinctions between the sites (federal versus provincial, remand versus sentenced, provincial differences in inmate demographics), the similarities in the interview findings support the validity of the data. For example, the consistency of inmates and staff developing and applying frames speaks to their trustworthiness in describing and explaining inmate or staff behaviour. The retrospective nature of the interviews in some instances is also a potential weakness, given the vagaries of memory, but in other ways it is a strength. Respondents often recalled or summarized experiences pertaining not just to their current custodial placement but also to other institutions, increasing our confidence that these findings are applicable to other correctional settings. Data analysis involved using the constant comparative method, whereby I stopped searching for themes when they became repetitive in the data. Indeed, while it was useful to travel to Matsqui as a non-prairie site, the respondents there most often did not add much to what had already been revealed to me about changes in prison life.

Morse and her colleagues (2008) believe that verification of qualitative data depends less on efforts to "audit" studies and more on the quality of the researcher's original design and sampling, and of research decisions made along the way. Thus, my decision to sample older, experienced inmates and staff (with a few younger gang inmates for that part of the study) was, to my mind, a successful means to address one of the original research questions. Also, there were several avenues I pursued based on the subjects' initial responses. Specifically, I added questions about female COs in male institutions as well as the influence of policy, architecture, and technology on prison life.

Triangulation through comparison to related research is an important strategy for validating or increasing confidence in the findings of qualitative or quantitative studies. While there are some unique findings in this study, my data are remarkably consistent with the extant prison research, and many of the changes over the past twenty-five years have been observed in other correctional jurisdictions. Some of the Canadian, American, British, and Dutch studies reviewed have found similar inmate and CO transitions and shifts in the inmate subculture, as well as similar changes in the communication between COs and inmates, and comparable impacts from policy on correctional staff behaviour. Likewise, prison gangs have presented remarkably similar problems in American jurisdictions as those reported here.

The applicability of the data across Canada can be questioned, given that this study has focused on western Canada. But one can then ask the same question of recent books by Rose Ricciardelli (2014b), Melissa Munn and Chris Bruckert (2013), and Elizabeth Comack (2008); are they generalizable past Ontario or Manitoba? This may well be an unreasonable restriction. Furthermore, the key evidence supporting generalizability is likely the consistency between many of this study's findings and those from other countries. The social isolation of inmates, the growth in interaction between inmates and COs, and the belief in procedurally just behaviours have all certainly been documented in other locales (Beijersbergen, Dirkzwager, Eichelsheim, et al., 2014b; Crewe et al., 2013; Liebling, 2004).

Finally, some reviewers may challenge the ability of qualitative interviewers to ferret out accurate motivations or depictions of behaviour; perhaps they were being duped by respondents who were not telling the truth or were fabricating accounts to put themselves in a favourable light – something that inmates may be more likely to do (see Comack's [2008] response to this criticism). This study has the advantage of having used interviews with thirty-seven inmates at four different facilities, thus increasing the chances that deception would be detected at some point (would all thirty-seven fake the same things?). The interviewer (me) had the advantage of having worked in corrections for fourteen years, including four spent in a correctional institution, and having had substantial past interview experience with both staff and inmates. I am confident that I have been able to sort through the data and identify the key findings and unanticipated results relevant to the original research questions.

Limitations of the Study and Future Research

This study was ambitious in that it tried to address changes in the institutional world for both staff and inmates in male institutions, and gain some insight into prison life today. Not all areas of importance in the field of corrections were addressed, and some topics did not receive the attention that perhaps they deserved. Female inmates – an important segment of the inmate population – were unfortunately not covered. I did interview a female inmate at Fort Saskatchewan Correctional Centre but decided the interview was insufficient to do any meaningful comparative analysis with males in the study. The experience of Aboriginal inmates was assessed, but not to the depth I would have liked. Central features of prison life, such as violence and illicit drug use, were discussed in this book, but not as systematically as others might have done. Case management staff, their relations with inmates, and the connection between preparation for release and dealing with everyday prison issues are all key components of prison life. Prison regimes and conditions and the efforts of non-correctional officer staff likely affect the perspectives of inmates, whose views on these things were not evaluated in this research. In the end, researching and writing a book requires making decisions based on the strength of the data, what the author thinks is important, and what will be of most value; hopefully, I have made a few proper decisions here.

Future research could more thoroughly investigate the influence of policy, architecture, and technology in shaping CO–inmate interactions based on the subjects' perceptions. These areas, especially technology, would benefit from more systematic study (Aas, 2004). Others have suggested that computers will depersonalize staff–offender relations, but I found the opposite. The work experience of female COs seems to have improved, but the most recent research in this area is not so positive (Samak, 2003). This area needs to be updated. Given the differing ratios of females to males working in provincial and federal prisons, this subject is ripe for a comparative study (i.e., does more women on the job improve the CO work environment?).

Given the problem of inmate isolation (i.e., few friends), treatment units like Ni-Miikana at Stony Mountain and friendship/mentor-based programs like the peer support program at Matsqui merit further study. These programs present as means to promote positive interaction between inmates (more "change talk," less "crime talk") and to encourage constructive transformation (Maruna, 2001). Prison gangs have been dealt with primarily using concentration and dispersal methods (Winterdyk & Ruddell, 2010). Research into these strategies might evaluate when either method is appropriate, and in what circumstances. Gangs are a pernicious concern, and their violence is too often lethal, necessitating ongoing scrutiny.

Much more needs to be done to see procedural justice applied effectively in institutions. There is strong consensus on what is appropriate or just behaviour by criminal justice agents, and a body of research is growing that shows associations with inmate well-being and more positive behaviour (Beijersbergen, Dirkzwager, Eichelsheim, et al., 2014b; Liebling, 2004, 2011). Yet complaints continue against police and COs, and studies such as this one still find too many workers engaging in counterproductive behaviours. A recent study by Alison Liebling and Helen Arnold (2012) found that a prison had regressed in staff–inmate relations, increasing fear among COs and staff. Legitimacy in a correctional institution is fragile.

An important first step is to establish procedural justice modules within training regimes and research whether that training transfers to the job (Cole & Latham, 1997). A mix of quantitative and qualitative approaches would be useful here. What is the likelihood that new officers will buy into the need for legitimacy, and what factors might preclude this? What is the influence of senior staff on the adoption of procedurally just behaviours, or the avoidance of disrespectful ones? A broad-based research project on procedural justice in Canada, including in the eastern provinces, could bring to light different approaches and help identify methods for achieving legitimacy in prison settings.

Some progress has been made in Canadian prisons over the past twenty-five years, but meaningful change is unlikely unless COs become more effective as agents of change. Instead of simply applying principles of procedural justice, COs need to realize their own potential to positively influence inmates. Being a CO and trying to influence offenders is challenging work, and there are good and bad ways to go about it. Prisons were originally intended to be places of reformation and change – problematic goals when one is managing security, preventing harm, and trying to stay safe. I believe that Canada's correctional institutions can become less violent and more humane places for offenders, and provide them with constructive ways to spend their time as well as opportunities for self-development. But if progress is to be made, ambition to move forward is needed on the part of correctional authorities and their staff.

Appendix: Interview Guide

Inmate Interview Questions (estimate: 2–3 hours)

1. Admission
   1.1. What was it like for you the first time you were admitted to prison?
   1.2. What was it like for you this last time?
   1.3. What about yourself has changed since you were admitted to prison?
   1.4. What about you has stayed the same, whether inside or outside prison?
2. Prison Life, General
   2.1. Tell me a bit about a typical day at this prison for you.
   2.2. What do you look forward to each day?
   2.3. What do you not look forward to?
   2.4. What is the most difficult thing about prison life for you?
   2.5 What has changed about prison life over the last twenty years (for older inmates)?
   2.6. How would you compare this prison to others you have been in? What is good about it, what is not good?
3. Relationships with Other Inmates
   3.1. Describe your relationships with other inmates. Do you have anyone you feel close to?
   3.2. Do you trust most other inmates? Why or why not?
   3.3. Do you spend much time with other inmates?

4. Relationships with Staff

    4.1. How do you get along with correctional officers?

    4.2. What makes a good correctional officer?

    4.3. What makes a bad correctional officer?

    4.4. How do you get along with case management staff?

    4.5. What makes a good case manager?

    4.6. What makes a bad case manager?

5. External Relationships

    5.1. Do you maintain contact with your family? How do you do this?

    5.2. Do you receive letters from people outside?

    5.3. Do you receive visits? Who visits you?

    5.4. How frequently do you maintain contact with people outside?

6. Programming

    6.1. How important are education or rehabilitation programs to you? How about for others in prison?

    6.2. What type of programs are you taking?

    6.3. What type of program(s) would you like to take?

7. Work

    7.1. Tell me something about your work life in prison.

    7.2. How important is work to you?

    7.3. What kind of work did you do when you were outside?

    7.4. What kind of work would you like to do?

8. Leisure Time

    8.1. What type of activities are you involved in during your spare time?

    8.2. What do you spend most of your time doing?

    8.3. What type of activities would you like to be involved in?

9. Violence

    When answering the following questions, please do not admit to committing any assault.

    9.1. Do you consider this prison to be violent?

    9.2. How much do you worry about being assaulted by another inmate?

    9.3. Have you been assaulted by anyone in the last three months?

    9.4. Have you been threatened by anyone in the last three months?

    9.5. What would you do to reduce violence or the threat of violence in this prison?

10. Drugs

> In the following section, please do not directly admit to any drug use or specific knowledge of drug users.

    10.1. Are drugs a problem in this prison?

    10.2. Are drugs easy to get in this prison?

    10.3. What types of drugs (have you heard) people can get in this prison?

11. Inmate Code

    11.1. In prison, there is rumoured to be an inmate code, or unwritten rules that you have to live by. Is this true? If so, what are the rules?

    11.2. How important is it to follow the rules of the inmate code?

    11.3. What type of inmate is respected in this prison?

    11.4. What is your opinion of what should happen to an informant?

12. Prison Gangs

    12.1. What impact do prison gangs have on day-to-day life in this prison? What kind of activities are they involved in?

    12.2. Do you belong to a prison gang? How did you join (recruit inside or outside, asked to join)?

    12.3. If not, were you recruited and refused?

    12.4. How much influence do prison gangs have in this prison?

    12.5. What kind of impact have prison gangs had on prison life over the past fifteen years?

13. Life after Prison

    13.1. Do you think much about what you will do when you are released?

    13.2. Are you doing anything to prepare yourself?

    13.3. What do you think correctional services could do to help you?

    13.4. Are you worried about getting back into the community? If so, what do you worry about?

    13.5. How likely do you think it is that you will avoid trouble when you are released?

Staff Questions (estimate: 2–3 hours)

1. Admission

    1.1. What was it like for you the first time you began working in prison?

1.2. What about yourself has changed since you began working in prison?

1.3. What about you has stayed the same, whether inside or outside prison?

2. Prison Life, General

2.1. Tell me a bit about a typical day at this prison for you.

2.2. What do you look forward to each day?

2.3. What do you not look forward to?

2.4. What is the most difficult thing about prison work for you?

2.5. What has changed about prison life over the last twenty years (for senior staff)?

2.6. How would you compare this prison to others you have been in? What is good about it, what is not good?

3. Relationships with Inmates

3.1. How do you get along with inmates?

3.2. What sort of relationship should correctional officers maintain with inmates?

4. Programming

4.1. How important are education or rehabilitation programs for inmates?

4.2. What type of programs do you think are most important?

5. Leisure Time

5.1. What type of activities do you observe inmates involved in during their spare time?

5.2. What type of activities should they be involved in?

6. Violence

6.1. Do you consider this prison to be violent?

6.2. How much do you worry about being assaulted by an inmate?

6.3. Have you been assaulted by anyone in the last three months?

6.4. Have you been threatened by anyone in the last three months?

6.5. What would you do to reduce violence or the threat of violence in this prison?

7. Drugs

7.1. In your opinion, are drugs a problem in this prison?

7.2. In your opinion, are drugs easy to get in this prison?

8. Inmate Code

    8.1. In prison, there is rumoured to be an inmate code, or unwritten rules that inmates live by. Is this true? If so, what are the rules?

    8.2. How important is it for inmates to follow the rules of the inmate code?

    8.3. What type of inmate is respected by staff in this prison?

9. Prison Gangs

    9.1. What impact do prison gangs have on day-to-day life in this prison? What kind of activities are they involved in?

    9.2. Are inmates recruited into gangs in this prison?

    9.3. How much influence do prison gangs have in this prison?

    9.4. What kind of impact have prison gangs had on prison life over the past fifteen years?

10. Changes

    10.1. What have been the most important changes in prison life over the past fifteen to twenty years (since you have started)?

    10.2. What changes have you seen in Correctional Officer staff? Program staff?

Notes

Introduction

1 On the one hand, increasingly, offenders or ex-offenders are identifying themselves as "prisoners" and have indicated that they consider the term "inmate" pejorative (e.g., see *Journal of Prisoners on Prisons*). On the other hand, "inmate" is a term commonly used in North American corrections- and justice-related research literature and is not intended by most administrators or academics as a repressive term. I fall into the latter camp and hope nothing derogatory is presumed by my use of this term in the book. I also find that "prisoner" is a term commonly used by staff in British, Australian, and New Zealand correctional systems, but have never found any demeaning intent by those organizations.

2 "Aboriginal" refers to Indigenous Canadians, such as First Nations peoples, Metis, Inuit, or Dene. Aboriginals used to be referred to as "Indians," then "Natives." Some of my Aboriginal faculty colleagues prefer the term "Indigenous peoples." I use "Aboriginal" and "Indigenous" interchangeably.

Chapter 1: Canadian Prisons and Their Problems

1 Some researchers feel that the amount of crime actually peaked in the 1970s and that the "increase" for crimes against persons in the 1980s was due to differences in what was reported and officially recorded by the police. New laws in 1983 made it easier to report domestic violence and sexual assault, and also made it simpler for police to lay charges for any type of assault (Kingsley, 1994). Consider that homicide, a good barometer of crime rates because it is always reported, held steady in the 1980s, diminished in the 1990s, and in 2012 hit its lowest point since 1967.

2 Custody use actually peaked in the early 1980s, and then declined despite an increase in reported crime. In the 1990s the custody rate bumped up again, and then did not sag until the late 1990s. It has been rising dramatically in Manitoba in the 2000s, one of the provinces represented in this study.

3 Canada was one of a number of nations introducing dispositions like conditional sentences during the late 1980s and 1990s (for a review, see Roberts, 2004). Conditional sentence offenders get dispositions of two years' custody (or less) that they can serve under community supervision. Conditions are more punitive than probation and include house arrest, curfews, and community work service. Enforcement is stricter than probation, and the onus is on the accused to show why they should be released once charged for violations. Penalties can include serving their original custody sentence. It is surprising that the introduction of conditional sentences did not have a larger impact on Canada's custody rate (Roberts 2004).

4 The federal committee chair was the former corrections minister during the Harris government's "slash and burn" years in Ontario, when private prisons were introduced and provincial parole eligibility reductions were engineered. Once elected, McGuinty's Liberal government rescinded all private prison contracts.

5 Elimination of statutory release would be a retrogressive step. Automatic release based on earned remission is a basic incentive in prisons throughout the world that dates back to the nineteenth-century Crofton system, which is premised on the common-sense idea that inmates can be motivated by incentives and rewards for good behaviour.

6 Security designation for remand inmates is largely moot: remand centre units are maximum security, thus even inmates held for minor crimes must all effectively serve "max" time.

7 The term "fish" to identify and stigmatize new admissions is still in common use in Canadian prisons.

8 Increasing numbers of inmates with mental disorders have posed challenges for federal and provincial authorities (Sapers 2014; Brown, Hirdes, & Fries, 2015). This issue is important, but I have not covered it because it is not directly related to the research reported here.

9 Meta-analysis utilizes strict criteria for including an empirical study (e.g., control or comparison group, random sample or assignment, appropriate indicator of institutional misconduct or recidivism, program criteria). Once appropriate studies have been identified, effect sizes are aggregated for a general summary of effects, and a relative program effect size. The Washington State Institute for Public Policy has a website dedicated to meta-analyses that rate the success of criminal justice interventions (http://www.cebma.info/wp-content/uploads/Drake-et-al-Evid-Based-Pub-Pol.pdf).

Chapter 2: The Prisons and the Interviews

1 Their status was confirmed by an Institutional Preventative Security Officer.

Chapter 3: How Inmates Understand Their Role

1 Subjects counted a young offender temporary detention or secure custody facility as custody; they did not include open custody (e.g., group home) as a first-time experience.

2   Goofs and nobodies were generally thought of as marginal players who do not understand prison life and are stigmatized by other inmates.

Chapter 5: How Correctional Officers Understand Their Role

1   CO gender was also a factor, but this will be discussed in more detail when we consider female officers in Chapter 8.

Chapter 8: Boundary Violations by Correctional Officers

1   Although these reports and legislation applied to federal corrections, the effects cascaded down to the provincial level. For example, this author remembers when he worked in provincial corrections in 1985 that a number of initiatives surrounding the disciplinary process and the "duty to act fairly" came into play. We were informed that these policies had all been developed in response to federal action after the *Martineau* decision.

2   "Tuning up" is slang for deterring an inmate from further misconduct by beating him. It has also been called "attitude adjustment."

3   In a strip search, one officer conducts the search while the other observes/provides back-up. For male inmate searches, two male officers are required.

Chapter 10: The Rise of Prison Gangs

1   An associate is a newer recruit who has yet to earn full gang member status.

2   The Deuce were once a mid-sized street gang but were taken over by larger gangs, usually the Manitoba Warriors. Some were in PC at HCC or in a transition unit at SMI at the time of the study.

3   SMI had a fatal deboarding incident in 2003, where a Native Syndicate inmate was violently "beaten out" of the gang and died due to his injuries.

Glossary: Correctional Terms and Inmate Argot

Bubble hound Male inmate who spends too much time talking to staff by their post (sometimes seated behind a glass bubble). Fairly new term used in Alberta provincial institutions.

CBT Cognitive behavioural therapy, a social psychological approach to programming that attempts to correct errors in thinking and target criminogenic risk/needs such as poor education or negative peers.

Correctional institution An umbrella term for Canadian prisons. Provincial institutions at one time used the term jail or the British "gaol," but now apply the term correctional centre (e.g., Headingley Correctional Centre) or remand centre. Federal facilities at one time exclusively used the term penitentiary, but now use the title "institution" (e.g., Matsqui Institution).

Crackhead A contemporary term denoting an inmate addicted to drugs (usually but not always crack cocaine) and determined to feed his addiction. Not to be trusted.

Dealer/supplier An inmate who distributes illicit drugs within the institution. Can be gang-affiliated or a lone operator.

Direct supervision A style of inmate management where correctional officers are to regularly interact with inmates and attempt to establish influence through relationships. In addition to being more knowledgeable about what is going on among inmates on the unit, officers are expected to know more about each inmate and any potential problems. Known as "dynamic security" in Canada's federal correctional system.

Dope fiend An inmate addicted to drugs and determined to feed his addiction. Not to be trusted. An old term that has been used for forty years.

Dynamic security Federal style of inmate management, also known as dynamic supervision. See *direct supervision*.

Gang associate In a prison gang, a newer recruit who has yet to earn full gang member status.

Goof A marginal inmate who is not socially skilled or tough, acts inappropriately, and is not respected within the institution. Susceptible to assault or exploitation by other inmates. Also used as an insult to denigrate another inmate or instigate a fight.

Incompatible An inmate who is targeted by other inmates for violence because of past conflicts in the community or institution. Often (but not always) gang-related. A relatively new term. Can include inmates who owe money for gambling, drug, or contraband debts.

Lifer An inmate serving a life sentence, usually for first or second degree murder.

Muscling Inmate intimidation of other inmates on a unit, usually for canteen or drugs.

Outlaw motorcycle gang Inmates affiliated with a community biker gang who continue this affiliation in the prison setting. Also called OMG.

Nobody An inmate of low status with either no friends or no friends of any consequence to other inmates. Susceptible to abuse or exploitation.

Panel mommy A female inmate who spends too much time talking to staff by their post (which is behind a big control panel). A fairly new term used in Alberta provincial institutions.

Phone bug An inmate incessantly on the telephone, typically phoning the same person over and over. They are most often observed to be calling a girlfriend or spouse.

Playing the heavy Denotes an aggressive inmate who is intimidating (muscling) other inmates on a unit.

Protective custody (PC) Placement where inmates are safe from predation by other inmates. Inhabitants include informants, sex offenders, and incompatible inmates targeted by others for assault because of past conflicts in the community.

Range A housing unit where inmates reside in their cells. Actually refers to an older, linear prison configuration, when large block tiers were in use. Although dated, inmates still like to use this term.

Rat An inmate who informs on other inmates to corrections staff.

Remand inmate An inmate held in custody awaiting trial. Typically held in custody for non-appearance. Also referred to as pre-trial detainees. They are accused, innocent until proven guilty, and not required to take treatment; however, many remands still participate in programs.

Rent Payment to an influential gang or group by a drug dealer for the privilege of dealing drugs. Also, might be paid by a "nobody" for protection, but according to my respondents, this is rare.

Security threat group (STG) Any group of three or more inmates who collude to violate institutional rules. This can involve intimidating or exploiting other inmates, or engaging in the drug trade or other aspects of the illicit *sub rosa* (underground) economy.

Sentenced inmate An inmate who has been found guilty and sentenced to a specific term of custody. Provincial sentences are less than two years; federal terms are two years and up.

Skinner A sex offender.

Solid An inmate who is knowledgeable about the informal and formal rules of the institution, will not act inappropriately, and is unlikely to inform on other inmates.

Storesman An inmate who trades in canteen goods or contraband such as illicit drugs. Interest is charged on canteen goods and contraband. Usurious rates are now common; a "two for one" exchange is frequently demanded.

***Sub rosa* economy** Underground (*sub rosa*), hidden contraband trade by inmates. Can include canteen, illicit drugs, or other items not authorized for inmates to possess in the institution. This phrase is most often used by researchers and some staff – not by inmates.

Transition units (TRUs) Units at Stony Mountain Institution at one time used to house inmates in danger from other inmates, or offenders who had become "incompatible." Included displaced gang members, inmates who could not pay gambling, drug, or contraband debts to other inmates, and other traditional protective custody inmates such as informants and sex offenders.

Tune-up A covert beating administered by correctional officers to troublesome inmates.

Unit A housing area where inmates reside in their cells.

References

Aas, K.F. (2004). From narrative to database technological change and penal culture. *Punishment and Society, 6*(4), 379–93. http://dx.doi.org/10.1177/1462474504046119

Adams, K. (1992). Adjusting to prison life. *Crime and Justice, 16*, 275–359. http://dx.doi.org/10.1086/449208

Anderson, E. (1999). *Code of the street: Decency, violence, and the moral life of the inner city.* New York: W.W. Norton.

Andrews, D., & Bonta, J. (2010). *The psychology of criminal conduct* (5th ed.). New York: Routledge.

Andrews, D., & Dowden, C. (2005). Managing correctional treatment for reduced recidivism: A meta-analytic review of programme integrity. *Legal and Criminological Psychology, 10*(2), 173–87. http://dx.doi.org/10.1348/135532505X36723

Andrews, D., Zinger, I., Hoge, R., Bonta, J., Gendreau, P., & Cullen, F. (1990). Does correctional treatment work? A clinically relevant and psychologically informed meta-analysis. *Criminology, 28*(3), 369–404. http://dx.doi.org/10.1111/j.1745-9125.1990.tb01330.x

Aos, S., Miller, M., & Drake, E. (2006). *Evidence-based adult corrections programs: What works and what does not.* Olympia: Washington State Institute for Public Policy.

Applegate, B. K., Surette, R., & McCarthy, B.J. (1999). Detention and desistance from crime: Evaluating the influence of a new generation jail on recidivism. *Journal of Criminal Justice, 27*(6), 539–48.

Arbour, L. (1996). *Commission of inquiry into certain events at the Prison for Women in Kingston.* Ottawa: Public Works and Government Services Canada.

Archambault, J. (1938). *Report of the Royal Commission to Investigate the Penal System of Canada.* Ottawa: King's Printer.

Arnold, H. (2005). The effects of prison work. In A. Liebling & S. Maruna (Eds.), *The effects of imprisonment* (pp. 391–420). Devon, UK: Willan.

Bales, W., & Mears, D. (2008). Inmate social ties and the transition to society: Does visitation reduce recidivism? *Journal of Research in Crime and Delinquency, 45*(3), 287–321. http://dx.doi.org/10.1177/0022427808317574

Bandura, A. (1977). Self-efficacy: Toward a unifying theory of behavioral change. *Psychological Review, 84*(2), 191–215. http://dx.doi.org/10.1037/0033-295X.84.2.191

Bateson, M., Nettle, D., & Roberts, G. (2006). Cues of being watched enhance cooperation in a real-world setting. *Biology Letters, 2*(3), 412–14. http://dx.doi.org/10.1098/rsbl.2006.0509

Beattie, K. (2006). *Adult correctional services in Canada.* Ottawa: Juristat.

Beetham, D. (1991). *The legitimation of power.* Basingstoke, UK: Palgrave Macmillan. http://dx.doi.org/10.1007/978-1-349-21599-7.

Beijersbergen, K.A., Dirzwager, A.J.E., Eichelsheim, V.I., van der Laan, P.H., & Nieuwbeerta, P. (2014a). Procedural justice and prisoners' mental health problems: A longitudinal study. *Criminal Behaviour and Mental Health, 24*(2), 100–12. http://dx.doi.org/10.1002/cbm.1881

–. (2014b). Procedural justice, anger, and prisoners' misconduct: A longitudinal study. *Criminal Justice and Behavior, 42*(2), 1–23. http://dx.doi.org/10.1177/0093854814550710

Beijersbergen, K.A., Dirkzwager, A.J.E., Molleman, T., van der Laan, P.H., & Nieuwbeerta, P. (2013). Procedural justice in prison: The importance of staff characteristics. *International Journal of Offender Therapy and Comparative Criminology, 59*(4), 1–22. http://dx.doi.org/10.1177/0306624X13512767

Beijersbergen, K., Dirkzwager, A., van der Laan, P., & Nieuwbeerta, P. (2012). Zoeken naar de juiste bouwstenen. *Tijdschrift voor Criminologie, 54*(3). 211–31.

Bell, D. (1953). Crime as an American way of life. *Antioch Review, 13*(2), 131–54. http://dx.doi.org/10.2307/4609623

Bennett, J., Crewe, B., & Wahidin, A. (2013). *Understanding prison staff.* Devon, UK: Willan.

Blaauw, E., Kerkhof, A., & Hayes, L. (2005). Demographic, criminal, and psychiatric factors related to inmate suicide. *Suicide and Life-Threatening Behavior, 35*(1), 63–75. http://dx.doi.org/10.1521/suli.35.1.63.59268

Boe, R., Nafekh, M., Vuong, B., Sinclair, R., & Cousineau, C. (2003). *The changing profile of the federal inmate population: 1997 and 2002.* Ottawa: Correctional Service of Canada.

Bonilla-Silva, E. (2006). *Racism without racists: Color-blind racism and the persistence of racial inequality in the United States.* Lanham, MD: Rowman and Littlefield.

Bottoms, A. (1999). Interpersonal violence and social order in prisons. *Crime and Justice, 26*, 205–81. http://dx.doi.org/10.1086/449298

Bottoms, A., & Tankebe, J. (2012). Beyond procedural justice: A dialogic approach to legitimacy in criminal justice. *Journal of Criminal Law and Criminology, 102*, 119–70.

Boyce, J. (2013). *Adult criminal court statistics in Canada, 2011/2012*. Ottawa: Juristat. http://www.statcan.gc.ca/pub/85-002-x/2013001/article/11804-eng.pdf

–. (2015). *Police-reported crime statistics in Canada, 2014*. Ottawa: Juristat. http://www.statcan.gc.ca/pub/85-002-x/2015001/article/14211-eng.htm

Britton, D. (2003). *At work in the iron cage: The prison as gendered organization*. New York: NYU Press.

Brown, G. (1849). Report of the Royal Commission to Inquire and Then Report upon the Conduct, Economy, Discipline, and Management of the Provincial Penitentiary. Ottawa: Journals of the Legislative Assembly.

Brown, G., Hirdes, J., & Fries, B. (2015). Measuring the prevalence of current, severe symptoms of mental health problems in a Canadian correctional population: Implications for delivery of mental health services for inmates. *International Journal of Offender Therapy and Comparative Criminology, 59*(1), 27–50. http://dx.doi.org/10.1177/0306624X13507040

Bruhn, A. (2013). Gender relations and division of labour among prison officers in Swedish male prisons. *Journal of Scandinavian Studies in Criminology and Crime Prevention, 14*(2), 115–32. http://dx.doi.org/10.1080/14043858.2013.845353

Buentello, S., Fong, R., & Vogel, R. (1991). Prison gang development: A theoretical model. *Prison Journal, 71*(2), 3–14. http://dx.doi.org/10.1177/003288559107100202

Cadwaladr, M. (1993). Breaking into jail: Women working in a men's jail. Master of Arts thesis, University of British Columbia, Vancouver, BC.

Campbell, M. (1997). Revolution and counter-revolution in Canadian prisoners' rights. *Canadian Criminal Law Review, 2*, 285–329.

Cao, L., Zhao, J., & VanDine, S. (1997). Prison disciplinary tickets: A test of the deprivation and importation models. *Journal of Criminal Justice, 25*(2), 103–13. http://dx.doi.org/10.1016/S0047-2352(96)00054-2

Carlson, W. (2001). *Breakfast with the devil: The story of a professional jail breaker*. Toronto: Insomniac Press.

Carrigan, D. (1991). *Crime and punishment in Canada: A history*. Toronto: McClelland and Stewart.

Cawsey, R. (1991). *Report of the Task Force on the Criminal Justice System and its impact on the Indian and Metis people of Alberta: Justice on trial*. Edmonton, AB: Author.

Chartrand, T., & Bargh, J. (1999). The chameleon effect: The perception–behavior link and social interaction. *Journal of Personality and Social Psychology, 76*(6), 893–910. http://dx.doi.org/10.1037/0022-3514.76.6.893

Chesney-Lind, M., & Pollock, J. (1995). Women's prisons: Equality with a vengeance. In J. Pollock-Byrne & A. Merlo (Eds.), *Women, law and social control* (pp. 155–76). Boston: Allyn & Bacon.

Clemmer, D. (1940). *The prison community*. Boston: Christopher Publishing.

Cochran, J. (2012). The ties that bind or the ties that break: Examining the relationship between visitation and prisoner misconduct. *Journal of Criminal Justice, 40*(5), 433–40. http://dx.doi.org/10.1016/j.jcrimjus.2012.06.001

Cochran, J., Mears, D., & Bales, W. (2014). Who gets visited in prison? Individual- and community-level disparities in inmate visitation experiences. *Crime and Delinquency.* http://dx.doi.org/10.1177/0011128714542503.

Cokley, K.O. (2002). Testing Cross's revised racial identity model: An examination of the relationship between racial identity and internalized racialism. *Journal of Counseling Psychology, 49*(4), 476–83. http://dx.doi.org/10.1037/0022-0167. 49.4.476

Cole, N., & Latham, G. (1997). Effects of training in procedural justice on perceptions of disciplinary fairness by unionized employees and disciplinary subject matter experts. *Journal of Applied Psychology, 82*(5), 699–705. http://dx.doi. org/10.1037/0021-9010.82.5.699

Comack, E. (2008). *Out there/in here masculinity, violence and prisoning.* Halifax, NS: Fernwood.

–. (2012). *Racialized policing: Aboriginal people's encounters with the police.* Halifax, NS: Fernwood.

Cooley, D. (1992). Prison victimization and the informal rules of social control. *Forum on Corrections Research, 4.* http://www.csc-scc.gc.ca/research/forum/e043/ e043l-eng.shtml

–. (1993). Criminal victimization in male federal prisons. *Canadian Journal of Criminology, 35,* 479–95.

Copes, H., Brown, A., & Tewksbury, R. (2011). A content analysis of ethnographic research published in top criminology and criminal justice journals from 2000 to 2009. *Journal of Criminal Justice Education, 22*(3), 341–59. http://dx.doi.org/10. 1080/10511253.2010.519714

Correctional Service of Canada (CSC) (2014). *Departmental performance reports.* http://www.csc-scc.gc.ca/publications/005007-4500-eng.shtml

Crawley, E. (2004). *Doing prison work.* New York: Willan.

Crewe, B. (2005a). Codes and conventions: The terms and conditions of contemporary inmate values. In A. Liebling & S. Maruna (Eds.), *The effects of imprisonment* (pp. 177–208). New York: Willan.

–. (2005b). Prisoner society in the era of hard drugs. *Punishment and Society, 7*(4), 457–81. http://dx.doi.org/10.1177/1462474505057122

–. (2006). Male prisoners' orientations towards female officers in an English prison. *Punishment and Society, 8*(4), 395–421. http://dx.doi.org/10.1177/1462474506067565

–. (2007). Power, adaptation and resistance in a late-modern men's prison. *British Journal of Criminology, 47*(2), 256–75. http://dx.doi.org/10.1093/bjc/azl044

–. (2009). *The prisoner society: Power, adaptation and social life in an English prison.* Oxford, UK: Oxford University Press. http://dx.doi.org/10.1093/acprof:oso/9780199577965.001.0001

–. (2011). Soft power in prison: Implications for staff–prisoner relationships, liberty and legitimacy. *European Journal of Criminology, 8*(6), 455–68. http://dx.doi.org/10.1177/1477370811413805

Crewe, B., Warr, J., Bennett, P., & Smith, A. (2013). The emotional geography of prison life. *Theoretical Criminology, 18*(1), 56–74. http://dx.doi.org/10.1177/

Crouch, B. (1985). Pandora's box: Women guards in men's prisons. *Journal of Criminal Justice, 13*(6), 535–48. http://dx.doi.org/10.1016/0047-2352(85)90082-0

Crouch, B., & Marquart, J. (1980). On becoming a prison guard. In B. Crouch (Ed.), *The keepers: Prison guards and contemporary corrections* (pp. 63–106). Springfield, IL: Charles Thomas.

Cullen, F. (2005). The twelve people who saved rehabilitation: How the science of criminology made a difference. *Criminology, 43*(1), 1–42. http://dx.doi.org/10.1111/j.0011-1348.2005.00001.x

DeLisi, M., Berg, M. T., & Hochstetler, A. (2004). Gang members, career criminals and prison violence: Further specification of the importation model of inmate behaviour. *Criminal Justice Studies, 17*(4), 369–83. http://dx.doi.org/10.1080/1478601042000314883

Demers, J. (2014). *Warehousing prisoners in Saskatchewan: A public health approach.* Regina, SK: Canadian Centre for Policy Alternatives, Saskatchewan Office.

Derkzen, D., Gobeil, R., & Gileno, J. (2009). *Visitation and post-release outcome among federally sentenced offenders.* Ottawa: Correctional Service of Canada.

De Viggiani, N. (2012). Trying to be something you are not: Masculine performances within a prison setting. *Men and Masculinities, 15*(3), 271–91.

Dhami, M., Ayton, P., & Loewenstein, G. (2007). Adaptation to imprisonment: Indigenous or imported? *Criminal Justice and Behavior, 34*(8), 1085–100. http://dx.doi.org/10.1177/0093854807302002

Di Placido, C., Simon, T., Witte, T., Gu, D., & Wong, S. (2006). Treatment of gang members can reduce recidivism and institutional misconduct. *Law and Human Behavior, 30*(1), 93–114. http://dx.doi.org/10.1007/s10979-006-9003-6

Dowden, C., & Tellier, C. (2004). Predicting work-related stress in correctional officers: A meta-analysis. *Journal of Criminal Justice, 32*(1), 31–47. http://dx.doi.org/10.1016/j.jcrimjus.2003.10.003

Draine, J., Wolff, N., Jacoby, J. E., Hartwell, S., & Duclos, C. (2005). Understanding community re-entry of former prisoners with mental illness: A conceptual model to guide new research. *Behavioral Sciences and the Law, 23*(5), 689–707. http://dx.doi.org/10.1002/bsl.642

Duffee, D. (1974). The correction officer subculture and organizational change. *Journal of Research in Crime and Delinquency, 11*(2), 155–72. http://dx.doi.org/10.1177/002242787401100206

Duwe, G., & Clark, V. (2013). Blessed be the social tie that binds the effects of prison visitation on offender recidivism. *Criminal Justice Policy Review, 24*(3), 271–96. http://dx.doi.org/10.1177/0887403411429724

Ehrhart, M. (2004). Leadership and procedural justice climate as antecedents of unit-level organizational citizenship behavior. *Personnel Psychology, 57*(1), 61–94. http://dx.doi.org/10.1111/j.1744-6570.2004.tb02484.x

Farabee, D. (2005). *Rethinking rehabilitation: Why can't we reform our criminals?* Washington, DC: Aei Press.

Farkas, M. (1997). The normative code among correctional officers: An exploration of components and functions. *Journal of Criminal Justice, 20*(1), 23–36.

–. (1999). Correctional officer attitudes toward inmates and working with inmates in a "get tough" era. *Journal of Criminal Justice, 27*(6), 495–506. http://dx.doi.org/10.1016/S0047-2352(99)00020-3

–. (2000). Inmate supervisory style: Does gender make a difference? *Women and Criminal Justice, 10*(4), 25–45. http://dx.doi.org/10.1300/J012v10n04_02

Farkas, M., & Manning, P. (1997). The occupational culture of corrections and police officers. *Journal of Criminal Justice, 20*(2), 51–68.

Farrar, W., & Ariel, B. (2013). *Self-awareness to being watched and socially desirable behavior: A field experiment on the effect of body-worn cameras and police use-of-force.* Washington, DC: Police Foundation.

Faulkner, P., & Faulkner, W. (1997). Effects of organizational change on inmate status and the inmate code of conduct. *Journal of Criminal Justice, 20*(1), 55–72.

Fauteux, G. (1956). *Report of the Committee Appointed to Inquire into the Principles and Procedures followed in the Remission Service of the Department of Justice Canada.* Ottawa: Queen's Printer.

Fong, R. (1990). The organizational structure of prison gangs: A Texas case study. *Federal Probation, 54*(4), 36–44.

Fong, R., & Vogel, R. (1994–95). Comparative analysis of prison gang members, security threat group inmates and general population inmates. *Journal of Gang Research, 2*(2), 1–11.

Forsberg, H., & Vagli, Å. (2006). The social construction of emotions in child protection case-talk. *Qualitative Social Work: Research and Practice, 5*(1), 9–31. http://dx.doi.org/10.1177/1473325006061535

Foucault, M. (1977). *Discipline and punish: The birth of the prison.* New York: Random House.

Franke, D., Bierie, D., & MacKenzie, D. (2010). Legitimacy in corrections. *Criminology and Public Policy, 9*(1), 89–117. http://dx.doi.org/10.1111/j.1745-9133.2010.00613.x

French, S. A., & Gendreau, P. (2006). Reducing prison misconducts: What works! *Criminal Justice and Behavior, 33*(2), 185–218. http://dx.doi.org/10.1177/0093854805284406

Gaes, G., Wallace, S., Gilman, E., Klein-Saffran, J., & Suppa, S. (2002). The influence of prison gang affiliation on violence and other prison misconduct. *Prison Journal, 82*(3), 359–85. http://dx.doi.org/10.1177/003288550208200304

Garfinkel, H. (1956). Conditions of successful degradation ceremonies. *American Journal of Sociology, 61*(5), 420–24. http://dx.doi.org/10.1086/221800

Garofalo, J., & Clark, R. (1985). The inmate subculture in jails. *Criminal Justice and Behavior, 12*(4), 415–34. http://dx.doi.org/10.1177/0093854885012004002

Gendreau, P., & Keyes, D. (2001). Making prisons safer and more humane environments. *Canadian Journal of Criminology, 43*, 123.

Gibbs, J. (1982). Disruption and distress: Going from the street to jail. In N. Parisi (Ed.), *Coping with imprisonment* (pp. 29–44). Los Angeles, CA: Sage.

–. (1987). Symptoms of psychopathology among jail prisoners: The effects of exposure to the jail environment. *Criminal Justice and Behavior, 14*(3), 288–310. http://dx.doi.org/10.1177/0093854887014003003

Gideon, L. (2010). Drug offenders' perceptions of the role of motivation in rehabilitation and reintegration. *International Journal of Offender Therapy and Comparative Criminology, 54*(4), 597–610. http://dx.doi.org/10.1177/0306624X09333377

Glaser, B.S., & Strauss, A. (1967). *The discovery of grounded theory: Strategies for qualitative research*. London: Weidenfeld and Nicolson.

Global News (2010, April 22). Saskatchewan's ombudsman warns of prison overcrowding. http://globalnews.ca/bc/saskatchewans+ombudsman+warns+of+prison+overcrowding/74484/story.html

Globe and Mail (2011, 14 December). Huge price tag for provinces attached to crime bill. http://www.theglobeandmail.com/news/politics/huge-price-tag-for-provinces-attached-to-crime-bill/article2271769/?service=mobile

Goffman, E. (1959). *The presentation of self in everyday life*. New York: Doubleday.

–. (1961). *Asylums: Essays on the social situation of mental patients and other inmates*. New York: Anchor Books.

–. (1963). *Stigma: Notes on the management of spoiled identity*. New York: Simon and Schuster.

–. (1974). *Frame analysis*. Lebanon, NH: Northeastern University Press.

Grant, B., & Ruddell, R. (2011). *Gang populations and ethnic diversity in Canadian penitentiaries*. Paper presented at the annual meeting of the American Society of Criminology, Washington, DC.

Grekul, J. (1999). Pluralistic ignorance in a prison community. *Canadian Journal of Criminology, 41*(4), 513–34.

Grekul, J., & LaBoucane-Benson, P. (2006). *"When you have nothing to live for, you have nothing to die for": An investigation into the formation and recruitment processes of Aboriginal gangs in western Canada.* Edmonton, AB: Public Safety Canada.

–. (2008). Aboriginal gangs and their displacement. *Canadian Journal of Criminology and Criminal Justice, 50,* 60–82.

Griffin, M., & Hepburn, J. (2006). The effect of gang affiliation on violent misconduct among inmates during the early years of confinement. *Criminal Justice and Behavior, 33*(4), 419–66. http://dx.doi.org/10.1177/0093854806288038

Griffiths, C., & Murdoch, D. (2014). *Canadian corrections.* Toronto: Nelson Canada.

Gruber, J.E. (1998). The impact of male work environments and organizational policies on women's experiences of sexual harassment. *Gender and Society, 12*(3), 301–20. http://dx.doi.org/10.1177/0891243298012003004

Hamilton, A., & Sinclair, M. (1991). *Report of the Aboriginal Justice Inquiry of Manitoba.* Winnipeg, MB: Queen's Printer.

Hannah-Moffat, K. (2005). Criminogenic needs and the transformative risk subject: Hybridizations of risk/need in penalty. *Punishment and Society, 7*(1), 29–51. http://dx.doi.org/10.1177/1462474505048132

Hannah-Moffat, K., & Klassen, A. (2013). Limiting the state's right to punish. In J. Winterdyk and M. Weinrath (Eds.), *Adult corrections in Canada* (pp. 247–68). Whitby, ON: de Sitter.

Harding, B., Linke, G., Van Court, M., White, J., & Clem, C. (2001). *2001 directory of direct supervision jails.* Washington, DC: US Department of Justice.

Harris, D.A. (2010). Picture this: Body worn video devices ("head cams") as tools for ensuring fourth amendment compliance by police. *Texas Tech Law Review, 43,* 357–7.

Harris, M. (2003). *Con game: The truth about Canada's prisons.* Toronto: McClelland and Stewart.

Harvey, J. (2007). *Young men in prison.* Devon, UK: Willan.

Hassine, V. (1999). In search of the convict code. In T. Bernard & R. McCleary (Eds.), *Life without parole: Living in prison today* (p. 6). Los Angeles: Roxbury.

Hemmens, C., Stohr, M.K., Schoeler, M., & Miller, B. (2002). One step up, two steps back: The progression of perceptions of women's work in prisons and jails. *Journal of Criminal Justice, 30*(6), 473–89. http://dx.doi.org/10.1016/S0047-2352(02)00170-8

Hepburn, J.R. (1985). The exercise of power in coercive organizations: A study of prison guards. *Criminology, 23*(1), 145–64. http://dx.doi.org/10.1111/j.1745-9125.1985.tb00330.x

Hough, M., & Roberts, J. (2005). *Understanding public attitudes to criminal justice.* New York: McGraw-Hill International.

Hughes, E.N. (1996). *Report of the Independent Review of the Circumstances Surrounding the April 25–26, 1996 Riot at the Headingley Correctional Institution.* Winnipeg, MB: Government of Manitoba.

Hulley, S., Liebling, A., & Crewe, B. (2011). Respect in prisons: Prisoners' experiences of respect in public and private sector prisons. *Criminology and Criminal Justice, 12*(1), 3–23. http://dx.doi.org/10.1177/1748895811423088

Hunt, G., Riegel, S., Morales, T., & Waldorf, D. (1993). Changes in prison culture: Prison gangs and the case of the "Pepsi generation." *Social Problems, 40*(3), 398–409. http://dx.doi.org/10.2307/3096887

Inciardi, J.A., Lockwood, D., and Quintan, J.A. (1993). Drug use in prison: Patterns, processes and implications for treatment. *Journal of Drug Issues, 23,* 119–30. http://dx.doi.org/10.1177/002204269302300108

Irwin, J. (1970). *The felon.* Berkeley, CA: University of California Press.

–. (1980). *Prisons in turmoil.* Boston, MA: Little, Brown.

–. (1985). *The jail.* Berkeley, CA: University of California Press.

–. (2005). *The warehouse prison: Disposal of the new dangerous class.* Los Angeles, CA: Roxbury.

Irwin, J., & Cressey, D.R. (1962). Thieves, convicts and inmate culture. *Social Problems, 10*(2), 142–55. http://dx.doi.org/10.2307/799047

Jackson, J., Bradford, B., Hough, M., Myhill, A., Quinton, P., & Tyler, T.R. (2012). Why do people comply with the law? Legitimacy and the influence of legal institutions. *British Journal of Criminology, 52,* 1–21.

Jackson, M. (2002). *Justice behind the walls: Human rights in Canadian prisons.* Vancouver, BC: Douglas and McIntyre.

–. (2004). Book review: Con game: The truth about Canadian prisons. http://justice behindthewalls.net/resources/news/congame.pdf

Jacobs, J. (1974). Street gangs behind bars. *Society for the Study of Social Problems, 21*(3), 395–409. http://dx.doi.org/10.2307/799907

–. (1977). *Stateville: The penitentiary in mass society.* Chicago: University of Chicago Press.

Jacobs, J., & Retsky, H. (1975). Prison guard. *Journal of Contemporary Ethnography, 4*(1), 5–29. http://dx.doi.org/10.1177/089124167500400102

Jenne, D., & Kersting, R. (1996). Aggression and women correctional officers in male prisons. *Prison Journal, 76*(4), 442–60. http://dx.doi.org/10.1177/0032855596076004005

Jensen, T., & Nafekh, M. (2011). *Evaluation report: Pathways healing units.* Ottawa: Correctional Service of Canada.

Jewkes, Y. (2005). Men behind bars. *Men and Masculinities, 8*(1), 44–63. http://dx.doi.org/10.1177/1097184X03257452

Jiang, S., & Winfree, L.T. (2006). Social support, gender, and inmate adjustment to prison life: Insights from a national sample. *Prison Journal, 86*(1), 32–55. http://dx.doi.org/10.1177/0032885505283876

Johnson, R. (2002a). Living in prison: The private culture of the prison. In S. Horne (Ed.), *Hard time: Understanding and reforming the prison* (3rd ed., pp. 164–96). Belmont, CA: Wadsworth, Cengage Learning.

–. (2002b). Prowling the yard: The public culture of the prison. In S. Horne (Ed.), *Hard time understanding and reforming the prison* (3rd ed., pp. 132–63). Belmont, CA: Wadsworth, Cengage Learning.

Johnson, S. (2003). *Custodial remand in Canada, 1986/87 to 2000/01*. Ottawa: Juristat.

Justice Canada (2011). Backgrounder: Safe streets. Communities Act. http://www.justice.gc.ca/eng/news-nouv/nr-cp/2011/doc_32637.html [no longer available]

Kauffman, K. (1981). Prison officers' attitudes and perceptions of attitudes: A case of pluralistic ignorance. *Journal of Research in Crime and Delinquency, 18*(2), 272–94. http://dx.doi.org/10.1177/002242788101800205

–. (1988). *Prison officers and their world*. Cambridge, MA: Harvard University Press.

Kelly, K., & Caputo, T. (2005). The linkages between street gangs and organized crime: The Canadian experience. *Journal of Gang Research, 13*(1), 17–32.

Kingsley, R. (1994). *Common assault in Canada*. Ottawa: Canadian Centre for Justice Statistics.

Klofas, J. (1990). The jail and the community. *Justice Quarterly, 7*(1), 69–102. http://dx.doi.org/10.1080/07418829000090481

Klofas, J., & Toch, H. (1982). The guard subculture myth. *Journal of Research in Crime and Delinquency, 19*(2), 238–54. http://dx.doi.org/10.1177/002242788201900207

Kong, R., & Peters, V. (2008). *Remand in adult corrections and sentencing patterns*. Ottawa: Juristat.

Kwan, S. (2009). Framing the fat body: Contested meanings between government, activists, and industry. *Sociological Inquiry, 79*(1), 25–50. http://dx.doi.org/10.1111/j.1475-682X.2008.00271.x

Lagace, D. (1994). Acceptance of female correctional officers in institutions for men: A Canadian perspective. Master of Arts thesis, Saint Mary's University, Halifax.

Lahm, K.F. (2009). Inmate assaults on prison staff: A multilevel examination of an overlooked form of prison violence. *Prison Journal, 89*(2), 131–50. http://dx.doi.org/10.1177/0032885509334743

Lambert, E. G., Lynne Hogan, N., & Barton, S.M. (2001). The impact of job satisfaction on turnover intent: A test of a structural measurement model using a national sample of workers. *Social Science Journal, 38*(2), 233–50. http://dx.doi.org/10.1016/S0362-3319(01)00110-0

Levinson, R., & Kitchener, H. (1966). Treatment of delinquents: Comparison of four methods for assigning inmates to counselors. *Journal of Consulting Psychology*, *30*(4), 364. http://dx.doi.org/10.1037/h0023588

Liebling, A. (2004). *Prisons and their moral performance: A study of values, quality, and prison life*. Oxford: Oxford University Press.

–. (2011). Distinctions and distinctiveness in the work of prison officers: Legitimacy and authority revisited. *European Journal of Criminology*, *8*(6), 484–99. http://dx.doi.org/10.1177/1477370811413807

Liebling, A., & Arnold, H. (2012). Social relationships between prisoners in a maximum security prison: Violence, faith, and the declining nature of trust. *Journal of Criminal Justice*, *40*(5), 413–24. http://dx.doi.org/10.1016/j.jcrimjus.2012.06.003

Liebling, A., Durie, L., Stiles, A., & Tait, S. (2004). Revisiting prison suicide: The role of fairness and distress. In A. Liebling & S. Maruna (Eds.), *The effects of imprisonment* (pp. 209–32). New York: Willan.

Liebling, A., Price, D., & Shefer, G. (2010). *The prison officer*. London: Routledge.

Lipsky, M. (1979). *Street level bureaucracy*. New York: Russell Sage Foundation.

Logan, C., & Gaes, G. (1993). Meta-analysis and the rehabilitation of punishment. *Justice Quarterly*, *10*(2), 245–63. http://dx.doi.org/10.1080/07418829300091811

Lombardo, L. (1985). Group dynamics and the prison guard subculture: Is the subculture an impediment to helping inmates? *International Journal of Offender Therapy and Comparative Criminology*, *29*(1), 79–90. http://dx.doi.org/10.1177/0306624X8502900107

–. (1989). *Guards imprisoned: Correctional officers at work* (2nd ed.). Cincinnati, OH: Anderson.

MacGuigan, M. (1977). *Report to Parliament by the Sub-committee on the Penitentiary System in Canada*. Ottawa: Government of Canada.

MacKenzie, D., & Hickman, L. (2006). *What works in corrections*. New York: Cambridge University Press. http://dx.doi.org/10.1017/CBO9780511499470.

Mahfood, V., Pollock, W., & Longmire, D. (2013). Leave it at the gate: Job stress and satisfaction in correctional staff. *Criminal Justice Studies*, *26*(3), 308–25.

Mahoney, T. (2011). *Homicide in Canada, 2011*. Ottawa: Juristat.

Manning, P. (2008). Goffman on organizations. *Organization Studies*, *29*(5), 677–99. http://dx.doi.org/10.1177/0170840608088767

Manson, A. (2004). Pre-sentence custody and the determination of a sentence (or how to make a mole hill out of a mountain). *Criminal Law Quarterly (Toronto)*, *49*, 292–350.

Marin, A. (2013). *Caught in the act: Investigation into the Ministry of Community Safety and Correctional Services' conduct in relation to Ontario Regulation 233/10 under the Public Works Protection Act*. Toronto: Ombudsman Ontario.

Marquart, J.W. (2001). Doing research in prison: The strength and weaknesses of full participation as a guard. In J.M. Miller & R. Tewksbury (Eds.), *Extreme methods: Innovative approaches to social science research* (pp. 35–47). Boston, MA: Allyn and Bacon.

Marquart, J., Barnhill, M., & Balshaw-Biddle, K. (2001). Fatal attraction: An analysis of employee boundary violations in a southern prison system, 1995–1998. *Justice Quarterly, 18*(4), 877–910. http://dx.doi.org/10.1080/07418820100095121

Marquart, J., & Roebuck, J. (1985). Prison guards and "snitches." *British Journal of Criminology, 25*(3), 217–33.

Marron, K. (1996). *The slammer: The crisis in Canada's prison system*. Toronto: Doubleday.

Martel, J., Brassard, R., & Jaccoud, M. (2011). When two worlds collide: Aboriginal risk management in Canadian corrections. *British Journal of Criminology, 51*(2), 235–55. http://dx.doi.org/10.1093/bjc/azr003

Martin, S.E., & Jurik, N.C. (1996). *Doing justice, doing gender: Women in law and criminal justice occupation*. Los Angeles, CA: Sage.

Maruna, S. (2001). *Making good: How ex-convicts reform and reclaim their lives*. Washington, DC: American Psychological Association. http://dx.doi.org/10.1037/10430-000

Mazerolle, L., Bennett, S., Antrobus, E., & Eggins, E. (2012). Procedural justice, routine encounters and citizen perceptions of police: Main findings from the Queensland community engagement trial. *Journal of Experimental Criminology, 8*(4), 343–67. http://dx.doi.org/10.1007/s11292-012-9160-1

McDonald, P. (2012). Workplace sexual harassment 30 years on: A review of the literature. *International Journal of Management Reviews, 14*(1), 1–17. http://dx.doi.org/10.1111/j.1468-2370.2011.00300.x

McIntosh, P. (2010). White privilege and male privilege. In E. Provenzo, (Ed.) *The teacher in American society: A critical anthology*, (p. 121–34). Thousand Oaks, CA: Sage.

Mears, D., Cochran, J., Siennick, S., & Bales, W. (2012). Prison visitation and recidivism. *Justice Quarterly, 29*(6), 888–918. http://dx.doi.org/10.1080/07418825.2011.583932

Mears, D., Stewart, E., Siennick, S., & Simons, R. (2013). The code of the street and inmate violence: Investigating the salience of imported belief systems. *Criminology, 51*(3), 695–728. http://dx.doi.org/10.1111/1745-9125.12017

Melnitzer, J. (1995). *Maximum, minimum, medium: A journey through Canadian prisons*. Toronto: Key Porter.

Miles, R. (1989). *Racism*. Milton Keynes: Open University Press.

Mohr, J. (1971). *Report of the Working Group on Federal Maximum Security Institutions Design*. Ottawa: Government of Canada.

Monture-Angus, P. (1999). Women and risk: Aboriginal women, colonialism, and correctional practice. *Canadian Women's Studies, 19*(2), 24–29.

Moore, B. (1977). *Concerning a riot at the Prince Albert Correctional Centre on the 21st and 22nd of June, A.D. 1977.* Regina: Province of Saskatchewan.

Morris, R., & Worrall, J. (2014). Prison architecture and inmate misconduct: A multilevel assessment. *Crime and Delinquency, 60*(7), 1083–109. http://dx.doi.org/10.1177/0011128710386204

Morse, J., Barrett, M., Mayan, M., Olson, K., & Spiers, J. (2008). Verification strategies for establishing reliability and validity in qualitative research. *International Journal of Qualitative Methods, 1*(2), 13–22.

Munger, K., & Harris, S.J. (1989). Effects of an observer on hand washing in a public restroom. *Perceptual and Motor Skills, 69*(3), 733–34. http://dx.doi.org/10.2466/pms.1989.69.3.733

Munn, M. (2013). Correctional workers. In J. Winterdyk & M. Weinrath (Eds.), *Adult corrections in Canada* (pp. 141–70). Whitby, ON: de Sitter.

Munn, M., & Bruckert, C. (2013). *On the outside: From lengthy imprisonment to lasting freedom.* Vancouver: UBC Press.

Murphy, K. (2005). Regulating more effectively: The relationship between procedural justice, legitimacy, and tax non-compliance. *Journal of Law and Society, 32*(4), 562–89. http://dx.doi.org/10.1111/j.1467-6478.2005.00338.x

Nafekh, M. (2002). *An examination of youth and gang affiliation within the federally sentenced Aboriginal population.* Ottawa: Research Branch, Correctional Service of Canada.

Neuman, L., & Wiegand, B. (2000). *Criminal justice research methods: Qualitative and quantitative approaches.* Needham Heights, MA: Allyn and Bacon.

Newbold, G. (2003). Rehabilitating criminals: It ain't that easy. In J.I. Ross & S.C. Richards (Eds.), *Convict Criminology,* (pp. 150–69). Belmont, CA: Woodsworth.

–. (2005). Women officers working in men's prisons. *Social Policy Journal of New Zealand, 25,* 105–17.

Nuffield, J. (1982). *Parole decision making in Canada.* Ottawa: Solicitor General of Canada.

Olatu, M. (2009). *Evalution report: Lifeline program.* Ottawa: Evaluation Branch, Correctional Service of Canada.

O'Leary, P., Tsui, M.-S., & Ruch, G. (2013). The boundaries of the social work relationship revisited: Towards a connected, inclusive and dynamic conceptualisation. *British Journal of Social Work, 43*(1), 135–53. http://dx.doi.org/10.1093/bjsw/bcr181

Ombudsman Office of Alberta. (1988). *Investigation into the use of urinalysis at the Fort Saskatchewan Correctional Centre.* Edmonton, Alberta: Author.

Ouimet, R. (1969). *Toward unity: Criminal justice and corrections. Report of the Canadian Committee on Corrections.* Ottawa: Queen's Printer.

Parliamentary Budget Office. (2012). The Fiscal impact of changes to eligibility for conditional sentences of imprisonment in Canada. Ottawa: Author. http://pbo-dpb. gc.ca/web/default/files/files/files/Publications/Conditional_sentencing_EN. pdf

Patton, M. (2002). *Qualitative research and evaluation methods.* Thousand Oaks, CA: Sage.

Perreault, S. (2009). *The incarceration of Aboriginal people in adult correctional services.* Ottawa: Juristat.

–. (2014). *Correctional services key indicators, 2012/2013.* Ottawa: Juristat.

Petersilia, J. (2003). *When prisoners come home: Parole and prisoner reentry.* New York: Oxford University Press.

Phelps, J. A., & Diamond, B. (1990). *Creating choices: The report of the Task Force on Federally Sentenced Women.* Ottawa: Correctional Service of Canada.

Pisciotta, A.W. (1996). *Benevolent repression: Social control and the American reformatory-prison movement.* New York: NYU Press.

Porter, L., & Calverley, D. (2011). *Trends in the use of remand in Canada.* Ottawa: Juristat.

Posner, C. (1991). An historical overview of the construction of Canadian federal prisons. *Forum on Corrections Research, 3,* 1–4.

Pratt, J. (2007). *Penal populism.* New York: Routledge.

Regan, P. (2010). *Unsettling the settler within: Indian residential schools, truth telling, and reconciliation in Canada.* Vancouver: UBC Press.

Reisig, M.D., & Mesko, G. (2009). Procedural justice, legitimacy, and prisoner misconduct. *Psychology, Crime and Law, 15*(1), 41–59. http://dx.doi.org/10.1080/10683160802089768

Review Panel. (2007). *Report of the Correctional Service of Canada Review Panel.* Ottawa: Public Safety and Emergency Preparedness Canada.

Ricciardelli, R. (2014a). An examination of the inmate code in Canadian penitentiaries. *Journal of Criminal Justice, 37*(2), 234–55.

–. (2014b). *Surviving incarceration: Inside Canadian prisons.* Waterloo, ON: Wilfrid Laurier University Press.

Ricciardelli, R., & Moir, M. (2013). Stigmatized among the stigmatized: Sex offenders in Canadian penitentiaries. *Canadian Journal of Criminology and Criminal Justice, 55*(3), 353–86. http://dx.doi.org/10.3138/cjccj.2012.E22

Roberts, J. (2004). *The virtual prison: Community custody and the evolution of imprisonment.* Cambridge: Cambridge University Press. http://dx.doi.org/10.1017/CBO9780511520976

–. (2005). Pre-trial custody, terms of imprisonment and the conditional sentence: Crediting "dead time" to effect "regime change" in sentencing. *Canadian Criminal Law Review, 9*(2), 191–213.

Roberts, J., & Gabor, T. (2004). Living in the shadow of prison: Lessons from the Canadian experience in decarceration. *British Journal of Criminology, 44*(1), 92–112. http://dx.doi.org/10.1093/bjc/44.1.92

Robinson, D. (1996). *Summary of findings of the 1995 CSC National Inmate Survey: Research brief.* Ottawa: Correctional Service Canada.

Ross, J. (2013). Deconstructing correctional officer deviance: Toward typologies of actions and controls. *Criminal Justice Review, 38*(1), 110–26. http://dx.doi.org/10.1177/0734016812473824

Ross, R. (1981). *Prison guard, correctional officer: The use and abuse of the human resources of prisons.* Toronto: Butterworths.

–. (1996). *Returning to the teachings: Exploring Aboriginal justice.* Toronto: Penguin Books.

Rothman, D. (1971). *The discovery of the asylum social order and disorder in the new republic.* Toronto: Little, Brown.

–. (1980). *Conscience and convenience: The asylum and its alternatives in progressive America.* Toronto: Little, Brown.

Rottman, D., & Kimberly, J. (1975). The social context of jails. *Sociology and Social Research, 59*(4), 344–61.

Roy, A. (2014). On-officer video cameras: Examining the effects of police department policy and assignment on camera use and activation. Master of Arts thesis, Arizona State University, Tempe.

Royal Commission on Aboriginal Peoples (RCAP). (1996). *Report of the Royal Commission on Aboriginal Peoples.* Ottawa: Queen's Printer.

Ruddell, R., & Gottschall, S. (2011). Are all gangs equal security risks? An investigation of gang types and prison misconduct. *American Journal of Criminal Justice, 36*(3), 265–79. http://dx.doi.org/10.1007/s12103-011-9108-4

Rynne, J., Harding, R., & Wortley, R. (2008). Market testing and prison riots: How public-sector commercialization contributed to a prison riot. *Criminology and Public Policy, 7*(1), 117–42. http://dx.doi.org/10.1111/j.1745-9133.2008.00495.x

Samak, Q. (2003). *Correctional officers of CSC and their working conditions: A questionnaire-based study.* Montreal: Confédération des syndicats nationaux.

Sapers, H. (2008). *A preventable death.* Special report of the Office of the Correctional Investigator. Ottawa: Office of the Correctional Investigator.

–. (2013). *Annual report of the Office of the Correctional Investigator, 2012–2013.* Ottawa: Office of the Correctional Investigator.

–. (2014). *Annual Report of the Correctional Investigator, 2013–2014.* Ottawa: Office of the Correctional Investigator.

Schmid, T., & Jones, R. (1991). Suspended identity: Identity transformation in a maximum security prison. *Symbolic Interaction, 14*(4), 415–32. http://dx.doi.org/10.1525/si.1991.14.4.415

–. (1993). Ambivalent actions: Prison adaptation strategies of first-time, short-term inmates. *Journal of Contemporary Ethnography, 21*(4), 439–63. http://dx.doi.org/10.1177/089124193021004002

Sherman, L. (1978). *Scandal and reform: Controlling police corruption.* Berkeley, CA: University of California Press.

Smith, M. (2006). *Erving Goffman.* London: Taylor and Francis. http://dx.doi.org/10.4324/9780203002346.

Smith, W. (2009). Theatre of use: A frame analysis of information technology demonstrations. *Social Studies of Science, 39*(3), 449–80. http://dx.doi.org/10.1177/0306312708101978

Söderfeldt, M., Söderfeldt, B., Ohlson, C.-G., Theorell, T., & Jones, I. (2000). The impact of sense of coherence and high-demand/low-control job environment on self-reported health, burnout and psychophysiological stress indicators. *Work and Stress, 14*(1), 1–15. http://dx.doi.org/10.1080/026783700417195

Sparks, J., & Bottoms, A. (1995). Legitimacy and order in prisons. *British Journal of Sociology, 46*(1), 45–62. http://dx.doi.org/10.2307/591622

Sparks, R., Bottoms, A., & Hay, W. (1996). *Prisons and the problem of order.* Oxford: Clarendon Press. http://dx.doi.org/10.1093/acprof:oso/9780198258186.001.0001.

Statistics Canada. (2014). Cansim – correctional services. http://www5.statcan.gc.ca/cansim/

–. (2015). *Adult correctional statistics in Canada, 2013/2014.* Ottawa: ON: Juristat. http://www.statcan.gc.ca/pub/85-002-x/2015001/article/14163-eng.htm

Steiner, B., & Wooldredge, J. (2008). Inmate versus environmental effects on prison rule violations. *Criminal Justice and Behavior, 35*(4), 438–56. http://dx.doi.org/10.1177/0093854807312787

Sunshine, J., & Tyler, T.R. (2003). The role of procedural justice and legitimacy in shaping public support for policing. *Law and Society Review, 37*(3), 513–48. http://dx.doi.org/10.1111/1540-5893.3703002

Sykes, G. (1958). *The society of captives.* Princeton, NJ: Princeton University Press.

Sykes, G., & Messinger, S. (1960). The inmate social system. In R. Cloward (Ed.), *Theoretical studies in the social organization of the prison.* New York: Social Science Research Council.

Szockyj, E. (1989). Working in a man's world: Women correctional officers in an institution for men. *Canadian Journal of Criminology, 31*, 319.

Taillon, J. (2006). *Offences against the administration of justice.* Ottawa: Juristat.

Tait, S. (2011). A typology of prison officer approaches to care. *European Journal of Criminology, 8*(6), 440–54. http://dx.doi.org/10.1177/1477370811413804

Teelucksingh, C., & Galabuzi, G.E. (2005). *Working precariously: The impact of race and immigrants' status on employment opportunities and outcomes in Canada.* Ottawa: Canadian Race Relations Foundation.

Thomas, C. (1977). Theoretical perspectives on prisonization: A comparison of the importation and deprivation models. *Journal of Criminal Law and Criminology, 68*(1), 135–45. http://dx.doi.org/10.2307/1142482

Tomkins, B.J. (2002). *Locked out: Inmate service and conditions of custody in Saskatchewan correctional centres.* Regina: Saskatchewan Ombudsman.

Trammell, R. (2009). Values, rules, and keeping the peace: How men describe order and the inmate code in California prisons. *Deviant Behavior, 30*(8), 746–71. http://dx.doi.org/10.1080/01639620902854662

Trammell, R., Raby, J., Anderson, A., Hampton, S., & Stickney, T. (2014). Maintaining order and following the rules: Gender differences in punishing inmate misconduct. *Deviant Behavior, 35*(10), 804–21. http://dx.doi.org/10.1080/01639625.2014.889992

Truth and Reconcilation Commission (TRC). (2015). *Honouring the truth, reconciling for the future: Summary of the final report of the Truth and Reconciliation Commission of Canada.* Ottawa: Government of Canada. http://www.trc.ca/websites/trcinstitution/File/2015/Honouring_the_Truth_Reconciling_for_the_Future_July_23_2015.pdf

Turnbull, S. (2014). Aboriginalising the parole process: "Culturally appropriate" adaptations and the Canadian federal parole system. *Punishment and Society, 16*(4), 385–405. http://dx.doi.org/10.1177/1462474514539538

Turner, V. (1995). *The ritual process: Structure and anti-structure.* Piscataway, NJ: Transaction Publishers.

Tyler, T. (1990). *Why people obey the law: Procedural justice, legitimacy, and compliance.* New Haven, CT: Yale University Press.

–. (2003). Procedural justice, legitimacy, and the effective rule of law. *Crime and Justice, 30*, 283–357. http://dx.doi.org/10.1086/652233

–. (2004). Enhancing police legitimacy. *Annals of the American Academy of Political and Social Science, 593*(1), 84–99. http://dx.doi.org/10.1177/0002716203262627

–. (2012). Why procedural justice matters. Paper presented at the International Conference on Community Courts, Washington, DC.

van Gennep, A. (1960). *The rites of passage.* Chicago: University of Chicago Press.

Vigil, J. (2003). Urban violence and street gangs. *Annual Review of Anthropology, 32*(1), 225–42. http://dx.doi.org/10.1146/annurev.anthro.32.061002.093426

Waldram, J. (1997). *The way of the pipe: Aboriginal spirituality and symbolic healing in Canadian prisons.* Peterborough, ON: Broadview Press.

Walmsley, R. (2014). World pre-trial/remand imprisonment list. http://www.prisonstudies.org/sites/default/files/resources/downloads/world_pre-trial_imprisonment_list_2nd_edition_1.pdf

Walters, S., & Lagace, D. (1999). Gender differences in occupational characteristics of Canadian correctional officers. *International Journal of Comparative and Applied Criminal Justice, 23*(1), 45–53. http://dx.doi.org/10.1080/01924036.1999.9678632

Weinrath, M. (2000). *Post-release success and early release potential for Manitoba inmates.* Winnipeg: Manitoba Justice.

–. (2009a). Inmate perspectives on the remand crisis in Canada. *Canadian Journal of Criminology and Criminal Justice, 51*(3), 355–79. http://dx.doi.org/10.3138/cjccj.51.3.355

–. (2009b). *A qualitative inquiry into inmate–staff relations, violence, drug use, prison gangs and programs, in Canadian federal and provincial correctional institutions.* Ottawa: Correctional Service of Canada.

Weinrath, M., Murchison, M., & Markesteyn, T. (2013). Justice as method: The evaluation of the Minobimasdiziwin prison gang intervention program. In K. Gorkoff & R. Jochelson (Eds.), *Thinking About justice.* Halifax, NS: Fernwood.

Weinrath, M., Swait, M., & Markesteyn, T. (1999). A comparison of prison gang members and non-members in a western Canadian province. Paper presented at the annual meetings of the Academy of Criminal Justice Sciences, Orlando, FL.

Weisheit, R., & Klofas, J. (1990). The impact of jail: Collateral costs and affective response. *Journal of Offender Counseling Services and Rehabilitation, 14*(1), 51–65. http://dx.doi.org/10.1300/J264v14n01_06

Wener, R. (2006). Effectiveness of the direct supervision system of correctional design and management: A review of the literature. *Criminal Justice and Behavior, 33*(3), 392–410. http://dx.doi.org/10.1177/0093854806286202

White, M.D. (2014). *Police officer body-worn cameras: Assessing the evidence.* Washington, DC: Office of Community Oriented Policing Services.

Willet, T. (1983). Prison guards in private. *Canadian Journal of Criminology, 25,* 1–18.

Wilson, D., Gallagher, C., & MacKenzie, D. (2000). A meta-analysis of corrections-based education, vocation, and work programs for adult offenders. *Journal of Research in Crime and Delinquency, 37*(4), 347–68. http://dx.doi.org/10.1177/0022427800037004001

Winterdyk, J., & Ruddell, R. (2010). Managing prison gangs: Results from a survey of US prison systems. *Journal of Criminal Justice, 38*(4), 730–36. http://dx.doi.org/10.1016/j.jcrimjus.2010.04.047

Winterdyk, J., & Weinrath, M. (Eds.) (2013). *Adult corrections in Canada.* Whitby, ON: de Sitter.

Wood, J., Moir, A., & James, M. (2009). Prisoners' gang-related activity: The importance of bullying and moral disengagement. *Psychology, Crime and Law, 15*(6), 569–81. http://dx.doi.org/10.1080/10683160802427786

Worley, R., & Worley, V. (2011). Guards gone wild: A self-report study of correctional officer misconduct and the effect of institutional deviance on "care" within the

Texas prison system. *Deviant Behavior, 32*(4), 293–319. http://dx.doi.org/10.1080/01639621003772738

Wormith, S., Ferguson, M., & Bonta, J. (2013). Offender classification and case management and their application in Canadian corrections. In J. Winterdyk & M. Weinrath (Eds.), *Adult corrections in Canada* (pp. 171–98). ON: de Sitter.

Wrong, D. (1994). *Problem of order: What unites and divides society.* Toronto: Maxwell MacMillan.

Young, M. (2013). Incarceration in Canada. In J. Winterdyk & M. Weinrath (Eds.), *Adult corrections in Canada* (pp. 61–84). Whitby, ON: de Sitter.

Zaitzow, B., & Houston, J. (1999). Prison gangs: The North Carolina experience: A summary of the findings. *Journal of Gang Research, 6,* 23–32.

Zamble, E., & Porporino, F. (1988). *Coping, behavior, and adaptation in prison inmates.* New York: Springer Verlag. http://dx.doi.org/10.1007/978-1-4613-8757-2.

Zimmer, L. (1986). *Women guarding men.* Chicago: University of Chicago Press.

Zimring, F., & Hawkins, G. (1991). *The scale of imprisonment.* Chicago: University of Chicago Press.

Zupan, L. (1991). *Jails reform and the new generation philosophy.* Cincinnati, OH: Anderson.

Jurisprudence

Martineau v. Matsqui Institution Inmate Disciplinary Bd., [1980] 1 S.C.R. 602.

R. v. Summers, 2014 SCC 26, [2014] 1 S.C.R. 575.

Solosky v. The Queen, [1980] 1 S.C.R. 821.

Weatherall v. Canada (Attorney General), [1993] 2 S.C.R. 872.

Index

Aas, Katja, 161

Aboriginal inmates, 7, 51, 83, 282n2(Intro); impact of Eurocentric assessments on, 52–53; limited access to cultural/spiritual programs, 5, 7, 51, 52–53, 66, 149–51, 157, 218–19, 235; Ni-Miikana Pathways unit (SMI), 97, 98, 219–21, 270; overrepresentation in prison system, 7, 48–49, 50; role of Elders in parole hearings, 51, 53. *See also* Aboriginal prison gangs

Aboriginal peoples: dispute resolution, 15; racialization of, 48–50, 52–53, 149–51. *See also* Aboriginal inmates; Aboriginal prison gangs

Aboriginal prison gangs, 38, 236, 238–39, 240; Deuce (street gang), 239, 284n2(Ch10); Indian Posse (prison gang), 196, 238–39, 240–41, 261; Manitoba Warriors (prison gang), 70, 196, 238, 239, 240, 250, 255, 260, 261, 264, 284n2; Native Syndicate (prison gang), 70, 238, 240, 257, 261, 284n3

academic programs. *See* vocational/academic programs

accused offenders. *See* remand inmates

administration. *See* penal administration

administrative segregation, 34–35, 40, 41, 42

African American inmates. *See* Black inmates

African gangs, 38, 237, 258

Albany Prison (England), 64

Alberta, 20, 43, 48; Edmonton Remand Centre, 261, 262; prison gangs, 239, 261–63, 353; remand inmates, 170, 232. *See also* Fort Saskatchewan Correctional Centre (AB)

anatomy of a set-up, 176, 177

Arbour Inquiry Report (1996), 6, 41, 184

Archambault Commission (1938), 16

architecture, 5–6; living units related to direct supervision, 6, 39–40, 42–44, 142, 159–60, 165–71, 173; traditional style related to direct supervision, 5–6, 43–44, 166

argot: definitions, 285–87
Arnold, Helen, 130–31
assaults. *See* violence
Auburn system, 15–16, 43–44

behavioural treatment. *See* cognitive-
    behavioural therapy
being strong: as inmate value, 86, 87
Black inmates, 50, 83, 151; African
    gangs, 38, 237, 258
body-worn video, 185, 197, 271
Bottoms, Anthony, 60; legitimacy
    model, 11, 61, 211
Brandon Correctional Centre, 43
British Columbia, 20, 21, 30, 43. *See
    also* Matsqui Institution (BC)
Brown Commission, 1849, 16
"bubble boys/hounds": definition,
    106, 285

Canada. Corrections and Conditional
    Release Act (1992), 6, 40, 184,
    187–88
Canada. Safe Cities and Communities
    Act (2012), 21
Canada. Ticket of Leave Act, 1897, 16
Canadian Charter of Rights and
    Freedoms (1982), 6, 40, 41
Canadian Human Rights Act (1977), 39
capital punishment, 14, 15, 39
CBT. *See* cognitive-behavioural therapy
CCRA. *See* Canada. Corrections and
    Conditional Release Act (1992)
cell extractions, 188–90, 192
children of inmates. *See* families of
    inmates
classification systems, 46–47; related to
    rehabilitation, 6–7, 14
clergy, 52

codes of conduct. *See* inmate code of
    conduct
cognitive-behavioural therapy, 7, 8,
    47–48, 210, 212, 214, 229–30, 235;
    definition, 285
COII positions, 161–64
colonial correction practices, 15–16
computer technology, 160, 161, 171–72,
    173, 275
conditional sentences, 5, 18, 20, 283n3
"cons," 101
Conservative government. *See* Harper
    administration
contact with families, 117; loss of
    contact, 80–81, 109, 117, 268; stress
    of contact, 113–17, 120–21, 268;
    telephone bugs, 117, 120–21; types
    of contact, 109–13
contact with friends (external), 109–14,
    117–21; loss of contact, 80–81,
    115–17
contraband trade, 99–100, 287; prison
    gangs and, 248–49. *See also* drug
    trade within prison
convict code. *See* inmate code of
    conduct
convict criminologists, 27, 37, 212–13
Cooley, Dennis, 30, 35
corporal punishment: historically
    related to public unrest, 14, 15; use
    in prisons, 16, 39, 189
correctional institutions: definition,
    285; as distinct settings, 60–61;
    Edmonton Remand Centre (AB),
    261, 262; history, 15–17, 39–42, 43–44,
    46–47. *See also* architecture; Fort
    Saskatchewan Correctional Centre
    (AB); Headingley Correctional
    Centre (MB); Matsqui Institution

(BC); penal administration; Stony
Mountain Institution (MB)
Correctional Investigator (Canada), 6,
39, 183, 189, 191; views on
Aboriginal programming, 53; views
on prison violence, 34–35, 194
correctional officers: accommodation
of prisoner needs, 129, 143–44, 146–47,
153; case management duties, 160,
161–64, 171–73, 269; corruption of
authority and, 41, 63, 174–83;
delegitimizing behaviour, 65, 145–46,
147–51, 153, 156, 158, 195–96, 197,
268, 271; discretionary behaviour,
62–63, 125, 129, 151, 153, 156, 176;
distancing from inmates, 136–37,
138, 174–83; distancing from
supervisors, 136–37, 138; education
and training, 4, 5, 132, 134, 138, 139,
176, 177, 183, 268, 269, 276; effects
of prison violence on, 124–25, 127,
130–31, 132–33; establishment of
authority, 61, 125, 134; frames, 12,
58, 137–38, 157, 182; hyper-
vigilance, 127, 131; interview
methodology, 70–72, 277–81; job
stress, 127, 130–37; judgmental/
punitive attitudes, 125–27, 145–47,
153, 157, 158, 268; misconduct,
174–209; recruits, 130–38, 179–83,
186–87, 268; relations with other
staff, 125, 130, 135–36, 137, 162, 183,
268, 276; subculture, 125–27,
183–95; transition to job conditions,
130–38; work ethic, 125–26, 145–49,
153, 156, 157, 163–65. *See also*
female correctional officers;
inmate-CO relations; violence
by COs

correctional policies: role of COs and,
160–61
Correctional Service of Canada: assault
statistics, 33–34
Correctional Service Review Panel
(2007), 21, 211
corrections administration. *See* penal
administration
COs. *See* correctional officers
courtesy. *See* respect
"crackheads," 121; definition, 100, 285
Crawley, Elaine, 130
Creating Choices report, 40
Crewe, Ben, 29–30, 91, 160–61
crime rates, 5, 8, 17–18, 19, 32,
282n1(Ch1)
Crofton system, 16
CSRP. *See* Correctional Service Review
Panel (2007)
Cullen, Frank, 210
custody rates, 8, 17–22, 32,
282n2(Ch1); remand, 8, 22–24,
232–33, 235

databases, 160, 161, 171–72, 173, 275
debt. *See* prison debts
Demers, Jason, 24
deprivation model, 25, 27, 37, 75
Deuce (street gang), 239, 284 Ch10n2
dignity, 61–62
direct supervision, 39–40, 157, 159–60;
definition, 42, 285, 286; evaluation
of, 44–45; related to architecture, 6,
39–40, 42–44, 142, 159–60, 165–71,
173; role of inmate-CO
communication, 148–49, 151–53,
161–65
discipline, 14
drug addiction. *See* drug use

drug-free units, 36

drug trade within prison, 9, 31, 35, 36, 117–18, 178–79, 285, 287; CO involvement, 177, 178–79, 182; prison gangs, 32, 238, 241, 248, 253, 259

drug use, 32–33; role in prison environment, 29, 32, 33, 35–36, 99–100, 104, 105, 117–18, 285; treatment programs, 36, 214

DS. *See* direct supervision

dynamic security. *See* direct supervision

earned remission, 17, 20, 29–30, 160–61, 283n5

Edmonton Remand Centre (AB), 261, 262

emotions: suppression by COs, 130, 131; suppression by inmates, 91, 93, 94

ethnic minorities: adjustment to prison, 88; racialization, 48–50. *See also* Aboriginal peoples

fairness. *See* procedural justice

families of inmates, 117; deaths in, 91; families of gang members, 112, 243–44, 252; private family visits, 111; supportiveness, 82, 108, 109. *See also* contact with families

Farabee, David, 211

Farkas, Mary Ann, 126, 128

Fauteux Commission (1956), 16

fear management: correctional officers, 130–31, 132–35, 137, 138, 139, 167, 168, 195, 209, 268, 276; inmates, 31, 78, 86, 87, 88, 90, 157, 276

federal correctional institutions, 79; violence within, 34–35. *See also* Matsqui Institution (BC); Stony Mountain Institution (MB)

female correctional officers, 45, 175, 182, 197–209, 275; harassment by male co-workers, 45, 175, 182, 199, 200–3, 209, 269; inmate attitudes towards, 106–7, 182, 199–200, 203–7, 209; staff attitudes towards, 207–8, 209

female inmates, 40–41, 176

First Nations. *See* Aboriginal peoples

"fish": definition, 26, 76, 283n7

Fort Saskatchewan Correctional Centre (AB), 66; architecture, 165–66, 170; correctional officer profile, 70–72, 209; inmate profile, 68–70; inmate relationships, 92–97; interview methodology, 67–72; prison gangs, 253, 261; programs, 232–33

Foucault, Michel, 14–15, 16, 211–12

frame analysis theory: applied to custodial conditions, 10–11, 55, 56–59, 73; Goffman, Erving, 10, 55, 56, 57–58, 75. *See also* correctional officers: frames; inmate frames

frame breaking, 11, 174. *See also* frame breaking by COs; frame breaking by inmates

frame breaking by COs, 174–75, 182, 197–99; crossing social boundaries, 175–83; harassment of female officers, 45, 100–203, 175, 182, 199, 209, 275; use of violence on inmates, 175, 183–96

frame breaking by inmates, 117, 120–21, 222–24; refusal to join gangs, 253–57

frame keying. *See* frame breaking

frames. *See* correctional officers: frames; frame breaking; inmate frames "fresh fish." *See* new inmates

friendship. *See* contact with friends (external); friendships within prison

friendships within prison, 97–98; CO-inmate friendships, 181–82; rarity within prisons, 92–94, 97, 101, 121, 268, 269, 271; shared pasts, 82–83. *See also* peer support programs

FSCC. *See* Fort Saskatchewan Correctional Centre (AB)

gambling, 99, 121, 248, 268

gang members, 83, 97; associates, 284n1Ch10, 286; exiting gangs, 246–47, 284n3Ch10; family relationships, 112, 243–44, 252; feelings of safety, 82–83, 243–45; programs, 260–61. *See also* prison gangs

gangs: interrelationships between types of gangs, 37, 38. *See also* gang members; prison gangs; street gangs

Gibbs, John, 77

Gideon, Lior, 213

glossary, 285–87

Goffman, Erving: frame analysis theory, 10–11, 55, 56, 57–58, 267; impression management, 90–91; stigmatizing rituals, 76

"goofs," 121; definition, 284n2, 286

Griffiths, Curt, 30

Grim Reapers (prison gang), 237–38

Harper administration, 20, 21, 24

Harris, Michael, 33, 42

Harris administration (ON), 283n3

Harvey, Joel, 78

Hassine, Victor, 29

HCC. *See* Headingley Correctional Centre (MB)

Headingley Correctional Centre (MB), 66; architecture, 166–69, 171; correctional officer profile, 70–72, 209; female correctional officers, 45, 207–8, 209; inmate profile, 68–70; inmate relationships, 92–97; interview methodology, 67–72; prison gangs, 38, 238–39, 253, 258, 261; programs, 232; remand inmates, 22–23; riot (1996), 166

history, 15–20; architecture, 42–44; corporal punishment, 14, 15, 16, 39, 189; security classifications, 46; services for Aboriginal inmates, 51–52

homicide, 32

human rights. *See* inmate rights

hyper-masculine values, 91, 106, 239; correctional staff, 130; prison gangs, 239–40, 253; program participation and, 224

IERT. *See* institutional emergency response teams

illicit drugs. *See* drug use

importation model, 25, 27, 37, 75

incarceration: as "badge of honour," 82, 83; initial incarcerations, 79–88. *See also* inmates

incarceration rates. *See* custody rates

incentives for good behaviour, 16; effects on inmate code of conduct, 29–30. *See also* earned remission

incompatibles, 34–35, 39, 245, 249–51, 257, 271–72, 287; definition, 286

Indian Posse (prison gang), 196, 238–39, 240–41, 261

Indigenous peoples. *See* Aboriginal
inmates; Aboriginal peoples;
Aboriginal prison gangs
indirect supervision, 5–6, 43–44,
148–49, 166
informing, 26, 102, 105–6, 121; about
assaults, 35, 105; about CO
misconduct, 183–84; avoiding
appearance of, 106; increased use of
by COs, 28, 29, 30, 58, 103–4,
151–52
inmate as hero, 117, 118
inmate as misunderstood, 117, 118–20
inmate code of conduct, 25–27, 75;
decline of, 27–32, 101–5, 121–22,
141–43, 151, 268, 272; doing one's
own time, 26, 28, 30, 31, 248;
inmate-CO dialog, 30, 103, 122,
140–45, 151–53, 161–65; minding
one's own business, 26, 27, 91, 102;
positive aspects, 27, 31, 75–76, 92;
respect among inmates, 26, 59, 85,
86, 87, 91, 100, 102, 103, 246, 268;
role in limiting hostility between
inmates, 92, 248, 249; stoicism, 26,
87, 91, 93, 106; street problems and,
26, 101, 102, 272
inmate-CO relations, 12–13, 50, 60,
100, 105–7, 133–38; inappropriate
familiarity, 177–81, 182; increased
dialog, 30, 58, 103, 122, 140–45,
151–53, 161–65, 175–83, 268–69,
271; intimate relationships, 177, 180,
181, 182; prison gangs, 154, 253,
254, 257–61; range walks, 161–63;
role of authority in, 62–64, 129, 143,
180; role of procedural justice in,
61–62, 128–29, 143, 268; shifts in,
58–59, 140–58; social distancing,

105–7, 136, 171, 175, 176–83, 253,
268. *See also* frame breaking by COs
inmate-external relations, 108–21, 123;
emotional expression and, 91, 94
inmate frames, 12, 58, 59; external
frames, 109–10, 117–20; frame
breaking, 117, 120–21, 253–57; gang
members, 118–19, 252–53, 254;
primary frame, 87–88, 92, 93, 100,
121, 252; program frames, 221–23
inmate grievance procedures, 40
inmate-inmate relations, 100, 122;
avoidance, 93, 95–96; distrust and
caution, 90–91, 92–97, 100, 101–2,
121–22; inmate-gang member
relations, 252–53, 254, 268; lack of
solidarity, 27–31, 101, 122, 271;
mutual respect, 26, 59, 85, 86, 87, 91,
100, 102, 103, 246, 268
inmate management, 5–6. *See also*
direct supervision; earned remission;
indirect supervision; penal
administration
inmate misconduct: related to
architecture, 170; related to
improved communications, 151;
related to procedural justice, 65, 74;
related to program participation,
211; related to visits from outside
prison, 108
inmate rights: effects of reports and
legislation, 6, 17, 39–42, 183, 184–86,
191–92, 196–97; protection from
CO violence, 186–95
inmates, 32, 282n1(Intro); female
inmates, 40–41, 176; incompatibles,
34–35, 39, 245, 249–51, 257, 271–72,
286, 287; interview methodology,
68–70, 277–79; involuntary transfer,

41, 262–63; slang definitions, 285–87; status, 25–26, 117–20, 121; street problems and, 26, 101, 102, 272; stress, 147–48; suppression of emotions, 91, 93, 94; traditional behaviour, 26. *See also* inmate code of conduct; inmate frames; inmate-inmate relations; inmate rights; lifers; new inmates; prison gangs; remand inmates; young inmates

inmate solidarity. *See* friendships within prison; inmate-inmate relations

inmate-staff relations, 7–8

inmate subculture. *See* inmate code of conduct; prison gangs

institutional culture. *See* living conditions

institutional emergency response teams, 189

involuntary transfers, 41, 262–63

Irwin, John, 27, 37, 77–78

Jackson, Michael, 41

Jacobs, John, 14–15

jobs in prison, 107

Johnson, Robert, 129

Jones, Richard, 78

juvenile detention, 79

Kent Institution (BC), 51

Kingston penitentiary: history, 15–16

Kingston's Prison for Women, 40–41; Arbour Report (1996), 6, 41, 184

legitimacy in criminal justice, 55; delegitimizing behaviour, 65, 145–46, 147–51, 153, 156, 158, 195–96, 197, 268, 271; related to wielding of

authority, 62–65, 143; role of correctional officers, 55, 60, 61, 62, 128–29, 142–58, 205–6

legitimacy model, 11, 55, 59–60

letters, 112–13, 119

Liebling, Alison, 62, 63–65, 143, 160, 269

lifers, 32, 286; Matsqui peer support program, 66–67, 86, 97–98, 122; solidarity, 30

living conditions, 3–4, 32; effect of drug use, 29, 35–36; effects of prison drug trade, 29, 32, 33, 35–36, 99–100, 104, 105, 117–18, 285; effects of prison gangs on, 258–59, 265; inmate movement, 250–51; punishment for rule violations, 62–64; as recurring issue, 17; remand centres, 22–24, 235. *See also* contraband trade; inmate code of conduct; programs

Lomabardo, Lucien, 126, 160

Long Lartin Prison (England), 64

Los Bravos (prison gang), 237–38

MacGuigan Commission Report (1977), 39–40, 184

mail, 112–13, 119

mandatory release, 17, 21, 284n5

Manitoba, 20, 43, 48, 209, 232, 282n2(Ch1); prison gangs, 38, 238–39. *See also* Headingley Correctional Centre (MB); Stony Mountain Institution (MB)

Manitoba Warriors (prison gang), 70, 196, 238, 239, 240, 250, 255, 260, 261, 264, 284n2

Marin, Andre. *See* Marin Report (2013)

Marin Report (2013), 184–86, 194
Marron, Kevin, 33
Martel, Joanne, 50, 52
*Martineau v. Matsqui Institution
 Review Board* (1980), 39, 184
Matsqui Institution (BC), 66;
 architecture, 165, 169–70; correctional
 officer profile, 70–72, 209; drug
 addiction, 99; inmate profile, 68–70;
 inmate relationships, 92–98; interview
 methodology, 67–72; lack of prison
 gangs, 242–43, 251, 253, 261;
 programs, 66–67, 92, 97–98, 270
medical model of offenders, 16–17
Melnitzer, Julius, 33
mental disorders, 32, 283n8; attitudes
 of COs towards, 147, 195; medical
 model and, 16–17; poor
 management and, 42
mentors, 86. *See also* peer support
 programs
methodology, 10–11, 66–73; data
 validity, 272–72; interviews, 67–68,
 277–91; limitations of the study,
 274–75. *See also* frame analysis
 theory
MI. *See* Matsqui Institution (BC)
minorities. *See* Aboriginal inmates;
 Black inmates; ethnic minorities;
 racialization
Mohr Report, 40, 42, 43
Murdoch, Danielle, 30

Native Syndicate (prison gang), 70,
 238, 240, 257, 261, 284n3
Netherlands Prison Project, 65
Newbold, Greg, 212–13
new inmates, 283n7; primary frame,
 87–88, 90–91; transition to

incarceration, 26, 27, 76–88,
 90–91, 108
Ni-Miikana Pathways unit (SMI), 97,
 98, 219–21, 270
"nobodies," 121; definition, 100, 284n2

Oakalla Prison (BC), 86
ombudsmen (provincial), 6, 40, 191,
 194. *See also* Marin Report (2013)
OMG. *See* outlaw motorcycle gangs
Ontario, 50; Harris administration,
 283n3; Marin Report (2013), 184–86,
 194; parole practices, 20, 283
oppositional subcultures, 26, 56, 125–27;
 COs, 56, 125–27. *See also* inmate
 code of conduct; prison gangs
Ouimet Report (1969), 17
outlaw motorcycle gangs, 286
overcrowding, 16, 21–22, 24, 53;
 related to trial delays, 24, 235

P4W. *See* Kingston's Prison for Women
"panel mommies," 106; definition, 286
parole, 20, 21, 46, 213; boards, 16, 20;
 officers, 154, 162, 173; role of
 Aboriginal Elders, 51, 53
pathways units, 66
PC. *See* protective custody
peer support programs, 66–67, 86, 88,
 97, 98, 122, 147, 219–21, 270, 275
penal administration, 17; arbitrary use
 of authority, 39–40, 41; classification
 systems, 6–7, 14, 46–47; duty to act
 fairly, 39, 40; effects of reports and
 legislation, 6, 17, 39–42, 183, 184–86,
 191–92, 196–97; integration of new
 inmates, 88; involuntary transfer, 41,
 262–63; overview of penal reform,
 16–17; prison gang management,

249–51, 258, 261–66; private prison contracts, 283n4. *See also* direct supervision; indirect supervision; programs; protective custody; record-keeping; sentences
penal populism: effect on custody rates, 8
penitence, 14, 15–16, 110
Pennsylvania system, 43–44
penology, 14
"phone bugs," 117, 120–21; definition, 286
PJ. *See* procedural justice
"playing the heavy," 286
policy recommendations, 5; direct supervision, 158, 173; inmate-CO interactions, 158, 173, 183; inmate relationships, 122–23; prison gang management, 266; programs, 235, 266; remand rates, 235; sexual harassment by colleagues, 209; staff training, 139, 158, 173, 183, 209; transition to incarceration, 88
prestige. *See* status
pre-trial custody. *See* remand inmates
pre-trial detention. *See* remand centres
Prince Albert Correctional Centre, 43
prison administration. *See* penal administration
prison debts, 29, 31, 84–85; related to violence, 35, 99, 248, 249, 251
prisoners. *See* inmates
prison gangs, 5, 9, 13, 33, 36–37, 275; affiliation statistics, 32, 38, 253; biker gangs, 237–38, 286; close friendships within, 92; contraband trade, 28, 99, 236, 237, 253; drug trade and, 32, 248; effects on inmate subcultures, 27–28, 29, 252–53; ethnic

affiliations, 9, 37, 38–39, 236, 237, 240, 258; loyalty requirements, 28, 245–46, 253; as modes of self-protection, 37, 243–45, 252; predatory nature, 37, 236, 237, 248–49, 252–53, 255–57, 259, 272; recruitment, 237, 239–42, 248, 252, 253–57, 284n1(Ch10); refusal to join, 254–57; relations with COs, 28, 154, 253, 254, 257–61; tensions between, 196; transition to incarceration and, 84, 85; violence, 32, 33, 37, 238–39, 241, 248–49, 253, 259, 260, 265, 272. *See also* Aboriginal prison gangs
prisons, 60–61. *See also* inmates; living conditions; staff
prison studies, 4–5
private family visits, 111
private prison contracts, 283n4
probation, 5; officers, 173
procedural fairness. *See* procedural justice
procedural justice, 11, 39–40, 55, 59–60, 61, 73–74, 143, 267, 275–76; in wielding of authority, 62–65, 128–29, 155–58, 268, 269
programs, 5, 6–7, 8, 107; admission orientation programs, 88; anti-social contexts related to effect of, 225–26; behavioral vs vocational, 8, 211–12, 216–18, 229–31, 270; difficulties with privacy and trust, 225; drug treatment, 36, 214; framing by COs, 222, 226–31, 234–35, 270; framing by inmates, 221–24, 234; gang members, 260–61, 265–66, 270, 272; impact of remand rates on, 232–34, 235; individual agency and, 213–15,

221–22, 234; inmate attitudes towards, 212–26, 268, 270; lack of quality programs, 215–16, 270; peer support programs, 66–67, 86, 88, 97, 98, 122, 147, 219–21, 270, 275; purposes of, 211–13; quality control, 228–29; success related to CO performance, 64–65

pro-social frames, 109–10, 122, 268

protective custody, 152, 249, 251, 252, 257; definition, 286; ex-gang members, 239, 245, 247, 249–51, 254; incompatibles, 34–35, 39, 245, 249–51, 257, 271–72, 286, 287

provincial correctional centres, 79. *See also* Fort Saskatchewan Correctional Centre (AB); Headingley Correctional Centre (MB)

provincial correction conditions, 20, 35; impact of Ouimet Report, 17; overcrowding, 21–22; remand inmates, 22–23

punitive laws and controls: prevalence, 15–16, 18–21

Quebec: parole practices, 20

racialization, 48–53, 149–51

racism, 48–53, 151; lack of respect for Aboriginal culture, 149–51

ranges: definition, 286

range walks, 161–63, 173

"rats." *See* informing

recidivism: related to programs, 7–8, 47–48, 211, 270; related to visits, 108

record-keeping, 14, 172, 191; databases, 160, 161, 171–72, 173, 275

rehabilitation, 4; classification systems and, 6–7, 14; established as guiding principle, 16; pro-social frames and, 110; treatment programs, 6–7, 8. *See also* programs

remand centres, 79, 283n6; poor living conditions, 22–24, 235; trial delays related to overcrowding, 24, 235

remand inmates, 77–78, 287; custody rates, 8, 22–24, 232–33, 235; external contacts and, 109; limited access to programs, 213, 215, 216, 232–34; stigmatization of, 77–78; studies on, 77; "two for one" credit, 23–24, 233

"rent": definition, 287

research on corrections, 9–10, 283n9; correctional officers, 124–31; future research recommended, 275–76; inmate relations, 90–92; legitimacy, 59–65, 142–43; policy change, 160–61; prison gangs, 210–12; programs, 210–12; seminal works, 14–15. *See also* methodology

respect: among inmates, 26, 59, 85, 86, 87, 91, 100, 102, 103, 246, 268; for correctional officers, 62, 205–6, 268; for inmates, 61–62, 65, 143–44, 153–56, 205–6. *See also* procedural justice

Ricciardelli, Rose, 31

riots, 39, 43, 65, 124, 166, 184; 1970s, 39

Risk, Needs, Responsivity models. *See* cognitive-behavioural therapy

RNR models. *See* cognitive-behavioural therapy

Ross, Jeffrey Ian, 174–75

Rothman, David, 211–12

rule enforcement: negotiation model of, 62–63

rule of law: role in correction services, 6, 17, 39–42, 181–92, 183, 184–85, 196–97

R v. Summers, 24

safety: related to direct supervision, 168–69; related to inmate rights, 42. *See also* violence

Sapers, Howard, 194

Saskatchewan: Aboriginal inmates, 48; overcrowded facilities, 21–22, 24; Prince Albert Correctional Centre, 43; Saskatoon Correctional Centre, 43

Schmid, Thomas, 78

security threat groups, 37, 287. *See also* prison gangs

segregation. *See* administrative segregation; protective custody

sentenced inmates, 287; living conditions, 22

sentences: conditional sentences, 5, 18, 20, 283n3; earned remission, 17, 20, 29–30, 160–61, 283n5; effects of federal policy on, 17–22; length, 17; statutory release, 17, 21, 284n5. *See also* parole

sex offenders, 121; gang membership, 252; inmate code of conduct and, 26, 29–30; programs, 66

sexual relationships: inmate-CO relationships, 177, 180, 181, 182

"skinners." *See* sex offenders

Slovenia: prison study, 65

smartness, 25, 87, 96

SMI. *See* Stony Mountain Institution (MB)

Smith, Ashley, 42

social distancing: effects of technological change on, 171–72, 173. *See also* inmate-inmate relations

solidarity among inmates. *See* friendships within prison; inmate-inmate relations

"solid" inmates: definition, 25, 287

Solosky v. The Queen (1980), 39

Sparks, Richard: legitimacy model, 11

Special Handling Units, 40

staff, 154; assault statistics, 33–34; exchange of information, 162–63; job satisfaction, 64–65; relationship with management, 65, 136–37, 166; safety, 42, 168–69. *See also* correctional officers; inmate-staff relations

state-raised youth, 27, 30–31, 103

static security. *See* indirect supervision

status: inmate as hero, 117–20; inmate as misunderstood, 117. *See also* respect

statutory release, 17, 21, 284n5

stereotypes: of correctional officers, 4, 149, 198; of prison life, 4–5, 149

STGs. *See* security threat groups

stigma of incarceration: external contacts and, 113–14; pre-trial custody, 77–78; social distancing and, 93; stigmatization by COs, 144–45; transition to incarceration, 76, 79, 81, 85, 87, 267–68

stigma of program participation, 221–22

stoicism, 26, 87, 91, 93, 106

Stony Mountain Institution (MB), 66; architecture, 165, 169–71; correctional officer profile, 70–72, 209; drug-free units, 36; inmate profile, 68–70; inmate relationships, 92–97; interview methodology, 67–72; prison gangs, 38, 237–38, 261,

284n2–3(Ch10); programs, 66, 97;
transitional units, 249–50, 251, 287
"storesmen," 99–100; definition, 287
street gangs, 9, 37, 38
strip searches, 284n3(Ch8)
subcultures. *See* inmate code of
conduct; oppositional subcultures;
prison gangs
sub rosa economy: definition, 287
suicide, 37, 42, 64; remand inmates, 77

tactics of talk. *See* inmate-CO
relations: increased dialog
Tait, Sarah, 128
technological change, 115, 171–72, 173;
computer technology, 160, 161, 171–72,
173, 275. *See also* video cameras
telephone calls, 114–15; emotional
impacts, 91; phone bugs, 117, 120–21,
286; recording of, 115
Texas Syndicate (gang), 37
theft within prisons, 101, 104, 106
tobacco. *See* contraband trade
Trammell, Rebecca, 28
transitional units, 249–50, 251, 287
treatment programs: drug treatment, 36
trial delays, 24
TRUs. *See* transitional units
trust, 121
"tune-ups": definition, 284n2(Ch8),
287. *See also* violence: use by COs
Turnbull, Sarah, 50, 51, 53
Tyler, Tom, 55, 59

underground economy. *See* contraband
trade
United States: lack of interest in
rehabilitation, 46
urinanalysis program, 36

video cameras, 171, 173, 185–86, 188–90,
192, 197, 269; body-worn cameras,
185, 197, 271
violence, 8–9, 188; as catalyst for
living-unit architecture, 42–43;
inmate anticipation of, 80; lack of
inmate solidarity and, 30; related to
historical spectacles of violence,
14, 15
violence among inmates, 31, 32,
33–35, 87–88; assault statistics,
33–35, 271; fighting related to
gaining respect, 87–88; informing
about, 35, 105. *See also* prison
gangs
violence by COs, 175, 183–95, 271;
aggressive control of inmates,
194–95
visits, 108–9; stresses of, 113–17. *See
also* contact with families; contact
with friends (external)
vocational/academic programs, 210,
211–12, 216–17, 230–31, 235

Waldram, Joseph, 7, 51–53
*Weatherall v. Canada (Attorney
General)* (1993), 41
Weinrath, Michael, 68, 72–73, 274
women. *See* female correctional
officers; female inmates
women's prisons, 40–41

young inmates: inmate subcultures
and, 27, 28, 30–31, 82–83, 105; state-
raised youth, 27, 30–31, 103;
transition to incarceration, 78, 79,
82–83, 84, 85–86
young offenders. *See* juvenile
detention; young inmates

LAW AND SOCIETY

Amanda Nettelbeck, Russell Smandych, Louis A. Knafla, and Robert Foster
Fragile Settlements: Aboriginal Peoples, Law, and Resistance in South-West Australia and Prairie Canada (2016)

Adam Dodek and Alice Woolley (eds.)
In Search of the Ethical Lawyer: Stories from the Canadian Legal Profession (2016)

David R. Boyd
Cleaner, Greener, Healthier: A Prescription for Stronger Canadian Environmental Laws and Policies (2015)

Margaret E. Beare, Nathalie Des Rosiers, and Abby Deshman (eds.)
Putting the State on Trial: The Policing of Protest during the G20 Summit (2015)

Dale Brawn
Paths to the Bench: The Judicial Appointment Process in Manitoba, 1870–1950 (2014)

Dominique Clément
Equality Deferred: Sex Discrimination and British Columbia's Human Rights State, 1953–84 (2014)

Irvin Studin
The Strategic Constitution: Understanding Canadian Power in the World (2014)

Elizabeth A. Sheehy
Defending Battered Women on Trial: Lessons from the Transcripts (2014)

Carmela Murdocca
To Right Historical Wrongs: Race, Gender, and Sentencing in Canada (2013)

Donn Short
"Don't Be So Gay!" Queers, Bullying, and Making Schools Safe (2013)

Melissa Munn and Chris Bruckert
On the Outside: From Lengthy Imprisonment to Lasting Freedom (2013)